## Public Policy and Politics

### Series Editors: Colin Fudge and Robin Hambleton

Public policy-making in Western democracies is confronted by new pressures. Central values relating to the role of the state, the role of markets and the role of citizenship are now all contested and the consensus built up around the Keynesian welfare state is under challenge. New social movements are entering the political arena: electronic technologies are transforming the nature of employment: changes in demographic structure are creating heightened demands for public services; unforeseen social and health problems are emerging; and, most disturbing, social and economic inequalities are increasing in many countries.

How governments – at international, national and local levels – respond to this developing agenda is the central focus of the *Public Policy and Politics* series. Aimed at a student, professional, practitioner and academic readership, it aims to provide up-to-date, comprehensive and authoritative analyses of public policy-making in practice.

The series is international and interdisciplinary in scope and bridges theory and practice by relating the substance of policy to the politics of the policy-making process.

# Public Policy and Politics

## Series Editors: Colin Fudge and Robin Hambleton

**Series Standing Order   (Public Policy and Politics)**

If you would like to receive future titles in this series as they are published, you can make use of our standing order facility. To place a standing order please contact your bookseller or, in case of difficulty, write to us at the address below with your name and address and the name of the series. Please state with which title you wish to begin your standing order. (If you live outside the UK we may not have the rights for your area, in which case we will forward your order to the publisher concerned.)

Customer Services Department, Macmillan Distribution Ltd, Houndmills, Basingstoke, Hampshire, RG21 2XS, England

# Urban Policy in Britain

### The City, the State and the Market

**Rob Atkinson**
**and**
**Graham Moon**

MACMILLAN

© Rob Atkinson and Graham Moon 1994

All rights reserved. No reproduction, copy or transmission of
this publication may be made without written permission.

No paragraph of this publication may be reproduced, copied or
transmitted save with written permission or in accordance with
the provisions of the Copyright, Designs and Patents Act 1988,
or under the terms of any licence permitting limited copying
issued by the Copyright Licensing Agency, 90 Tottenham Court
Road, London W1P 9HE.

Any person who does any unauthorised act in relation to
this publication may be liable to criminal prosecution and
civil claims for damages.

First published 1994 by
MACMILLAN PRESS LTD
Houndmills, Basingstoke, Hampshire RG21 2XS
and London
Companies and representatives
throughout the world

ISBN 0–333–56746–3
ISBN 0–333–56747–1

A catalogue record for this book is available
from the British Library.

10   9   8   7   6   5   4   3
03   02   01   00   99   98   97

Edited and typeset by Povey–Edmondson
Okehampton and Rochdale, England

Printed in Hong Kong

# Contents

# List of Tables

# List of Abbreviations

| | |
|---|---|
| BIC | Business in the Community |
| BUD | British Urban Development |
| CAT | City Action Team |
| CBI | Confederation of British Industry |
| CCP | Comprehensive Community Programme |
| CDP | Community Development Project |
| CPS | Centre for Policy Studies |
| CURDS | (Newcastle) Centre for Urban and Regional Development Studies |
| DES | Department of Education and Science |
| DHSS | Department of Health and Social Security |
| DLO | Direct Labour Organisation |
| DoE | Department of Employment |
| DoI | Department of Industry |
| DTI | Department of Trade and Industry |
| EC | European Community |
| ECU | European Currency Unit |
| ERDF | European Regional Development Fund |
| ESF | European Social Fund |
| EZ | Enterprise Zone |
| FIG | Financial Institutions Group |
| FP | Free Port |
| GLC | Greater London Council |
| GDO | General Development Order |
| GEAR | Glasgow Eastern Area Renewal Project |
| GLEB | Greater London Enterprise Board |
| HAT | Housing Action Trust |
| HCPAC | House of Commons Public Accounts Committee |
| HMCE | Her Majesty's Customs and Excise |
| HMSO | Her Majesty's Stationery Office |
| IAS | Inner Area Studies |
| IEA | Institute for Economic Affairs |
| IMF | International Monetary Fund |
| IRC | Industrial Reorganisation Commmittee |

| LDCC | London Docklands Development Corporation |
| LEB | Local Enterprise Board |
| LGPLA | Local Government, Planning and Land Act |
| LLMA | Local Labour Market Area |
| LRG | London Regeneration Consortium |
| MDC | Merseyside Development Corporation |
| MHLG | Ministry of Housing and Local Government |
| MoD | Ministry of Defence |
| MSC | Manpower Services Commission |
| NEB | National Enterprise Board |
| NF | National Front |
| NAO | National Audit Office |
| OPCS | Office of Population Censuses and Surveys |
| RDG | Regional Development Grant |
| RSG | Rate Support Grant |
| SDA | Scottish Development Agency |
| SDO | Special Development Orders |
| SPZ | Simplified Planning Zone |
| TEC | Training and Enterprise Council |
| TVEI | Training and Vocational Education Initiative |
| UDC | Urban Development Corporations |
| UDP | Unitary Development Plan |
| UP | Urban Programme |
| URA | Urban Regeneration Agency |
| WMEB | West Midlands Enterprise Board |

# Guide to Reading the Book

Britain today is a predominantly urban society; the majority of the population living or working in cities. These cities are continually changing and adapting in the face of economic pressures; at times they prosper, and at other times they decay. 'Urban policy' is centrally involved in these changes. It seeks to foster prosperity or, more often, to bring about a return to prosperity and moderate the impact of decay. It is inevitably contentious. For some commentators it is inadequate, for others it constitutes unwarranted interference by government. Local government has not always wanted the same from urban policy as central government. We can even question whether or not there is actually such a thing as urban policy; whether it is 'urban'; and whether it is a 'policy'. These conflicts and debates form the subject matter of this book.

The book focuses on the development and evolution of British urban policy since 1945. Its central theme, and one which distinguishes it from others on a similar theme, is a focus on the growing importance of the private sector in the framing and practice of urban policy. When, after the 1987 United Kingdom general election, the then Prime Minister, Margaret Thatcher, announced that her Government was to give specific attention to the inner cities, the result, *Action for Cities*, favoured an approach in which the economic fortunes of urban areas were to be revived by the private sector; the market rather than state planning was to be the key instrument. This represented the culmination of a trend evident for over a decade and traceable throughout the period since 1945.

The structure of the book is straightforward. The first chapter considers the concept of urban policy. It begins with a discussion of the nature of 'the urban'. It then outlines key theoretical perspectives concerning policy, describing pluralist, New Right and Marxist analyses. Finally, it sets out a framework for policy analysis. The two latter sections provide reference points to which subsequent chapters return.

The following three chapters provide a chronological analysis of urban initiatives in the period prior to 1979. Chapter 2 considers the physical approach to urban problems evident throughout the 1950s and 1960s. It notes the changing fortunes of the private and public sectors through the period and the relative lack of coherence regarding approaches to urban problems. Chapter 3 assesses the emergent urban initiatives of the late 1960s and the conflict between area-based and structurally-based approaches to urban decay. Chapter 4 reviews the milestone 1977 White Paper, *Policy for the Inner Cities*, in the context of contemporary politics. Although these chapters stand on their own as statements about pre-1979 urban initiatives, the reader requiring a full understanding of the periods to which they refer will need to refer also to Chapters 8, 9 and 10, where contextual material concerning town and country planning, local government and race is covered.

The core of the book comprises three chapters on the post-1979 period. In Chapter 5 we consider the extent to which New Right theoretical positions underpinned the actions of the post-1979 Conservatives and examine the application of these principles to the subject of urban regeneration. Chapters 6 and 7 make an admittedly crude but convenient distinction between the initiatives which were inherited by the post-1979 Conservatives, and those which they created themselves; the distinction is not complete, nor is it always clear, but it does allow us to break up what would otherwise be a very long chapter indeed. Chapter 6 considers the inheritance and the ways in which the Conservatives reframed and restructured existing approaches to urban problems. Chapter 7 focuses on the initiatives which were originated after 1979 and presents an overall assessment of post-1979 Conservative urban policy.

Three further chapters present the material referred to above on thematic topics related to urban regeneration. Much day-to-day urban policy is effectively carried out through the town and county planning system. Chapter 8 considers the gradual marketisation of that system and its realignment with private-sector needs. Chapter 9 focuses on the role of local government in addressing urban problems and examines central–local conflicts. As we shall see in Chapters 2 and 3, the presence of minority ethnic groups in inner city areas was intimately associated with the emergence of early urban initiatives; in Chapter 10 we review the extent to which urban policy has been and continues to be a 'race issue'.

Chapter 11 concludes the book. It provides an overview of British urban policy using the framework for policy analysis set out in Chapter 1 and addresses the subject of the overall coherence of urban policy. It also speculates briefly on the likely future of urban policy in the context of continuing economic crisis and confusion over Britain's ties with the European Community.

In writing this text we have drawn on our experiences of teaching urban policy to undergraduates and postgraduates in social policy, politics, sociology and geography. Our own backgrounds span these disciplines and, in our experience, there is a considerable amount of common ground in the material which they cover. We have accordingly sought to integrate perspectives across these disciplines in the firm belief that a full understanding of urban policy requires an analysis of its socioeconomic, sociopolitical and spatial contexts. We would anticipate a readership drawn from courses at both undergraduate and postgraduate levels.

The academic debts which we have incurred in the preparation of this text have, of course, been considerable. We would like to thank first the many students on whom we have tried out ideas over the past ten years. Second we wish to acknowledge the help, encouragement and assistance of Stephen Savage and Steven Kennedy. Finally, we dedicate this book to our parents and to Liz, Tomáš and Laura with thanks for their forbearance, support and love.

ROB ATKINSON
GRAHAM MOON

# 1   Analysing Urban Policy

In this first chapter we shall address some necessary preliminaries to the study of urban policy. We shall:

- Consider the term *urban*. An understanding of the meanings associated with this ill-defined term are essential in the study of a field labelled 'urban policy'.
- Outline three distinct *analytical traditions*: pluralist, Marxist and New Right. These approaches, and their subvariants, provide concepts which allow real-world urban policies to be analysed and evaluated.
- Propose a framework for *policy evaluation*; this will provide the basis for subsequent chapters focused on the assessment of specific urban policies.

## The urban

We all think we know what urban areas are and what their existence entails. They are extensively built-up concentrations of population and employment which have usually developed over a considerable period of time. They will often have both manufacturing industry and office-based employment and will undoubtedly have substantial shopping provision. They may well be a seat of government or administration. Areas of cities, or even whole cities, may be characterised as run-down, decayed or depressed. These areas are the battlegrounds on which debates about how to address 'urban problems' are played out.

Despite this popular understanding, the precise meaning of the term 'urban' has been a continued and increasingly esoteric concern within the social sciences for many years. For some social scientists the term has simply been an unproblematic taken-for-granted prefix denoting a specialist area of study, such as 'urban politics' or 'urban geography', focused on cities or towns. For others the term is redundant; the UK is so overwhelmingly urbanised that it is no

1

longer appropriate or possible to distinguish distinct urban areas (Castells, 1977). Between these two extremes lie two definitional traditions: empirical and theoretical. The two have often overlapped and have increasingly converged.

*Empirical approaches*

Pinch (1985) proposes three criteria for distinguishing urban areas: *physical, administrative* and *functional* definitions. Each has as its objective the identification of the geographical boundary of an urban area: the demarcation of an area on a map. Various empirical, measurable indicators are used to achieve this goal; some of greater and others of lesser sophistication.

Physical definitions of urban areas involve the identification of continuously built-up areas of residential, industrial or service-use land. Such definitions are straightforward on a superficial level but surprisingly complex in practice. The terms 'continuous' and 'land' require firm explication. In the National Land Use Classification, for example, urban land consists of permanent structures and their surrounding 'grounds', transport corridors and associated features, industrial and other works, and the areas surrounded by these land uses. The 1981 Census took this simple definition and, with the aid of Ordnance Survey maps, identified urban areas in Britain which comprised continuous areas of over 20 hectares, at least four coterminous census enumeration districts, and a minimum population threshold of 1000 people. Similar approaches emphasising non-agricultural land uses and population thresholds have been used in other countries. The OPCS analysis (Office of Population Censuses and Surveys 1984) revealed 2231 urban areas in Britain, of which 302 had populations in excess of 20 000. It also confirmed that the population of England and Wales is concentrated in urban areas: 25 per cent of the population lived in four areas, each with over one million residents, and 52.4 per cent lived in the sixty areas, each with populations greater than 100 000.

Administrative definitions of urban areas rest upon the identification of a local government area as being, in some sense, urban. In the simplest of cases this may relate merely to the name given to an area. For example, prior to the 1972 reorganisation of local government in England and Wales (Dearlove, 1979), most of the largest cities and towns had special powers and were designated *county boroughs*; smaller towns were labelled *urban districts*, and other areas were *rural districts*. A similar division was possible in Scotland using 'counties of cities' and large and small *burghs*. These titles provided a convenient way of identifying urban areas, indeed empirical studies exploring the countervailing concept of 'rurality' often excluded such areas from their analysis (e.g. Cloke, 1977). After 1974, when the local government reforms came into effect, these simple distinctions were no longer possible although many local authorities retained titles with urban resonances such as city, town or borough, and certain authorities were specifically identified as being 'metropolitan' – another urban epithet.

Urbanisation processes were one factor which caused the abolition of the pre-1972 system of local government. Increasingly, the old urban and rural designations ceased to have any real meaning as people commuted to urban areas from wider and wider regions. Such commuting patterns are central to the third geographical approach to the identification of urban areas: functional definitions. These embody two concepts. First, taking it for granted that paid work in much of modern Britain is centred on urban areas, it is possible to identify functional areas within which the broad focus of commuting is towards a common core or set of cores. Second, attention may focus on the quantity and quality of services and employment opportunities underlying the attractiveness of a particular settlement and, in part, determining its position in the urban hierarchy. Crudely, urban settlements are characterised both by more functions and by particular functions: perhaps the most deeply-rooted basis to popular attempts to define functional urban areas has been the possession of a cathedral or a weekly market, the key characteristic that distinguishes a city or town from a less important settlement.

Functional regions, the fields of influence of urban settlements, are not a new research area. The Redcliffe–Maud Report (Redcliffe–Maud, 1969) based its recommendation that British local government should be reorganised on a city-region basis on the concept of the functional region. The standard metropolitan statistical area in the USA embodies similar ideas and, in 1980, comprised urban settlements with a population of over 50 000, the county surrounding that settlement and adjacent counties with over 75 per cent non-agricultural land use, and clear commuting links with the central city. Recent work on functional regions in Britain has been dominated by the work of the Newcastle Centre for Urban and Regional Development Studies (CURDS) (Chamption *et al.*, 1987, ch. 7). Working originally with the British 1971 Census and subsequently with the 1981 Census, the CURDS team identified 280 functional regions or local labour market areas (LLMAs) in Britain. A classification of these areas according to regional location, hierarchical status, urban size and employment structure identifies just 52 LLMAs which are essentially rural (Table 1.1). The remainder are functional urban regions, of which 20 dominate metropolitan areas (which also include subdominant LLMAs).

TABLE 1.1   The CURDS classification of local labour market areas

| Class | No. of LLMAs |
| --- | --- |
| **Metropolitan** | |
| *Dominant* | |
| London | 1 |
| Conurbation | 5 |
| Provincial | 5 |
| Subregional | 9 |
| | |
| *Subdominant* | |
| London cities | 7 |
| London towns | 23 |
| Conurbation cities | 13 |
| Conurbation towns | 22 |
| Small northern | 24 |
| | |
| **Freestanding** | |
| Southern cities | 12 |
| Northern cities | 13 |
| Southern service towns | 22 |
| Northern service towns | 12 |
| Southern commercial towns | 14 |
| Northern commercial towns | 19 |
| Southern manufacturing towns | 13 |
| Northern manufacturing towns | 14 |
| | |
| **Rural** | |
| South | 19 |
| North | 33 |

Freestanding LLMAs are also identified; these comprise the town and city regions away from the major conurbations. Clearly the functional approach is not without problems. It uses the labour market as its spatial base, defining it in terms of commuting patterns; other bases would produce different results. It is essentially static in that it depends on data collected at ten-yearly intervals and thus fixes notions of urbanisation rather than seeking to capture the dynamic process of urban change. Nevertheless, the concept of a substantially urbanised Britain is largely confirmed by functional definitions.

*Sociological approaches*

If it is difficult to identify just where urban areas begin or end, then it is even harder to identify the sociological meaning which we attach to 'the urban'. Short (1984) distinguishes two historic perspectives: a *positive* and a *negative* image. In the former case, urban places are perceived as liberating, open, tolerant settings in which dynamism thrives and potential is limitless. Such an image has profound resonances with popular conceptions of the booming London of the mid-1980s. In contradistinction, negative images are those portrayed in the engravings of Doré or cautionary Victorian tales; urban settlements are corrupt and evil, with the teeming urban masses being a threat to social order.

The rooting of these images in social theory has been extensively reviewed by Saunders (1981) and Smith (1979). The former focuses particularly on the founders of sociological theory, noting the role of 'the urban' in the development of industrial capitalism. Smith, in contrast, concentrates more on sociocultural theories such as Wirth's notion of urbanism (Wirth, 1938) in which urban life was seen as transitory, socially disorganised and lacking a sense of community as a consequence of the complexity of urban labour divisions and social organisation. A central aspect of Wirth's work was a concern to identify the distinctive essence of the city. His ideas, which carry echoes of Short's historic urban images, underpin the notion of the *rural–urban continuum* which contrasts stable, integrated, homogeneous rural societies with mobile, disorganised cities with their greater population size and density (Pahl, 1966).

This perspective has been found wanting in recent work in urban studies; simple characterisations of metropolitan or rural life have been rejected. Instead contemporary sociological analyses now pursue a somewhat different trajectory. The neo-Marxist tradition of the late 1970s and early 1980s argued that, with the development of industrial capitalism, it had become inappropriate to distinguish the urban from the rural. Western society, dominated by industrial enterprises focused on urban centres, had become overwhelmingly urban in its socioeconomic organisation (Saunders, 1985). The social relations in this society could no longer be meaningfuly separated into 'urban' or 'rural'. If the urban did have a role in Western society it was as a locus for the organisation of *collective consumption*: the provision of otherwise uneconomic services by the state in its efforts to secure the reproduction of the labour power of concentrated populations (Castells, 1977). Only in non-Western societies, characterised by a developing rather than a developed industrial capitalism, could a rational distinction continue to be drawn between the urban and the rural.

This perspective of a unified urban society has continued to dominate sociological thinking regarding the possibility of defining the urban. The perspective has, however, been modified. The completely 'non-spatial urban sociology' has now been rejected. In its place has come a recognition of the importance of geography in structuring the nature and experience of urban life. Perspectives as diverse as Harvey's geographically aware neo-Marxism and Giddens' concept of *locale* (Harvey, 1989a; Giddens, 1984) have stressed the extent to which processes taking place in urban settings act together in such a way that the whole exceeds the sum of the parts. Thus, for example, although there may be consensus on a macro level that Western society is overwhelmingly urban, there is also a realisation that, in specific geographical settings within that society, there are distinctive articulations of socioeconomic processes, some of which are 'urban' in the traditional, popularly understood sense of the word.

*Synthesis*

Geographical and sociological attempts to isolate the meaning of the term 'urban' have come to three broad conclusions:

- It is impossible to draw a line round an area on a map and call it urban. The most sophisticated geographical approach, the

functional area perspective, indicates that cities' spheres of influence extend far into their surrounding countryside.
- The processes which led to the creation of urban areas, the requirements of nineteenth century industrial capitalism, are now universal in Western society, with the result that the existence of a predominantly urbanised society can be proposed at a theoretical level and confirmed at an empirical level.
- There remain locality-specific manifestations of social and economic relations in particular parts of the urban system.

It is this third area which has provided the focus for urban policy. Policies have been developed for the inner city, for the urban fringe, for depressed regions and so on; for fragments of the broader urban system. The crux of the sociological perspective, however, is that, although there may indeed be such areas, an understanding of them can only be achieved by considering both their local setting and their regional, national and international structural context. The failure to do this, as we shall see, has been a criticism levelled at much of British urban policy as it has evolved measures restricted to administrative empirical definitions of urban, promoted almost nineteenth-century notions of the city as the fount of progressive enterprise, and generally failed to link local and structural processes.

## Theoretical approaches

There are a multitude of theories available to us in our attempt to understand the way in which policy has evolved in Britain. In this section we will focus on three general approaches to the study of policy. We provide an introduction to the basic ideas of each with the objective of outlining competing theoretical attempts to account for the forms which policy, specifically urban policy, has taken.

### Pluralism

Pluralism in its classic post-war form emerged in the United States during the 1950s and was particularly closely identified with the work of Robert Dahl, who has remained central to its evolution down to the present day (Dahl, 1961, 1982). In the context of the 1950s, pluralism represented an attempt to theorise and explain the nature of Western liberal democracies at the height of the Cold War. Pluralism, at least in part, served the function of distinguishing free Western societies from the totalitarian colossus of the USSR and its Eastern European satraps.

The central contention of pluralism in its many guises was that there were no overwhelming concentrations of power in liberal democratic societies; power was widely dispersed and no one won or lost all of the time. The existence of regular and frequent democratic elections was one key mechanism which allowed *participation* by the population, held governments to account and kept them in check. Furthermore, the multiplicity of competing *pressure groups* ensured that at all times every citizen had access to the means to express his/her views and to campaign for or against changes. For every pressure group advocating a particular view there was an opposing group counterbalancing its views (e.g. trade unions and business groups). Power was thus dispersed rather than concentrated.

In 1950s pluralism the state acted as a neutral umpire or weathervane reflecting the preferences of citizens. It had no interests of its own, it merely pursued the interests of its citizens. The notion of *intensity of preference* meant that no one group would ever gain a position of complete dominance. Instead, groups would compete with one another, with each group exhibiting a different level of intensity of preference on each issue. In this 'pluralist heaven' nobody would lose all of the time and nobody would win all of the time. Power, and by extension, resources, should be evenly distributed throughout society.

This basic pluralism came under severe pressure, first of all from élite theorists such as Mills (1956), then from theorists such as Bachrach and Baratz (1963) and, more recently, from Marxists (Manley, 1983). Clegg (1989) provides details of these debates. The *élite theorists* argued that power was highly concentrated, with society being divided into, and dominated by, three key sectors: the military, the economy and the political. The massive growth in these sectors during the twentieth century had produced a corresponding growth in the scale and power of their organisations. As a result, those individuals who occupied key organisational positions at the apex of each sector formed powerful élites which were interlinked through a series of personal and social ties as well as the desire to maintain their own power. According to Mills (1956) this *power élite* took the key decisions which determined the nature and shape of society. They determined the context in which everything else occurred. Mills was prepared to acknowledge that pluralism, as described by Dahl, operated at what he called 'the middle levels of power', but only within this more general context. When taken with the arguments of Bachrach and Baratz (1963) that pluralism focused (wrongly) on a single observable 'face' of power and ignored non-decision-making and the 'mobilisation of bias', these arguments forced a theoretical rethink by pluralists. The events in US society at the time – the civil rights movement and the anti-Vietnam protests – further served to confirm that a large section of the USA population was systematically and permanently excluded from access to power and decision-making (Dunleavy, 1977).

Out of these debates emerged what has been variously referred to as *neo-pluralism* (Dunleavy, 1981a) and *pluralism II* (Manley, 1983). It was accepted that the 'pluralist heaven' no longer existed, if it ever did, and that access to power was limited. However, neo-pluralists would not accept that there was a single power élite or a ruling class. Power might be concentrated in the hands of a relatively small number of groups and individuals, but those groups and individuals were in competition with one another, thus preventing any total concentration of power (Dahl, 1982). These élite groups were also open to entry by any individual. It was accepted that the state was not, or no longer, a neutral umpire; that it had interests of its own; and that it was systematically biased in favour of capital (Lindblom, 1977). This did not mean it was simply a tool of any single group, whether a power élite or ruling class. Not only was there competition between groups to influence the state but there was also competition between groups within the state. The rise of experts, professionals, departments, state and local governments, and other interests within the state meant that it too contained within its institutions and organisations a series of competing interests which, when articulated with those outside the state, preserved some measure of power dispersal. Added to all this must, of course, be the existence of democratic elections and a multi-party system which further ensured a degree of competition.

When applied to policy, the theories of classical pluralism suggest that every interest is counterbalanced by another and things change very slowly, if at all, in a step-by-step fashion. However, on the relatively rare occasions when pluralism has been applied to urban decision-making in the UK, the results have not been altogether encouraging. Power, decisions and outcomes have been found to reflect dominant social interests. Pluralism has rationalised this finding as the outcome of the democratic process in action, reflecting the changing needs, demands and choices of independent but interacting participants in the process, including city residents, developers, property speculators, industrial and service firms, central and local government and a host of associated pressure groups (Fagence, 1977; Saunders, 1974, 1978; Newton, 1976). Thus, for pluralists, urban change reflects:

- the interaction of a myriad of decisions by individuals and organisations;
- responses to changing conditions and new opportunities.

Urban policy, intended to control such change, has to be a matter of controls and incentives designed to appeal to the interests of involved agencies and individuals.

*Marxism*

Unlike pluralism, which has served as both an explanation and justification of Western liberal democracies, Marxism has been concerned to provide an explanation, critique and alternative to such systems. Essentially it argued that all societies are divided into classes which inevitably enter into conflict with one another over the ownership of the means of production and the allocation and ownership of what is produced. In capitalist societies, the fundamental class struggle is between the *bourgeoisie* and the *proletariat*. The former own the means of production, which we can equate with capital, and constantly strive to maintain their position in society through the subordination of the proletariat or working class. The latter is constantly struggling to throw-off capital's domination. In this scenario the state is not viewed as being in any way neutral, in fact it is viewed as 'a committee for managing the common affairs of the whole bourgeoisie' (Marx and Engels, 1968, p. 37).

For Marxists all conflicts within capitalist societies are *ultimately* reducible to class conflicts although more recently they have been prepared to acknowledge that the class structure of capitalist societies is more complex than Marx and Engels suggested (Poulantzas, 1975): not all social conflicts are *immediately* reducible to class conflicts; issues such as gender, race, space and the *role of the state* have been increasingly recognised as valid but super-structural determinants of social conflicts. The debate between Miliband and Poultanzas (Miliband, 1970, 1973; Poulantzas, 1969, 1973) rejected the simplistic view that the state was simply an instrument of capital and merely existed to ensure its continued domination. The state, it was argued, was relatively autonomous; it had the ability to act with a degree of independence in order to guarantee the continued dominance of capitalist sociopolitical and economic relations. As such it opened up the way for Marxists to begin to consider the operations of state institutions and organisations (Smith, 1988; Ham and Hill, 1984, pp. 32–6) and their part in maintaining and expanding capital accumulation (Fine and Harris, 1979; Harvey, 1982).

When applied to an understanding of the city, Marxism has produced a range of interesting analyses. In particular, Marxist analyses have suggested:

- that urban decline has its roots in a wider economic decline;
- that the role of local government, particularly with regard to urban areas, needs to be understood in terms of the wider needs of capitalism (Cockburn, 1977; Duncan and Goodwin, 1988).

More generally Marxists have seen cities as playing an absolutely crucial role in the post-war expansion of capitalism (Castells, 1977; Pickvance, 1976; Harvey, 1978). These analyses have rarely been unproblematic; the role of urban areas has often been reduced to one of ensuring the continued reproduction of capitalism and the conditions essential for further capital accumulation. The analysis of the internal structure of cities was largely reduced to an assessment of such effects of economic forces as property speculation. Very little attention was given to political and social forces such as urban government, parties and pressure groups. It is in this latter area that Marxism has proved particularly weak, especially when it has sought to match its theoretical contentions to empirical evidence.

*The New Right*

Many of the key thinkers of the New Right advocated their ideas for a number of years without attracting serious attention. Friedrich von Hayek argued for a free market and minimal state in the 1930s and his seminal book, *The Road to Serfdom*, was published in 1944. Other theorists, such as Milton Friedman, James Buchanan and Gordon Tullock have been arguing for their particular brands of New Right theory since at least the early 1960s. However, the economic and social crises which beset Western societies from the late 1960s onwards created conditions favourable to the emergence of the New Right as a major and influential social and political force (Kavanagh, 1990, ch. 4). Its rise was intimately connected with its opposition to the social democratic consensus (the relatively peaceful coexistence of right- and left-wing political parties), to Keynesian demand-focused economics and to the interventionist welfare state (Cowling, 1990; King, 1987; Brittan, 1980; Bogdanor, 1983; Kavanagh, 1990, ch. 3).

In talking about the 'New Right' there is a great danger of providing it with a coherence which it does not possess. There are several distinct strands to the broad area of political thought which has come to be known by the label 'New Right'. In this book we will use the term as an 'umbrella category' covering market-oriented ideas which gained the political high ground during post-1979 Conservative governments. The perspective can be divided into two broad groups: neo-liberals and neo-conservatives. It is the former which we will largely be concerned with in this book, but the latter have also been influential in certain policy areas relevant to urban policy so will be given a brief consideration.

*Neo-liberalism*

Many of the themes, if not the substance, of neo-liberal thinking can be traced back to the classical political economists, in particular to Adam Smith. The neo-liberals place a great deal of emphasis on issues such as *freedom, choice, the free market, minimal state intervention* and the primacy of *the individual* (Joseph and Sumption, 1979). Green (1987) identifies four basic 'schools' of thought:

1.   The Austrian School, best represented by Hayek, and particularly concerned to identify and preserve the conditions conducive to the maximum amount of *individual liberty* and *personal choice*. In *The Road to Serfdom* Hayek argued that state intervention, collectivism and planning would produce a

totalitarian society. Capitalism, with minimal state intervention and a free market, was identified as the system most likely to create and encourage freedom – any situation in which a person has a choice, no matter how unpalatable that choice (Hayek, 1960). Capitalism will be of benefit to everyone, not only in terms of freedom, but also materially if wealth creators are allowed to operate unhindered (Hayek, 1960, ch. 1). Thus the perspective is *anti-egalitarian*. Furthermore, democracy is viewed with a degree of caution as it contains the ever-present danger that majorities will oppress minorities and that politicians will interfere on behalf of special interests. Hayek therefore proposes to limit the power of governments, suggesting that the market alone is an appropriate mechanism for registering consumer choice. Such an approach is sympathetic to 'supply-side economics', which aim to removing bottlenecks in the economy (such as restrictive practices in the capital and labour markets), to allow producers to supply consumer demands (Thompson, 1986).

2.    The Chicago School, best represented by Milton Friedman and '*monetarism*', and adopted, during the early 1980s, by the Conservative government. Monetarism argues that the money supply should expand in line with production. If it expands faster than production there will be 'too much money chasing too few goods' and the result will be inflation (Thompson, 1986). The Chicago School places an emphasis upon the *market* as the primary provider of goods and services, perhaps more so than the Austrians. It is hostile to almost any state provision and has a preference for provision by the private sector with a residual state empowering those on low incomes via negative income tax and/or vouchers. It too is anti-egalitarian.

3.    The Virginia School of Public Choice, sometimes referred to as simply the Public Choice School and best represented by Buchanan and Tullock (1965) who use neo-classical economics to explain the behaviour of politicians and bureaucrats. In essence, all individuals are assumed to behave as if they were rational utility maximisers. As a result, state services are provided in the interests of their providers, not their clients; politicians and bureaucrats aim to increase their power and security by expanding programmes and 'buying' votes to win elections. Thus, in competitive party democracies, there is an inherent tendency to expensive state 'overload' (King, 1975). The answer is, once again,

to return as much as possible to the market and, where this cannot be done, to introduce 'pseudo-market' disciplines and place *constitutional limitations* on the activities of politicians and bureaucrats. This School has been particularly influential *vis-à-vis* the reform of public service and its ideas have been introduced into the UK via the Institute of Economic Affairs who, in tandem with the Adam Smith Institute, were able to exercise some influence over the development of policy during the Thatcher administrations.

4.    The anarcho-capitalist school, perhaps best represented by Robert Nozick, although other key figures are Murray Rothbard and David Friedman. This is the most diverse of the four groupings. Given their particular emphasis upon *unrestrained freedom* and, in some cases (e.g. David Friedman), a total absence of a state and any general societal rules not agreed to and made by all individuals subject to them, their influence on governmental thinking has been minimal.

What is clear from the above is that there are three notions which are crucial to neo-liberalism: freedom/liberty, a limited or minimal state; and the free market. The first is the most important of the three, the other two being seen as essential to the existence and defence of freedom. Neo-liberal concepts of *freedom* mean the absence of coercion; the choice between a low paid and dangerous job or starvation still constitutes freedom of choice. For neo-liberals, state actions would be a threat to freedom, a coercion; they should be avoided at all costs. According to Hayek (1960: p. 12): 'The task of a policy of freedom must . . . be to minimize coercion or its harmful effects, even if it cannot eliminate it completely'. This leads to the notion of the *minimal state*. The state is seen as essential to the creation of a general environment in which individuals can exercise their freedom via the 'rule of law'. At the same time it is also the greatest threat to freedom. For Hayek (1944), the growth of collectivism threatens to undermine freedom and lead to 'serfdom'. Thus the role of the state must be limited and its actions strictly controlled and rendered compatible with a *free market* (Hayek, 1960, pp. 222–4; Friedman, 1962; ch. 2). According to Hayek and Friedman, the free market, and therefore capitalism, offers the best system for guaranteeing freedom because it is based upon individual choice, allows individuals to pursue their own self-interest and provides a mechanism for co-ordinating the needs of the millions of free, self-interested individuals who make up society. If the state interferes in this co-ordinating mechanism it risks not only encroaching upon individual freedom but also undermining society's key means of production and growth.

### Neo-conservatism

Neo-conservatives, it quickly becomes clear, are an even more diverse and less organised body than the neo-liberals (Cowling, 1990; Scruton, 1980). However, again, there are certain common themes. In particular there is an emphasis upon *authority*, *tradition*, *stability*, *order* and *morality*. Ironically, they do not see the problems of post-war societies as stemming from a lack of freedom but from 'too much freedom' (Worsthorne, 1988) and human imperfection (O'Gorman, 1986, p. 1). They perceive a breakdown of law and order, decline of morality and general disintegration afflicting modern society. Unlike the neo-liberals, they see solutions in collectivities and the duties of the individual towards the collectivity. Thus the greatest influence of neo-conservatives on government policy has been in areas such as 'family' policy, on which a leading neo-conservative, Ferdinand Mount, was an adviser to Mrs Thatcher (Mount, 1982). They have also been able to exercise some influence upon areas such as law and order and immigration control. This emphasis has clearly been on display at many Conservative Party Conferences since the 1960s.

It need hardly be said that there are considerable conflicts between neo-conservatives and neo-liberals, particularly over the issue of individual freedom and to a lesser extent over the role of the market and the state. However, they are united, in a general sense, by their anti-egalitarianism and opposition to the welfare state. Indeed, neo-conservatives will accept that the state's role and public expenditure should be considerably reduced, that people should become more self-reliant, and that any state services should be selective (i.e. means tested) rather than universal (Marsland, 1988). This basis for a temporary alliance manifested itself, in the 1980s, in what has been termed *Thatcherism*. This combination of neo-liberalism and neo-conservatism, presented in a populist manner and constrained by the exigencies of a competitive party system, a liberal democracy and pre-existing institutions, organisations and social and political forces, was riddled with contradictions (e.g. between freedom and authority), potentially and inherently unstable, yet able, with its amorphous character, to shift ground quite effortlessly.

Thatcherism, if indeed it can be said to exist at all, has generated a great deal of debate. Arguments have ranged from seeing it as a coherent set of ideas, beliefs and policies (Hall and Jacques, 1983) to suggestions that it lacks any coherence at all (Riddell, 1983; Keegan, 1984). For us, neither extreme is correct. Thatcherism may lack the coherence of other '-isms' but it played a key role in setting the policy agenda from the mid-1970s onwards. Even after Mrs Thatcher's personal political demise, it continued to define many basic boundaries of political and social debate in Britain.

*New Right urban policy*

The main urban policy proposals emerging from the New Right have focused on a general reduction of state intervention, privatisation, contracting-out and the facilitation of free-market enterprise and the entrepreneurial spirit. Specific attention has been levelled at two areas:

- Local government has been generally criticised for interfering in the market. It has been suggested that it should greatly reduce its role as a service provider and become an *enabler* or *facilitator* (Ridley, 1988).
- More direct criticism has centred on the planning system. It has been suggested that it should be largely dismantled in order that 'the market' might operate unhindered with the private sector determining the pace and nature of urban change (Brindley *et al.*, 1989; Thornley, 1991).

By allowing markets to operate freely, New Right urban policy claims everyone will benefit in the long run through the *trickle-down effect*, the gradual percolation of economic benefits throughout society (Hayek, 1960). Firms may choose to leave urban areas initially but, as they find costs rising elsewhere and falling within cities, they will move back. Over time any unevenness will be eradicated by the natural ebb and flow of the market. Strictly speaking, any formal regional or urban policy would be anathema.

## A framework for urban policy analysis

The final task which we have set ourselves in this introductory chapter is to provide a consistent basis for the assessment of urban policies. The criteria which we will employ are not exclusive to the assessment of urban policy; indeed, we recognise that they are equally applicable to other areas of public policy. Our approach recognises that what constitutes a 'policy' is by no means straightforward (Barrett and Fudge, 1981). Indeed, we suggest that policy is an analytical construct conceived by researchers rather than something necessarily recognisable by policy-makers (Heclo, 1972). Furthermore, following Barrett and Fudge (1981), we reject the artificial separation of policy formulation and policy implementation with its attendant assumption that policy is formulated by central government and implemented by local authorities. Policy is a complex and ambiguous phenomenon. Given these arguments, we will base our approach on the following interlocking questions:

### 1. What is the problem-focus of the urban policy?

It is generally accepted that, for the last fifteen or so years, urban policy has been concerned with urban decline. For much of the period between 1945 and 1977 there was little awareness of such a decline; indeed, attention was focused on the planned decentralisation of jobs, industry and population away from urban areas. This raises the issue of how something becomes defined as a 'problem' and then gets on the policy agenda (Edelman, 1977; Heclo, 1972).

### 2. How is the problem-focus to be explained?

By this we mean the identification and understanding of the causal mechanisms which produce a problem. The concept of 'deindustrialisation' (Martin and Rowthorn, 1986) could be employed to explain Britain's industrial decline on a general level, serving as a starting point for understanding urban economic decline. At a somewhat more specific level, the notion of an urban–rural shift (Keeble, 1980; Fothergill and Gudgin, 1982) could be employed to help explain the loss of jobs and industry in British cities since the 1950s. Finally each city would need to be placed in the context of its locality (Cooke, 1989; Harloe *et al.*, 1990). The recognition that the causes of a problem are multiple also involves the acknowledgement that analysis, and action, must proceed at a variety of levels: international, national, regional and local. This requires the development, and co-ordination, of strategies which address a problem in its full complexity.

### 3.   What is the aim of the policy?

This should be defined clearly if a consistent and coherent policy is to be developed. In a general sense it can be argued that current, Conservative, urban policy aims to reverse urban decline but also that the government has a variety of other objectives including economic regeneration, territorial crisis management, reducing the powers of Labour-controlled urban local authorities and facilitating a social restructuring which will create Conservative electoral majorities in inner city areas. These latter objectives may not be stated overtly and the analyst may need to infer their existence; nor are they necessarily mutually consistent.

### 4.   How is the aim to be achieved?

The means by which urban policies might achieve their aims are legion. A coherent policy should offer a clearly defined, goal-focused set of measures: for example grants, concessions or prohibitions, constituting identifiable policy outputs.

### 5.   How is the policy to be resourced?

If a problem is to be tackled in a serious and genuine manner, policies must have adequate inputs. Proper resourcing, primarily of a financial nature, does not have to come only from the public sector; it may also come from the private and voluntary sectors. What is crucial is that it is definitely available for deployment.

### 6.   How will the policy be managed?

Given the multi-causal nature of most urban problems, action will require the co-operation of several Whitehall departments as well as co-operation between central and local government and between public and private sectors. Thus there must be adequate arrangements to ensure that not only do these various bodies co-operate over urban policy, but also that other policies which they may be pursuing do not conflict with it. Furthermore, the bodies involved must also develop organisational structures which are equal to the problem and capable of managing policy implementation.

### 7. Does the policy have political support?
Without political will, all the declarations of good intent by a government will be worthless. In a sense political will is the *sine qua non* of the whole process under discussion. Without it, and its maintenance, there is no likelihood of a problem being tackled successfully. Because something becomes defined as a problem and then appears on the policy agenda it does not necessarily mean that the government intends to take serious action to deal with the problem. This issue – '*symbolism*' (Edelman, 1977) – means that we should not accept at face value government claims regarding a policy (Heclo, 1972; Barrett and Fudge, 1981).

### 8. Is there an adequate legislative basis?
Sufficient legislative mechanisms should be available to allow the policy to have a chance of success. These may take the form of a particular Act, or series of Acts, or the amendment of existing legislation to give participating agencies powers adequate to the pursuance of the policy and to ensure that legal impediments to action are minimised. Such powers and legislation should effectively facilitate the efficient delivery of policy outputs.

### 9. What are the measures for monitoring?
Monitoring and evaluation procedures should be integral to an effective policy, ensuring that it is actually achieving its aims and objectives. Perhaps more controversially, but importantly in the light of New Right concerns for consumer choice, this process should also provide mechanisms whereby the needs and views of those affected by a policy can be fed into the policy process.

Beyond these basic questions of policy analysis we come to the issue of policy outcomes. Most policies, including urban ones, involve the taking of decisions which will often lead to the allocation of resources and will have both direct and indirect effects or outcomes. For instance, a decision to rezone land from agricultural to housing use to satisfy development pressures in the urban fringe will have the obvious effect of greatly increasing the value of the land to the landowner. It will also provide new housing for those who can afford it and possibly release housing elsewhere for others. But land and amenity values of those living in or near the rezoned areas will be affected and new demands placed on services. There will be winners and losers. Thus the question 'who benefits?' must be added to our list. This question cannot simply be answered by examining the direct effects of a policy, nor will the outcomes necessarily be unambiguous. Furthermore, although up to this point we have largely focused on the impact of policy on individuals, one of the perspectives which will be developed in this book is the notion that policies frequently have predictable effects on particular social groups. By this we mean that the winners and losers are largely determined by class, race and gender.

**Conclusion**

In this chapter we have considered three basic themes: what we mean by the word 'urban', what we mean by the term 'policy', and the approach which we will use to examine 'urban policy'. We have confronted an extensive literature and provided an inevitably somewhat superficial summary of three major areas of social scientific enquiry. Despite this shortcoming a number of key themes have been identified. First, in a strict sense, there is little logic in talking about a specifically urban policy as the object of such policy is, at least in Western society, a chaotic conception. Second, if any clear message emerges from either the research on the definition of the urban or from the different policy models, it is that the root of urban problems lies in the operation of the capitalist economy. It follows that urban policy measures designed to alleviate such problems will, with due regard to a particular policy model, seek to curtail or facilitate that capitalist economy. In the chapters that follow we will employ the frameworks set out in the preceding sections to investigate the changing policy models underlying British urban policy.

# 2 Post-War Urban Problems and the Rediscovery of Urban Poverty

This chapter considers the period from 1945 to the mid-1960s and sets out the background from which a coherent British urban policy began to emerge in the late 1960s. Prior to this time urban issues were conceptualised and tackled in a very different manner; urban policy as defined in Chapter 1 and discussed in later chapters did not exist in a form which would be recognised today. Urban problems were largely seen in *physical* terms. They were to be tackled by the redevelopment of the city and by the dispersal of urban problems through the creation of new towns and the fostering of regional policy.

This chapter covers:

- The physical approach to urban problems: housing supply and quality, urban growth and industrial change.
- The sociopolitical challenges to this approach and its assumptions: the re-emergence of urban poverty as a policy theme in the mid-1960s, social pathology and area-based policies, issues of racial difference and tension, and the Kennedy–Johnson urban policy measures in the United States of America and their alleged galvanising effect on British policy.
- An assessment of the theoretical basis and policy coherence of the approaches pursued during the period.
- The immediate determinants of the emergence of co-ordinated, specifically urban initiatives in the later 1960s.

## The physical approach to urban problems

Following the Second World War, Britain faced a multitude of economic, social and political problems. The costs of victory had

21

been high, not only in terms of lives lost, but also in economic and physical terms. In 1945 the economy of the United Kingdom was in tatters (Morgan, 1985) and the fabric of its major cities had suffered severe damage. Donnison (1967) estimated that 200 000 houses had been destroyed and over 500 000 rendered uninhabitable. There was clearly a need to rebuild both the economy and the cities.

At the same time there was also a desire to create a better post-war world in which the cities would be transformed and the conditions which had characterised the Depression of the inter-war period would be banished. A war-induced perception of the effectiveness of concerted collective action suggested that the achievement of this vision could be attained by *planning, co-operation* and *state involvement* making a return to the non-interventionist policies and politics of the 1930s impossible. Although wartime experience fostered this vision, it was also an acceleration of developments apparent in the 1930s, such as regional policy.

The resounding electoral success in 1945 of the Labour Party set the seal on these developments. The Labour government built upon the achievements and promises of the war to establish a universal 'welfare state', guarantee full employment and accept a greatly expanded and more interventionist role for government. Importantly, most Conservatives also accepted the legitimacy of these developments, although, as Gamble (1974, p. 64) has noted, their acceptance was based upon the assumption that this was a once-and-for-all reconstruction process, not the beginning of a new orthodoxy. Thus the scene was set for the thirty-year post-war consensus between the two main British political parties.

By the time of the 1950 election Labour politicians believed that, even if they had not yet completely conquered unemployment and want, they had at least put in place the political and policy machinery to overcome it. An important article of faith, articulated particularly well by Anthony Crosland in *The Future of Socialism* (1964), was the argument that *primary poverty* had been vanquished. As a consequence of this assumption, contemporary urban problems were seen as being *residual*, the result of largely physical causes: the nature of the housing stock, unconstrained urban growth, and industrial decline. We will examine each of these in turn.

*The housing stock*

The 1945 Labour Government inherited a housing problem characterised by two facets. First, there was not enough housing; rising birth-rates and changing social expectations ensured a housing shortage. Second, a significant proportion of the housing stock, particularly in urban areas, was in extremely poor condition. The Second World War had exacerbated these problems, but they were essentially the same as those facing pre-war policy-makers.

The pre-war policy tradition had been rooted in the 'sanitary approach' involving honourable but ineffective attempts to regulate overcrowding and amenities in an almost exclusively private sector housing market. The sanitary approach was predicated on the notion that poverty stemmed from poor housing and that the conditions in which the urban poor lived were a consequence of their housing and not of poverty. Initial efforts to encourage private landlords to improve the conditions of their properties were of limited effect and an alternative strategy of government involvement in housing construction developed in a piecemeal fashion, mainly during the inter-war years. The municipal housing constructed during this period was mainly built to address the housing shortage among the working classes; slum clearance: that is, the demolition of slums, only received coherent attention as late as the Housing Act, 1930.

In 1945, with cities devastated by war and with a Labour Government committed to collective solutions, the relatively recent concepts of clearance and the construction of municipal housing were of considerable influence. The solution to the housing condition problem was considered to be simple: demolish the old unsanitary or unstable dwellings and redevelop the sites with new housing under the ownership and management of local authorities. The solution to the housing shortage problem was similar: build new council homes on green-field sites.

*Housing shortage*
However, it was the housing shortage problem which claimed the lion's share of government attention in the years immediately after

the Second World War. For the first two years after the war attention was largely directed to the repair of war-damaged dwellings and the solution of the most pressing housing needs through the construction of temporary prefabricated houses – some of which were still in use forty-five years later. In 1947/8 however new building really began to take off. At first, over 80 per cent of these new houses were constructed by the public sector; indeed, 1952 and 1953 were the highpoints for municipal housing starts (McKay and Cox, 1979). Subsequently a closer balance evolved between the sectors and the reborn private (owner-occupied) sector ultimately accounted for a clear majority of the post-war growth in the United Kingdom housing stock.

The 1945 Labour government's continuation of wartime rent controls severely constricted the private rental sector which had dominated in the pre-Second World War inner city slums. Rent controls undermined the already precarious profitability of private-sector landlordism and any incentive to promote improved housing conditions disappeared. The housing condition problem began to grow and officially re-emerged with the Conservative's Housing Repairs and Rents Act, 1954, which reinstituted the earlier system of *slum clearance* and contributed considerably to the subsequent development of high-density inner city public sector housing estates constructed to rehouse displaced families (McKay and Cox, 1979).

### Housing quality

The assault on the housing condition problem through the medium of slum clearance continued throughout the 1950s. By the early 1960s, however, it was becoming increasingly clear that there was no accurate count of the number of slum properties in the UK. In assessing progress towards the target of clearance, central government relied almost completely on local authority estimates of the number of obsolescent dwellings. Frequently these were simply estimates of the number of houses which the authority believed they could afford to clear and replace within a reasonable period of time (Berry, 1974; Merrett, 1979). Whatever the reality, the housing condition problem was thought to be large and widespread. A continuing programme of clearance was required. The cost of this programme was enormous and, in emphasising the physical manifestations of poor housing conditions, the possibility was neglected that the appalling conditions under which large sections of the population were housed might have social causes.

In essence, physical approaches to housing issues addressed symptoms and not causes. Inherent in the approach was a belief that, simply by eradicating all the insanitary housing, a once-and-for-all solution could be achieved. There was, however, a gradual realisation during the 1950s that the housing condition problem was not disappearing and that, notwithstanding a cultural urge to 'modernise', there was a constant need to repair, renovate and replace the housing stock (Berry, 1974; Atkinson, 1989). Given the cost of the clearance programme and its increasingly apparent futility in the face of the persistence of poor housing, it was inevitable that the 'physical approach' would begin to be questioned. By the mid-1960s, as we shall discuss later in this and the following chapter, more emphasis began to be placed upon the cheaper alternative of (area) improvement (Merrett, 1979; Gibson and Langstaff, 1982; Atkinson, 1989) (see also Chapter 3).

*Urban growth*

The major British cities in 1945 were largely the product of the virtually unconstrained operation of nineteenth-century industrial capitalism. They had developed in a haphazard way, experiencing booms and slumps, over several centuries, and comprised a poorly-planned mixture of housing and industry. Despite an emerging and developing planning system (Rydin, 1993), inner city housing was often of very high density, and control on suburban development had been limited. In the period after 1945 the process of suburban expansion accelerated and threatened villages and countryside immediately adjacent to towns, providing the perfect context in which one shibboleth of pioneer planners could occur – the planned *dispersal* of urban populations.

Dispersal was, of course, a physical strategy. It was intended to have two consequences. First it would facilitate reduced population densities in inner cities, which could then be redeveloped at lower densities. Second, by encouraging movement to areas beyond the immediate proximity of cities, it would promote efforts to contain the urban environment and assist regional growth. It could also be allied to measures to improve the quality of the housing stock and increase the economic efficiency of the urban built environment. Two measures encapsulate the aspirations of the dispersal strategy: the development of land-use planning and the new towns policy.

*Land-use planning*

A desire to plan and design towns more rationally and to prevent urban sprawl was a key objective of the immediate post-Second World War period. In particular, the haphazard 'ribbon-development' which characterised the inter-war years was to be avoided. This objective was to be achieved by means of the Town and Country Planning Act, 1947 and associated legislation (Cherry, 1974; see also Chapter 8). The system set up by the 1947 Act allowed planning authorities to control the type of developments which could legally take place. The legislation worked through the twin tools of land use planning and development control.

Inherent in the land use planning legislation was a strong emphasis on the protection of the countryside. Measures were instituted which sought to preserve the character of rural areas surrounding Britain's towns and to stop almost all new development (Hall *et al.*, 1973). A key strategy was the *green belt*, an encircling cordon facilitating the containment of urban areas. In the green belt, agricultural land use would be the norm, along with a certain amount of recreation. The provisions of the 1947 Act enabled the London green belt identified in the 1944 Greater London Development plan to become a reality. At the same time a green belt around Glasgow was instituted and the policy was later adopted by several other major urban areas. Perhaps because of its preservationist flavour, the green belt was one of the few interventionist planning measures to find favour with the Conservative governments of the 1950s.

Scant consideration was given to the social and political aspects of the green belt system for urban containment. Somewhat inevitably it emerged that the groups who benefited most were the middle class residents of the green belt who found their environment protected against further incursions and their property prices greatly increased. Those who got least were the inner city working class populations whose areas were subject to slum clearance; the containment of the city by the green belt may have partially encouraged the shift to high-density high-rise redevelopment in the inner city. It certainly gave rise to cases where people and firms moving out of the city had no choice but to move a considerable distance from the city (Young and Willmott, 1962).

*New towns*
The dispersal of people and jobs to 'new towns' beyond the immediate proximity of cities may appear initially to be a very radical idea. However, it reflected a long-established anti-urban tradition and developed the ideas of the Garden City Movement which, from the late nineteenth century onwards, had exercised considerable influence over the development of town and country planning. These ideas, which saw planned decentralisation of population and industry to garden cities as the solution to problems of industrial and population over-concentration (Howard, 1946), were put into practice via developments at Welwyn and Letchworth and provided an influential input to the wartime Reith Report, which recommended a government-financed and -delivered programme of new town construction, and to the 1944 Greater London Plan, which proposed ten new towns as receptors for London overspill.

The New Towns Programme was formally initiated by the New Towns Act, 1946 (Thomas and Creswell, 1973; Cordon, 1977). Fourteen were built soon after 1947, generally around an existing village nucleus rather than on totally green-field sites (Table 2.1). Initial planned population sizes were between 25 000 and 80 000 and, in keeping with the ethos of reduced settlement density, an emphasis was placed on a dispersed urban design. Other factors given attention included the need for a balanced social mix and a self-generating and self-contained labour market. Control was vested in government-appointed *new town development corporations* with considerable powers to enable and finance development.

Following the defeat of the immediate post-war Labour administration, the nature of new towns changed. The Town Development Act, 1952, introduced the concept of the *expanded town* under which certain small town local authorities agreed to take people decanted from larger urban areas. The anti-interventionist Conservative governments of the 1950s designated only one actual genuine new town development, at Cumbernauld in central Scotland. In the 1960s, however, the policy was revitalised and, although elements of the aim of decentralisation were retained, regional development became a guiding force behind most designations. Furthermore,

**TABLE 2.1   First generation new towns**

| New Town | Date | 'Parent'/Function |
|---|---|---|
| Stevenage | 1946 | London/decentralisation |
| Crawley | 1947 | .. .. |
| Hemel Hempstead | 1947 | .. .. |
| Harlow | 1947 | .. .. |
| Newton Aycliffe | 1947 | County Durham/deindustrialisation |
| East Kilbride | 1947 | Glasgow/decentralisation |
| Hatfield | 1948 | London/decentralisation |
| Welwyn | 1948 | .. .. |
| Peterlee | 1948 | County Durham/deindustrialisation |
| Glenrothes | 1948 | Fife/deindustrialisation |
| Bracknell | 1949 | London/decentralisation |
| Basildon | 1949 | .. .. |
| Cwmbran | 1949 | South Wales/deindustrialisation |

higher densities and increased centralisation also became the norm. Towards the end of the period covered by this chapter the emphasis shifted still further: new towns at Northampton and Peterborough were grafted on to existing developments.

The major urban areas of Britain all undoubtedly lost population during the 1950s and 1960s (Drewett *et al.*, 1976). Although ultimately some two million people came to live in new towns (Blake, 1977), it is difficult assess the extent to which this fall in urban population was a result of the new towns programme or a consequence of broader processes of suburbanisation and counter-urbanisation which became more marked in the 1970s (see Chapter 3). Certainly, beyond the major conurbations, many cities continued to expand through the development of suburban housing estates. An evaluation of the new towns programme is, however, beyond the scope of this book.

New towns provide another clear example of a physical solution to urban growth; the social and economic causes of urban problems were not addressed and nor were the social consequences of new town development. The removal of a mainly young and working-class population from an inner city to a new town environment where retail, leisure and even, occasionally, work, opportunities were often developed rather later than housing had considerable impact on both receiver and sender communities; in particular, little attention was given by policy-makers to the social impact on inner cities (Young and Willmott, 1962; Cordon, 1977).

*Industrial change*

In 1945 Britain retained its traditional industrial geography. Steel was made in Sheffield, ships in Newcastle, pots in Stoke and cars in Coventry. The industrial geography which had developed with the Industrial Revolution and which had taken on the methods of mass production had evolved into a complex of regional and local specialisation (Massey, 1984). This geography had survived the world economic crisis of the 1930s and the Second World War, but only just; during the period covered by this chapter it would be fundamentally challenged. The evolution of the world capitalist economy would bring the first manifestations of the large scale *restructuring* of manufacturing industry which was to characterise the 1970s and 1980s. The period would also see the beginnings of the rise of the service sector. In this section we consider two issues related to this theme: urban transport planning and regional planning.

*Urban transport planning*
Although suburban industrial estates had been developed during the inter-war period, most industry in urban areas intermingled in a relatively unplanned fashion with residential, retail and office developments. In the immediate post-Second World War period of reconstruction this was of little importance. In the 1950s, however, it became clear that the rebirth of the economy required an effective transportation and distribution network; Britain's dilapidated cities were based on a network developed essentially for the horse. This was no longer effective at either moving people to and from work or leisure, or at moving goods to or from shops or factories.

Although car ownership quintupled during the period covered by this chapter, the road network received little attention until the early 1960s. By that time, Britain's cities were becoming increasingly congested. The Buchanan Report provided a much needed input of policy (Ministry of Transport, 1963). Central to the document was the promotion of a free flow of traffic. This was to be achieved by segregating pedestrians from road traffic through the use of pedestrian walkways and segregated pedestrian precincts, and the construction of urban motorways giving access to a national network. Three points can be made. First, the Buchanan proposals placed a heavy emphasis on private road transport; public transport and rail-based solutions were neglected. Second, pedestrian segregation created dead areas at night and motorway policies created physical barriers; the social geography of the city was altered. Finally, the creation of urban motorways gave further impetus to clearance policies. Properties were often scheduled for clearance years in advance of road construction, producing *planning blight*; in some cases, long-standing communities were destroyed (Grant, 1977). Urban transport planning, like other physical solutions to urban problems, was therefore undertaken with little consideration of its social impact, or indeed any realisation that, far from remedying existing traffic problems, the chosen solutions often merely encouraged even greater volumes of traffic.

*Regional planning*

One consequence of industrial specialisation was vulnerability to the swings of the market economy. In areas dominated by declining industries, this vulnerability could be catastrophic. The Second World War had shown that industry could be redistributed throughout the country, thus state intervention and some form of planning had gained a degree of legitimacy and it was this solution which was chosen as the strategy for addressing industrial decline.

Building upon the hesitant steps towards a form of regional policy begun in the 1930s (Parsons, 1986) and the recommendations of the 1940 Barlow Report (HMSO, 1940), attempts were made to redirect industry from the South East to the Northern regions, Scotland and Wales. This approach involved two strategies: incentives to encourage firms to locate in *development areas*, and regulations such as *Industrial Development Certificates* (and later *Office Development Permits*) to force businesses that wished to expanded to move out of southern cities (McCrone, 1973).

The links between regional policy and the type of land use planning described in the previous section were never developed. As Cherry (1974) noted 'planning was a matter of providing for orderly development, and a question of town design' (p. 109); broader considerations of industrial restructuring were not considered.

Indeed, the responsibility for land-use planning and industrial planning lay with different government departments which had their own priorities, bodies of knowledge and modes of operation. Co-ordination was rarely attempted. Furthermore, the effectiveness of the approach in terms of its ability to enforce recommendations was limited. As Morgan (1985) has noted, 'relations with private . . . industry . . . were not marked by anything that could coherently be described as planning . . . It had nothing that resembled the dirigiste economic strategy of de Gaulle's popular front government in France in 1945–6' (p. 30). The state never adopted a directive approach to industrial location; at best, attempts were made to influence the behaviour of firms.

Keeble (1976) has suggested that British regional policy had a significant effect on the relocation of industry; however, his views have been challenged by Massey (1984), who argues that changes in corporate organisation have been equally important in bringing about industrial decentralisation. Regional policy was therefore of questionable effectiveness in ameliorating the effects of uneven development within the British economy and did little to tackle and solve the causes of that unevenness (Parsons, 1986; Pickvance, 1981, 1986).

## Challenges to the physical approach

The physical approach may have seemed, at first, to be a comprehensive and coherent strategy to deal with the urban problems facing post-war Britain. In fact, it was nothing of the sort. At best, the initiatives described above represented a hotch-potch of well-intentioned but often contradictory legislation. At worst, they disguised the true nature and scale of problems and set in motion unforeseen and unwanted consequences. Most impor-tantly the social aspects of urban problems were largely ignored, and opportunities to develop a coherent approach to urban decay were missed.

Following on from the previous section, we will now turn to the challenges to the physical approach. These challenges essentially concern the 'rediscovery of urban poverty' and the strategies for its amelioration. We will consider the concept of social pathology, the 'area approach' to urban problems, the role of race in the genesis of urban policy, and the catalytic impact of United States' urban policy. First, however, we will re-examine the central tenet of the physical approach: that urban poverty had been eradicated.

### The abolition of primary poverty

As we noted at the start of this chapter, the prevailing consensus in the immediate post-Second World War era assumed that 'primary poverty' had largely been abolished by the achievement of full employment and the establishment of the welfare state. Crosland (1964, p. 59) asserted:

> Primary poverty has been largely eliminated; the 'Beveridge revolution' has been carried through; and Britain now boasts the widest range of social services in the world, and, as a result the appellation 'Welfare State'. It is true that considerable areas of social distress, not mainly due to primary poverty and of a character not always foreseen by pre-war socialists, still remain. But this is a new and different question. The historic objective has, in Britain, largely been attained; and the traditional means of universal, indiscriminate social services are in any case not always the most appropriate to the more subtle social problems which remain.

Full employment had played a major role in the eradication of primary poverty. The benefits of economic growth, which was assumed to be permanent, were thought to have 'trickled down' to almost all members of the population. As the economy grew, so living standards for all would steadily rise and everyone would gain access to the 'affluent society'. For those remaining areas of social distress, welfare state policies could be developed.

Social analyses conducted at the time reflect this rosy viewpoint. Social science in the 1950s was dominated by notions such as embourgeoisement and citizenship, which contended that the economic, political and social reforms of the post-war era had significantly altered the nature of British Society (Zweig, 1961; Marshall, 1965; Goldthorpe *et al.*, 1969). Research appeared to assume that everyone had benefited from the welfare state.

*Social pathology*

Ironically, at the very moment Crosland was proclaiming the eradication of primary poverty and the triumph of the welfare state, research was being carried out which seriously challenged his thesis (Townsend, 1962; Wedderburn, 1962; Abel-Smith and Townsend, 1965). This research demonstrated that the incidence of poverty was much greater than had previously been acknowledged.

This rediscovered poverty was initially interpreted in the light of the prevailing theory of *social pathology*. This perspective contended that, given the far-reaching nature of welfare state policies, the causes of any residual poverty had to be the 'pathological' behaviour of the people or communities who remained in poverty. This effectively directed attention away from systemic failures and structural inequalities and on to the more limited issue of how to deal with the individuals/groups still living in poverty. In effect, it became a question of how best to change peoples' behaviour.

*The 'area approach'*

While welfare-state policies, working through means tests or individual need assessments, generally worked at the level of the individual, the various studies of continuing poverty indicated that the implicated people tended to concentrate in discrete areas of the city. Such areas were characterised by *multiple deprivation*, linking social and economic disadvantage. Not surprisingly, the spatial concentration of poverty led policy makers towards spatially-based strategies for addressing the problem. This *area approach*, when allied with the social pathology perspective, entailed the targeting of policies and resources on to areas with the express aim of combating the problems therein.

Eventually, area-based social pathology policies came to address simultaneously several of the problems evident within the selected areas. In this way the first truly urban policies, the Urban Programme and the Community Development Programme, emerged in 1968 in the United Kingdom. The first area policies, however, addressed just one social pathology: educational disadvantage. This policy area was one of the key areas in the post-war meritocracy; it was through education that any remaining inequalities would be further reduced and it was education which would be one of the driving forces of economic growth (Crosland, 1964).

The publication of the Plowden Report (HMSO, 1967) confirmed evidence that working-class children, particularly in urban areas, were significantly and systematically underachieving when compared with their suburban middle-class counterparts. In the social pathology tradition, it argued that urban working-class children, on entering school, brought with them significant disadvantages originating in their home circumstances (poor housing, lack of parental interest, 'anti-academic' attitudes). These were then compounded by poor school buildings and large classes. The report recommended the targeting of additional resources on *educational priority areas* and the payment of deprived-area allowances to teachers on the basis of a formula which took account of key parental, home and child development data. Although only some of the Plowden proposals were ultimately adopted, owing to financial retrenchment in which it was assumed that any new spending would have to come out of efficiency savings, it provided evidence that area-based positive discrimination policies could be developed in Britain. It was, however, fundamentally flawed: it failed to give adequate consideration to the structural causes of failure at school or even of the role of the school (McKay and Cox, 1979, p. 236).

In a general, empirical sense, the area approach is also flawed. Using a definition of deprivation involving eighteen indicators drawn from the Census of Population, Holtermann (1975) attempted to examine the distribution of multiple deprivation in British cities. Her results (Table 2.2) indicate the extent to which multiple deprivation characterised conurbations. However, she also noted that significant numbers of deprived people lived within areas that would not, in aggregate terms, be defined as deprived. It is such people that area-based initiatives neglect.

### The race 'problem'

The measures proposed in the Plowden Report had, in fact, been preceded by an earlier area-based education policy: *Section 11 grants*. These stemmed from the Local Government Act, 1966, and were for English language teachers in areas where there were significant numbers of black or Asian schoolchildren. This policy

TABLE 2.2 Multiple deprivation in British cities, 1971

|  | Conurbation | Non-Conurbation |
|---|---|---|
| Percentage EDs in Great Britain | 42.9 | 57.1 |
| Percentage worst 5% of EDs: | | |
| household lacking exclusive use of amenities | 63.6 | 36.4 |
| unskilled manual workers | 51.3 | 48.7 |
| lacking car | 71.7 | 28.3 |

Note: ED = (Census) Enumeration District.
Source: Calculated from Holtermann (1975).

involved relatively little expenditure and gave no recognition to the broader disadvantages experienced by black or Asian groups, or the importance of non-white culture. It did, however, identify a key emerging element in the 'pathology' of inner cities in the 1960s.

McKay and Cox (1979, p. 234) suggest that Britain's non-white population grew from 74 500 in 1951 to 595 100 in 1969. Daniel (1968) makes a possibly more realistic suggestion that in 1950 there were around 100 000 black people in the UK; by 1969 with immigration and population growth this figure had risen to just over 1 million. The vast majority of this growth was concentrated in Britain's seven major conurbations and larger urban areas (Robinson, 1989). Within these areas black people concentrated in specific districts due both to choice and to constraint in the housing and employment markets (Daniel, 1968; Ohri and Faruqi, 1988; Robinson, 1989).

Most black immigrants initially came to the UK as a form of migrant labour force, to do the dirty, low-paid and unsociable jobs which the white labour force would not do (Phizacklea and Miles, 1980). Increasingly during the 1950s new arrivals found themselves competing for jobs and housing with members of the white working class. Their presence was then reconstructed as a threat to jobs and to British culture and society. Certain Conservative politicians

overtly campaigned for controls on immigration and were covertly
supported by sections of the British government and media (Carter
*et al.*, 1987). The Notting Hill and Nottingham riots of 1958
provided the ideal opportunity to finalise the process whereby 'race'
became defined as a problem; an element in the social pathology of
cities.

In the 1960s, while most attention focused on immigration
control, 'liberal' opinion argued that something, however small,
should be done to improve the lot of black and Asian people already
in the United Kingdom. Immigrants, and their children, were still
perceived as being a problem, but one which could be dealt with
largely by a process of assimilation and education: by them
abandoning their languages, cultures and social mores and
unambiguously accepting the culture and norms of white Britain
(for more detail on education see Carr-Hill and Chadha-Boreham,
1988). Immigration control was justified by a commitment to
improve the lot of existing immigrants, while positive discrimination
was small scale and discreet as the government was fearful of the
electoral consequences should it be seen to be overly preoccupied
with the needs of immigrants.

Given the concentration of black and Asian people in urban
areas, some form of area-based general urban initiatives would
inevitably include many within its net while avoiding overt targeting.
From this perspective the genesis of urban initiatives can be seen, at
least partially, as a shrewd response to black and Asian needs and
white liberal opinion which, simultaneously, avoided alienating the
white working-class vote that was so essential to the Labour Party's
electoral fortunes. We shall revisit this paradox in subsequent
chapters and in detail in Chapter 10.

*United States' urban policy*

The contention that, following the rediscovery of urban poverty in
Britain, the gradual emergence of urban policy owed much to policy
developments in the United States has received considerable
attention elsewhere (Higgins, 1978; Loney, 1983). Britain's urban
initiatives, it is claimed, were influenced by experience in the United
States. The 'War on Poverty' initiated by President Johnson in his
1964 State of the Union address but originated during the Kennedy
administration provides the main parallel.

The war on poverty was an attempt 'to equip the poor to compete more effectively in the market place' (Loney, 1983, p. 27). As in Britain, the rediscovery of poverty after the complacency of the Eisenhower years during the 1950s played a part in the genesis of the programme. More important in the United States' context, however, was the race issue; the civil rights movement was instrumental in drawing attention to the severe problems which existed in the ghetto areas of the inner cities (Harrington, 1962). The 1960s Democrat administrations, to an extent reliant on the black vote, committed themselves to action. The 1964 Economic Opportunity Act initiated a number of employment-related measures such as *Head Start*, which aimed to give deprived pre-school children an introduction to the skills so essential to them if they were to have any chance of shaking off the generations of poverty lying behind them and becoming part of the 'affluent society'. Higgins (1978) notes that this programme was so popular that it had more than five times the anticipated take-up. The Economic Opportunity Act also created the *Community Action Program*. This provided federally-funded community action teams which were expected to co-ordinate local services and mobilise self-help in inner-city communities. The *Model Cities Program* of 1966 modified the Community Action Program and brought it under local government control (Marris and Rein, 1973, p. 261).

Quite significant levels of funding were made available for the war on poverty. Higgins (1978, pp. 49–50) notes that in the financial year 1966, $627.6m was allocated to deal with a variety of problems including housing, training and health. As would later be the case in Britain, the policies reflected the social pathology approach and aimed to ameliorate the immediate problems of the urban poor. Underlying this perspective was the *culture of poverty* theory (Lewis, 1966) which assumed that the poor were in essence the cause of their own problems; the behaviour and culture, of both individuals and communities, was the root cause of urban problems. There is very little evidence that any of the programmes attempted to analyse, define or tackle systematically the problem of poverty in terms of structural inequalities.

Given these assumptions and shortcomings it always seemed unlikely that any significant diminution in poverty would be achieved. For a while, policy served as a form of territorial crisis management and legitimation (Piven and Cloward, 1972) but when, in 1968, US cities began literally to explode into racial violence it appeared that the programmes had failed and, by the end of the 1960s, they were being wound down. Interestingly, while British urban initiatives were undoubtedly influenced by the United States experience, there is little evidence that the lessons of those experiences were heeded (Loney, 1983, pp. 25–7).

## Assessment

We can make sense of these developments in a variety of ways. A neo-liberal would see the development of planning frameworks such as regional policy and population, and industrial dispersal as a misconceived and unwarranted form of intervention in the market. For Hayek, town planning is permissible only to the extent that it facilitates the market. It becomes a threat when 'it is motivated by the desire to dispense with the price mechanism and to replace it by central direction' (Hayek, 1960, p. 350). However, in the period under discussion such ideas were mainly confined to the fringes of politics and had little or no influence on political events or the development of policies.

Marxists tended to see the policies covered above as being closely associated with the post-war consensus and as attempts to make capitalism work more efficiently. Decentralisation policies and town planning policies were viewed as part of an attempt to manage capitalism and ameliorate its worst excesses. Rees and Lambert (1985, p. 102) argue that the development of regional policy was determined by a need to respond to 'Britain's deteriorating domestic economy' and the political pressures eminating from industrial capital. Castells (1977, p. 277) argued that 'new towns were above all a response to the urban (social and functional) crisis of the London region'. The policies outlined above could do little to resolve the fundamental contradictions of the capitalist mode of production and would merely displace the effects on to the poorest and least powerful groups in society.

There were few explicit attempts to analyse the developments we have outlined above in overtly pluralist terms. However, a pluralist would have undoubtedly seen these developments as the interaction of a variety of competing organisations and pressure groups with the state 'holding the ring'. Thus regional policy could be seen as a response to the demands of depressed regions for a fairer share of national employment. However, Simmie (1974, p. 137), in an examination of participation in the planning process, noted:

> Those who participate in town planning, and consequently influence the distribution of those resources for which it is responsible, do not form a representative cross-section of society.

Newton's (1976) excellent study of local politics in Birmingham also supports this general conclusion, suggesting the existence of a modified form of élitism, with middle-class groups and interests receiving preferential treatment (see also Saunders, 1974).

Table 2.3 presents an overall assessment of the policies of the period from 1945 to the mid-1960s, using the policy appraisal framework from Chapter 1. There was an *ad hoc* conception of the urban with no systematic attempt to define urban problems. The problems were conceptualised in terms of imbalances and the solution was a larger role for central and local government which would provide overall direction and the resources for (re)development which, on the whole, would actually be carried out by the private sector. With regard to urban problems and their causation, the social dimension was entirely ignored and the emphasis was firmly on the physical. Explanations tended to stress overconcentration of industry and population in cities but also saw cities as suffering from an almost inevitable ageing process which meant that certain areas (or forms of housing) had come to the end of their natural lives and needed replacing. With regard to regional problems this was simply a problem of imbalance which could be rectified by government forcing or encouraging firms to relocate.

There is no evidence of any clearly defined strategy which integrated the various elements we have discussed; indeed, industrial and land-use planning took place entirely separately. The only overarching concern seems to have been a desire to modernise British society. The physical rejuvenation of cities seems to have been part of that wider vision. At the same time the provision of better accommodation also accords with the idea of a post-war settlement which hoped to deliver better living standards to the mass of the population. The mechanisms utilised to realise the approach were clearance/rebuilding, regional policy, new towns and land-use planning, all of which stressed the physical rather than the social

TABLE 2.3   **Physical urban policy: an assessment**

|  | Physical Urban Policy |
| --- | --- |
| Conception of 'urban' | *Ad hoc* definition; urban nature of problem of little relevance |
| Theoretical approach | Mix of *laissez-faire* liberalism and central direction. State direction with private sector support |
| Nature of problem | Rundown and decrepit state of British cities |
| Explanation | Obsolescence of urban fabric; maldistribution of people and jobs |
| Aim of Policy | Modernisation and redistribution |
| Mechanisms | Clearance, regional policy, new towns, town and country planning |
| Resourcing | Variable and unplanned |
| Management | Mainly local; some national direction; New Town Corporations |
| Political support | Consensual though partisan attitudes towards private sector |
| Legislation | Town and country planning legislation |
| Monitoring | Very limited |

dimension. The costs of these major redevelopment and relocation policies were largely borne by central government but it was assumed that an expanding economy would provide the necessary finance to underwrite them.

Central government largely structured and ran regional policy, although its operation was significantly affected by demands from the regions. For New Towns, central government set up the framework and then appointed a New Town Commission, non-accountable to local interests and voters, to run development. With the passing of the 1952 Expanded Towns Act localities were given a greater say but, after the return of a Labour government in 1964, the programme was more closely integrated into regional policy utilising the notion of the 'growth poles'. Other approaches occurred within a legislative framework established by the centre which favoured particular forms of development. However, local government was frequently left to determined the location and pace of development.

While both political parties supported the initiatives we have outlined, there were minor differences. The Conservative government elected in 1951 turned from the more centrally directed new towns programme of its Labour predecessor to a more locally influenced programme and it also created the financial subsidy structure which produced the switch away from general needs building favoured by the Labour Party, to clearance and rebuilding. The Conservatives also gave the private sector a greater role, most notably through an increase in owner-occupation, and attempted, unsuccessfully, to rejuvenate the private rented market. Such differences, unlike those which were to emerge in the 1970s and 1980s, occurred within a generally accepted framework. As regards the monitoring and evaluation of these programmes there seems to have been none at all.

### Conclusion: an emerging urban policy?

As we have seen in the preceding pages, despite the absence of clear policy there was a general recognition, by the mid-1960s, that poverty and disadvantage still existed in the United Kingdom despite the establishment of the welfare state and the achievement of full employment. New problems, notably racial, were also emerging to bemuse politicians and policy-makers, and policies being developed in the United States were providing possible pointers for future action. By the second half of the 1960s governments were also increasingly being forced to acknowledge that the problems of Britain's cities could not be solved simply by physical measures. The emergent new approach entailed area-based policies focused on one or more aspects of social pathology.

The impetus for this shift in policy emphasis did not come from politicians. Only Enoch Powell and others on the right appeared much concerned about cities, and this was a concern inspired largely by perceived threats to the 'British nation'. There were, however civil servants who were interested in urban issues – most notably Derek Morrell (a Home Office civil servant) and a group of associated individuals (Higgins *et al.*, 1983, ch. 2; Loney, 1983, ch. 2). These civil servants, noting developments in the USA, were aware of an emerging and potentially large policy area related to urban poverty. Through their participation in inquiries and interdepartmental working teams they were conscious of the opportunities for the participating departments although there was also a genuine motivation to improve the lot of the urban poor (Higgins *et al.*, 1983, pp. 14–17).

When Enoch Powell, a former Conservative minister, made his infamous 'rivers of blood' speech in 1968 about immigration, planning was well under way for both the Urban Programme and the Community Development Project (Fuller and Stevenson, 1983). Powell's speech, however, served as a catalyst, forcing politicians, most notably the then Prime Minister, Harold Wilson, to take an interest in urban issues. Urban policy offered the prospect of some relief to the problems faced by urban inhabitants and had the added advantage of benefiting an important part of Labour's electoral constituency at a time when the Labour government was experiencing a series of crises and doing particularly badly in opinion polls. Wilson, ever the consummate politician, immediately offered his party's support for the new initiatives.

# 3 First Steps: Urban Initiatives and Urban Problems in Early 1970s Britain

The first urban initiatives emerged in Britain in the late 1960s. The programmes initiated at that time, the *Urban Programme* and the *Community Development Projects* were firmly in tune with the prevailing social pathology approach and operated through area-based measures. Notwithstanding these initiatives, many urban problems continued to be addressed by physical approaches. This chapter covers:

- The experiences of the early urban initiatives and their successors in the period up to the mid-1970s. We will reflect on the lessons they suggested for future urban initiatives and show how the assumptions that underlay them, notably the social pathology approach, were undermined by the experience of the urban initiatives themselves.
- The demise of the remaining physical measures associated with problems of housing, urban growth and industrial change, and discuss the themes of counterurbanisation and deindustrialisation; issues central to the emerging views on the structural base of urban policy.
- An assessment of the theoretical basis and policy coherence of the approaches pursued during the period.
- The ideological and politicoeconomic context in which urban policy found itself in the mid-1970s. This context was to play a crucial role in determining the parameters within which urban policy would both operate and develop in subsequent years.

## The early urban initiatives

Chapter 2 discussed the background to the emergence of the first urban initiatives: the Urban Programme and the Community

43

Development Projects which were initiated in 1968 in the aftermath of Enoch Powell's 'rivers of blood' speech (Edwards and Batley, 1978; Lawless, 1979, ch. 6, 1986; Higgins *et al.*, 1983; Loney, 1983). There have also been suggestions that the then Prime Minister, Harold Wilson, was directly responsible for initiating both projects. As we pointed out in Chapter 2, however, planning for the initiatives had begun some time before Powell's dramatic political intervention; there may be some truth in the assertion about Wilson, although Higgins *et al.* (1983, pp. 50–1) suggest that Wilson may have 'borrowed' the idea from an earlier interdepartmental working team. What is more certain is that the direct antecedents of the initiatives were the 'liberal' perspective on the perceived 'race problem' (see Chapters 2 and 10), electoral expediency in Labour's inner city heartland, policies in the United States and civil service commitment. We will now examine the experiences of the two initiatives, particularly the latter, and the conclusions which were drawn from them.

*The urban programme*

In essence, the Urban Programme (UP) served as a filler of gaps in existing provision. Higgins *et al.* (1983, pp. 47–8) point out that, from 1968 to 1978, the UP was: 'a set of arrangements for the part-funding by central government of projects in any local authority . . . that could demonstrate "special social need"'. As the then Home Secretary, James Callaghan, noted in the Commons:

> The purpose of this programme is to supplement the Government's other social and legislative measures to ensure as far as we can that all our citizens have an equal opportunity in life. (Hansard, 22.7.1968, no. 768, col. 41)

The programme involved *positive discrimination* in favour of selected groups or areas and typically took the form of small-scale projects emphasising experimentation, self-help, co-ordination of existing services and the promotion of rapid results.

The programme as a whole was funded and administered by the Home Office and may be seen as an attempt to portray that department in a more liberal light. Eligible local authorities could apply to the Home Office and if successful receive a 75 per cent grant towards the costs of a particular project. The total amount available to local authorities was limited to £22 million over four years (Higgins *et al.*, 1983, p. 56; Edwards and Batley, 1978, p. 34, 55–7), hardly a generous level of funding, although total expenditure did rise to around £30 million *per annum* by 1976/7.

Initially there were no specific instructions as to what types of projects the government would prefer to support and encourage. These emerged as a result of discussions by an interdepartmental working team (Edwards and Batley, 1978, pp. 134–8; Higgins *et al.*, 1983, pp. 58–9). The prime criteria for approval seem to have been race; visible effect at lowest cost; and the enthusiasm and commitment of the relevant central government department: in other words a *laissez-faire* approach with little central direction, suggesting that the centre had little or no idea of what the problems were or what it wanted to achieve. In essence, a local authority had to be able to demonstrate *special need* in order to qualify for funding. However, exactly what constituted special need remained rather vague and may at best be loosely equated with the presence of multiple deprivation, however defined and measured (Edwards and Batley, 1978, pp. 48–55).

It is difficult to define and identify any coherent principles underlying the UP. It could be argued that race (and by implication immigration) was a central issue, but it was played down until at least 1973 (Stewart and Whitting, 1983) for fear of a 'white backlash' (see Chapter 10). Thus, as Higgins *et al.* (1983, p. 58) argued:

> No one had a clearly formulated view of what urban deprivation was or what the major problems of the inner cities were that required remedial action. A precision of problem definition was acutely lacking, and though the Prime Minister's speech had mentioned a wide range of problems there was no means of rationally setting priorities. In the absence of a problem-defined strategy, administrative expedience filled the vacuum.

The early projects were dominated by pre-school initiatives. The Department of Education and Science was eager to promote such schemes and encouraged Local Education Authorities to take advantage of available monies. It was also alert to the issue of positive discrimination, especially as Educational Priority Areas had just been launched. In subsequent years the scope of the projects was to widen greatly to include youth and community projects (frequently directed at black youth), and environmental improvements.

It could be argued, drawing on the United States' experience, that the one thing that UP projects had in common was that they might be interpreted as part of a conflict displacement strategy designed to act as a pressure valve to prevent tensions in run down inner city areas from reaching boiling point. From such a perspective they also had a social control function, identifying and rewarding acceptable forms of behaviour (Bridges, 1975). While such a contention may be overstated (see Higgins *et al.*, 1983, pp. 19–20), the issue of social control is not entirely irrelevant. In their assessment of black experience of the Urban Programme, Stewart and Whitting (1983, p. 18) noted that:

> The major concerns felt by ethnic groups are about racism, discrimination and relations with the police. Thus for many groups the Urban Programme, if understood at all, is at best a source of funds for useful community based activity and at worst a diversionary smokescreen to divert attention from the absence of a serious commitment to a multi-racial society.

## The Community Development Projects

The Community Development Project (CDP), like the UP, was also influenced by civil servants, academics and the US experience. They were essentially small-area projects located within deprived local authorities and designed to focus limited resources on 'deviant' individuals and communities who had, by reason of choice or accident, slipped through the welfare net or not taken advantage of the opportunities offered by full employment (Lawless, 1979, ch. 6). In each authority a specific area containing 'deviant populations' was identified and an *action team* then focused on the area's population.

A little more thought appears to have gone into the CDPs, but their setting up and operation appears to have been no more methodical than the UP – of which, strictly speaking, they formed a part. In fact, it appears that, at a meeting with CDP planners, Prime Minister Wilson plucked the figure of £25 million per annum out of the air as a suggested level of funding for the projects (Higgins, 1978, p. 43). In the event, the CDPs cost around £5 million over a period of nine years (Higgins *et al.*, 1983, p. 12) and, as with the UP, there seems to have been no systematic attempt to relate funding to objectives.

Local authorities played an important role in the CDPs, but once again central government provided 75 per cent of the finance. While the Home Office acted as the central co-ordinating body, each CDP had an *action team* and a *research team*. The action team was located in the chosen area while the research team was placed at a nearby university or polytechnic. The underlying basis of this functional separation was the notion that the action team would attempt to encourage the people in their area to improve the situation in which they found themselves and the research team would monitor developments and pass on research data and lessons to the Home Office and the relevant local authority. In practice it proved an unworkable relationship.

Twelve CDPs were set up in a variety of, mainly urban, locations suffering from deprivation. There were no clearly identifiable and agreed criteria underlying the selection process. Moreover, in no way were the most deprived areas identified. It would appear (see Higgins, 1978, pp. 44–8 for more details) that some local authorities were selected because of their sitting (Labour) Member of Parliament: Highfields, for example was in the Coventry constituency of Richard Crossman, the then Social Services Secretary. Others were chosen for their location: Southwark, for example, was close to the Houses of Parliament. Cardiff, then Home Secretary James Callaghan's constituency, declined to be selected on the grounds that having a CDP would stigmatise it as a 'deprived' area.

The CDPs take on a somewhat greater degree of coherence if we see them as *action research* experiments designed to discover the causes and nature of urban problems (Edwards and Batley, 1978; Lawless, 1979: ch. 6; 1986, ch. 2; Higgins *et al.*, 1983, ch. 2; Loney, 1983). But even from this, more generous, perspective they still pose immense problems. If the CDPs were an experiment designed to unveil the nature and causes of urban deprivation, then they required clearer experimental design and, more importantly, someone to control the experiment; they required direction from the centre and an organisational structure which would ensure that the results of the co-ordinated work of action teams and research teams were widely circulated among the CDPs and assimilated by policy-makers both at the centre and locally. There is little evidence of this having occurred. Initially teams frequently complained of a lack of central guidance and direction from the Home Office which, after an early burst of enthusiasm, showed a general lack of interest in their activities. Relations between action and research teams rarely appear to have been close and, at the local level, the relationship between action teams and local authorities was often frosty, if not antagonistic (Lawless, 1979, pp. 117–26).

The premature death of Derek Morrell, the civil servant cited in the previous chapter as an advocate of area-based approaches, may have been partly responsible for these problems of direction; he appears to have been one of the few civil servants at the Home Office who was seriously concerned with the CDPs. However, he was alive when they were initiated without coherent guidelines. Following his death, the CDPs encountered a succession of civil servants as 'head' of the project. For many, a posting to the CDP desk was seen as a diversion from their career paths; the Home Office's major concerns were law and order, and immigration control. The CDPs were a neglected backwater and anyone who spent time there was losing out in the upward mobility stakes. As a result, the local CDPs were largely left to their own devices.

A second problem for the CDPs concerned the impact of the area approach on existing local politics. When they were initially set up, the action teams frequently included behaviourial psychologists and social workers, reflecting the underlying belief that the problems within each team's area, however defined, stemmed from the pathological behaviour of individuals and communities. In an era when local government was dominated by corporate management techniques (Bains, 1972; Dearlove, 1979), a remedy merely required a better targeting of local authority activities and resources. Such an approach had the advantage of confining the problem to discrete spatial areas and limiting the financial commitments of both central and local government. However, it disturbed the status quo; many local authorities, given their entrenched political and committee structures, reacted with hostility when even a minor redistribution of resources was suggested.

A third, and more important, problem related to the nature and shortcomings of the social pathology model. Social pathology was central to the CDPs at the time of their inception. The underlying approach is perhaps best summed up in a National CDP Report, which noted that the CDP assumed that:

> problems of urban deprivation had their origins in the characteristics of local populations – in individual pathologies – and these could best be resolved by better field coordination of the personal social services combined with the mobilisation of self-help and mutual aid in the community 'even among those experiencing most difficulty in standing on their own feet'. (CDP, 1974, p. 1)

Many of the CDP teams subsequently rejected this perspective. The lack of central control and direction may have accelerated this rejection but, in the long run, it probably could not have been prevented. It came about because, when the projects were set up, many of their workers were individuals schooled in the community and student radicalism of the 1960s; it was highly unlikely that they would meekly and uncritically accept a role and a problem definition which blamed the victim, completely exonerated society and reduced poverty to a residual problem. Indeed, very soon after their establishment, some of the CDPs began to question social pathology and, once this occurred, it was then only a small step to questioning the area-based approach, particularly as, on an empirical level, it soon became apparent to the project workers that the CDP areas were indistinguishable from those surrounding them and thousands of others throughout Britain's urban (and rural) areas.

The search for alternative explanations began and culminated in the adoption, by many of the teams, of an explicitly Marxist theory which saw urban poverty (and other forms of deprivation) as an inevitable by-product of *uneven capitalist development* (CDP, 1977a; Forrest *et al.*, 1979). According to the CDP, it was:

> clear that the problems of these areas were firmly tied to much more basic structural problems in society and that the solution does not consist in the poor pulling themselves up by their bootstraps, but in sufficient political will being directed toward fundamental and far reaching social change. (CDP, 1977b, p. 5)

The new explanation of urban decline thus looked to regional, national and international economic and political forces, and unemployment was identified as a key feature of these areas. As a result, teams adopted a *structural explanation* rather than the individually-based social pathology explanation. In such a context the area approach was rendered largely redundant as both an explanatory variable and as a viable strategy to revive economic fortunes. The forces which determined an area's decline were now recognised as originating outside it and to have nothing to do with a local population's behaviourial characteristics (for more detail on the problems of the area approach see Higgins, 1978, pp. 111–15; Hamnett, 1979; Eyles, 1979).

The consequence of the adoption of this diagnosis by the majority of CDP teams was that their practical activities turned towards encouraging residents in their areas to oppose the activities of the capitalist state (e.g. the Housing Finance Act, 1972) and make greater demands on their local authorities. This exacerbated the problems of conflict between the teams and the local authorities and it hardly needs to be said that the adoption of such an approach also made the CDPs extremely unpopular with central government. It is perhaps one of the greatest of ironies that the Home Office found itself funding a bunch of Marxists.

Despite the apparent independence of the teams, financial control remained with central and local government. This provided the means by which the CDPs could be curbed. In 1975 the then Labour government allowed local authorities with CDPs in their areas to withdraw their 25 per cent funding. In 1976 central funding for the CDP Information and Intelligence Unit was terminated; this effectively ended the CDPs, and by 1978 they were all defunct.

*Comprehensive Community Programmes and the Inner Area Studies*

There is no doubt that the CDPs produced valuable research on the nature of urban problems in Britain's cities. However, given the explicitly Marxist nature of much of this work, it was viewed with great suspicion and apprehension by the government. No British government would be likely to accept the diagnosis that, crudely put, capitalism was the problem and its abolition the solution. But, like the equally problematic Community Action Programme in the United States (see Chapter 2), important questions were raised which could not be ignored. Two initiatives were developed to address these questions: the Inner Area Studies and the Comprehensive Community Programmes.

## The Inner Area Studies

In 1972 the then Secretary of State at the Department of the Environment (DoE), Peter Walker, set up the Inner Area Studies (IAS). These studies numbered six in all. Three were concerned with local government decision-making and its impact on environmental problems, and focused on Oldham, Rotherham and Sunderland. The other three gave detailed attention to relatively small inner-city communities in Liverpool (Toxteth), Birmingham (Small Heath) and London (Lambeth). The emphasis in all the studies was on research and the development of an understanding of the causes of urban deprivation.

Unlike the CDP research element, the IASs were carried out by carefully selected teams of consultants. Their reports, however, were not unlike those of the CDPs, indicating the extent to which, by the early 1970s, there was a general realisation that the social pathology approach was misleading as well as inadequate. At the same time, however, there was a retreat from the wilder Marxist assertions of the CDPs in favour of a more pragmatic approach emphasising structural factors yet retaining an area-based concern. This position was, perhaps, best expressed in the report of the Birmingham IAS (Llewellyn-Davies and associates, 1977, p. 215) which argued that:

> Our analysis of the problems of inner areas and their causes has confirmed our belief that the roots of urban deprivation do not lie in personal inadequacy but in societal forces which create situations of such serious disadvantage and deprivation for many people that they may properly be termed 'victims'. It follows that the focus of inner area policy must be to effect basic changes in the way our society functions in order to achieve a more equitable distribution of resources, and indeed this is the main thrust of our argument. Nonetheless, we cannot pursue the goal of redistribution without recognising that there remains the urgent need, and responsibility, to compensate those who now suffer deprivation and disadvantage, and that this need will remain for as long as poverty and severe structural inequality persist.

By the end of 1976, feedback from the research carried out by these teams was making an impact on government thinking, helping force an acknowledgement of the inadequacy of the social pathology approach and the associated urban initiatives as well as a recognition of the centrality of economic factors in the causation of inner city decline. This created the theoretical and policy context in which the initiatives covered in the next chapter could be developed.

*Comprehensive Community Programmes*

The IASs were a departure from previous initiatives in that they were run by the Department of the Environment rather than the Home Office. However, the latter body maintained its involvement with urban policy. A *Home Office Urban Deprivation Unit* was created with the express aim of researching urban deprivation and, in 1974, the new Labour government launched the Home Office-led Comprehensive Community Programmes (CCPs) (Higgins *et al.*, 1983, ch. 4; McKay and Cox, 1979, 249–50; Lawless, 1986, pp. 40–6; Sills *et al.*, 1988, pp. 25–6).

In essence, the CCPs were an attempt to apply contemporary techniques of corporate management to urban problems. Teams would be located in local authorities and they would play a central role in carrying out research, identifying problems, prioritising them and then persuading authorities to redirect resources and energies to their solution (for more detail see Hambleton, 1977; Spencer, 1980, 1981). Emphasis was placed on understanding and solving local problems by reference to their national context and to central–local and public–private sectoral relations. Pilot areas for an estimated ninety CCPs were identified and two were formally launched, in Gateshead and Motherwell (Rees and Lambert, 1985, p. 131). However, by the time they were established (1978), the Labour government had already launched its White Paper *Policy for the Inner Cities*, and CCPs were either sidelined or absorbed into this new initiative. As a result, they then quietly faded from the policy scene, having provided a first glimpse of the subsequently important notion of '*partnership*'.

Before their final fading, however, responsibility for the CCPs was transferred to the DoE. Although this left the UP and the discredited CDPs under the control of the Home Office, it clearly located the 'new' urban initiatives with the DoE. Competition between the two departments increased the difficulty of developing a coherent and consistent strategy, but the DoE was in the ascendant. Integration into the DoE enabled the former urban initiatives to be linked to mainstream urban policy legislation in the housing, transport and planning fields; later policies were to flow largely from this department.

### The demise of the physical approach

The UP, CDPs, CCPs and IASs were a departure from the physical approach to urban problems. They increasingly sought to co-ordinate action across a number of traditionally discrete policy areas; they also incorporated social, and latterly economic analyses of urban decline. Parallel with the rise of this new approach came the demise of the old, physical, approach to urban problems.

*The housing stock*

In inner cities, the clearest manifestation of the physical approach to urban problems had been slum clearance and council-led redevelopment. Although this was an extremely expensive course of action it, in one form or another, dominated central government plans for most of the 1950s and well into the 1960s. Clearance was never, however, the only strategy. The Labour Housing Act, 1949 had instituted *improvement grants* for owner occupiers, and the scheme was extended in the Conservative's Housing Repair and Rent Act, 1954 and House Purchase and Housing Act, 1959. By 1962, the Ministry for Housing and Local Government (MHLG) was encouraging local authorities to tackle their housing problems by a judicious mixture of both clearance and improvement (MHLG, 1962a). This latter approach received a further boost in the Housing Act, 1964, which incorporated an aim to achieve an increase in house improvement from 130 000 a year to 200 000.

Improvement was, however, still a subsidiary tactic in the overall strategy. As the 1965 White Paper *The Housing Programme 1965–70* (HMSO, 1965) made clear, the government still believed clearance and rebuilding to be the best way to proceed, and maintained the fiction that the problem of bad housing could be solved. The White Paper argued that:

once the country has overcome its huge social problem of slumdom and obsolescence, and yet met the need of the cities for houses to let at moderate rents, the programme of substantial council housing should decrease. The expansion of the public programme now proposed is to meet exceptional need . . . The expansion of owner-occupation on the other hand is normal; it reflects a long term social advance which should gradually pervade every region. (HMSO, 1965, p. 8)

This position is interesting. Not only does it demonstrate the continuing emphasis on clearance and the belief in a 'once-and-for-all' solution of the housing problem, it also introduces a sea-change in the politics of housing: owner-occupation is portrayed, even by a Labour government, to be the tenure of the future. Local authority housing was seen as a short-term expedient.

The 1967 House Condition Survey suggested that the optimism of the 1965 White Paper was misplaced. It confirmed that the scale of housing problems was much greater than previously acknowledged. Rapid construction of systems-based low- and high-rise council housing was one response; others involved attempts to promote fair rents in the private-renting sector, and low-cost mortgages. At the same time, however, came the first major down turn in the post-war world economy. In the UK this coincided with a period of crisis ushered in by the Wilson government's long overdue decision to devalue sterling and rein in the rate of growth in public expenditure.

Given the massive costs involved in council-house building, it was inevitable that this programme would come under pressure to cut costs. The publication, in 1968, of the White Paper, *Old Houses into New Homes*, and the subsequent Housing Act, 1969, signalled the beginning of the end for the physical approach as primacy gradually switched from clearance and rebuilding over the period 1968 to 1974. In keeping with the spirit of the times, the new approach was to be area-based. The 1969 Act introduced *General Improvement Areas* in which take-up of improvement grants was to be encouraged. Merrett (1979, p. 139) has pithily summed up the thinking behind the change and the duplicity involved in the advancement of area improvement:

The cunning of the ancient thief is nothing beside that of the civil servants who authored [the White Paper]. For it promised everything. The scale of improvement was to rise; the scale of clearance was to rise; yet the total of public investment in housing was to remain static. The answer to this riddle is not contained in the paper but all three commitments are only mutually consistent if local authority housebuilding for general needs was to be slashed.

By 1974 slum clearance had almost ceased and council building had been greatly reduced. The private sector had little intention of stepping in to fill the breach in cities, or anywhere else, once the owner-occupation bubble had burst as economic crisis loomed. Improvement had gained ascendancy and, by 1974, a central element of the 'physical approach' had been undermined.

## Urban growth and industrial change

At the same time doubts began to emerge over the value of the programmes entailing the decentralisation of people and industry from the inner cities. Unemployment began to rise towards one million in the early 1970s and, for the first time in many years, became a problem at the centre of the political agenda. Furthermore, the CDP and IAS research pointed to a considerable growth in urban unemployment. It was only a relatively small step from this to questioning the wisdom of decentralising job opportunities from the cities.

### Counterurbanisation

By 1974–6 evidence was clearly emerging which suggested that, since the early 1950s, there had been a major movement of industry and population out of Britain's urban areas (Begg *et al.*, 1986). This movement had been first to the city suburbs and later it had fuelled the expansion of small, free-standing rural towns and even remote rural areas. It left behind an increasingly vulnerable unskilled, ageing, low-income urban population (Redfern, 1982; Champion and Townsend, 1990, ch. 4) and an industrial base which had seen its heyday in the late nineteenth century and was increasingly vulnerable to overseas competition, and thus closure (Cambridge Economic Policy Review, 1982, ch. 3). The conurbations were heavily affected:

A common feature of all conurbations in the post-war period is a loss of both population and employment. Within conurbations, the most rapid decline has occurred in the centre. In the six inner conurbation areas on aggregate the population of working age declined by nearly 30 per cent and employment by 20 per cent between 1951 and 1976. Employment of inner city residents. . .declined by about a third. (*Cambridge Economic Policy Review*, 1982, p. 40)

This phenomenon became known as the *urban–rural shift* or *counterurbanisation* (general reviews are provided by Keeble, 1980; Elias and Keogh, 1982; Fothergill and Gudgin, 1982; Goddard and Champion, 1983; and Cross, 1990).

In this situation there seemed little point in encouraging industry to decentralise, and both the new town and regional policies were questioned (Parsons, 1986). Regional policy, so long the jewel in the crown of post-war industrial policy, was now argued to have actively contributed to the rundown of Britain's urban areas (Keeble, 1976). Additionally, its effectiveness was brought into question when unemployment also began to increase in the regions and the apparently intractable problem of regional disparities, which had characterised the 1930s, and which many believed that post-war policy had solved, reared its ugly head once again (Parsons, 1986). Notwithstanding these doubts, both the parties in power during the late 1960s and early 1970s maintained a regional policy. Perhaps through reasons of electoral expediency the emphasis was placed on attracting industry to *Development Areas* which were extended to cover much of northern Britain, including all the major conurbations except London and Birmingham. New town policy was less resilient: Stonehouse new town near Glasgow was abandoned in favour of inner city regeneration within that city, and population forecasts for the 'third generation' of new towns were revised downwards.

### Deindustrialisation

Much of the research carried out on industrial decline points out that, while industry and population were certainly moving out of cities, by far the worst cause of job loss was *in situ* closure (Dennis, 1978). This in turn has been related to the fact that those cities experiencing particular decline were highly dependent upon obsolescent nineteenth-century industries. This process has been termed *deindustrialisation* (Blackaby, 1979; Martin and Rowthorn, 1986). In essence it refers to both the absolute decline of manufacturing industry in the UK and its relative decline *vis-à-vis* other sectors (e.g. the service sector).

Rowthorn (1986) argues there are three possible general explanations for the phenomenon:

1. Every economy goes through a *life cycle* and, in the mature stage, consumer demand for services can only be satisfied at the expense of the manufacturing sector, which then declines. Britain reached maturity in the mid-1950s (Rowthorn, 1986, pp. 8–15).

2. A second explanation relates to external trade and how an economy pays its way in the world economy. From the mid-nineteenth century to the mid-1950s the UK was a 'workshop' economy and needed to import massive quantities of raw materials; in turn this required the export of equally massive quantities of manufactured goods in order to create a large trade surplus to pay for more raw materials, and so on. Since the 1950s the structure of the economy has become less simple and, with the growth of the service sector, there is no longer any need to have a large manufacturing sector (Rowthorn, 1986, pp. 15–19).

3. The final explanation is the *failure thesis*. This argues that since the 1880s Britain has failed to compete with other industrial economies (e.g. the USA, Germany and Japan) and, as a result, its manufacturing sector has gone into terminal decline. How this failure is explained remains a moot point and depends upon one's political position. Possible theses would include excessive trade union power, incompetent managers, too much state intervention, and a financial sector which is orientated overseas and deprives industry of investment (Rowthorn, 1986, pp. 19–26).

We have neither the time nor the space to probe too deeply into the concept of deindustrialisation. It should be clear that there is no general agreement over its definition, its implications, its measurement (see the essays in Blackaby, 1979) or whether it even matters (see Massey, 1988). However, in the crisis atmosphere of the mid-1970s, the concept seemed to crystallise the problems which were facing Britain as a whole, and its cities in particular.

**Assessment**

The New Right perspective on the arguments set out above would be that the consequences of excessive state intervention were coming home to roost. The market was reasserting itself, for example through the urban–rural shift, and the state could do little or nothing to counteract these developments. Indeed, as we. shall conclude below, just at the time the state was beginning to acknowledge that urban problems had social and economic dimensions and were not spatially discrete, its capacity to counteract these forces was diminishing.

For Marxists, urban problems were the inevitable by-product of capital accumulation: wealth and poverty were intimately related (CDP, 1977b). The concept which began to emerge as crucial to the explanation of continued (urban) poverty was uneven capitalist development (CDP, 1977b; Forrest *et al.*, 1979). This was so powerful that the best the state could do was to ameliorate the consequences; in the conditions of the early to mid-1970s even this ability was severely constrained.

Pluralist theorists found themselves increasingly challenged and marginalised by the re-emergence of Marxist and New Right accounts. Where attempts were made to analyse urban processes using pluralist theory the results suggested that access to decision-making processes was very limited (Simmie, 1974; Newton, 1976). Neo-pluralism acknowledged that not all interests or groups were able to participate or influence the decision-making process. Indeed, some interests were deliberately excluded and the distribution of resources and benefits accrued to already 'privileged' groups. According to Simmie (1981, p. 306) a 'primarily corporatist power structure' dominated decision-making and policy implementation.

Table 3.1 applies the policy assessment criteria which we outlined in Chapter 1 to the urban initiatives covered by this chapter. In terms of conception of 'the urban' there appears to have been very little change from the situation we outlined at the end of Chapter 2. Problems, when acknowledged, were seen to be spatially concentrated and marginal to society as a whole. This was accentuated by the 'theoretical approach' which informed thinking at the time – social pathology, which blamed the individuals and communities for the poverty they were experiencing. As a result, at least initially, governments were convinced that they were dealing with small-

**TABLE 3.1   Early urban initiatives: an assessment**

| | Early Urban Initiatives |
|---|---|
| Conception of urban | Largely *ad hoc*; urban problems spatially concentrated and marginal |
| Theoretical approach | Social pathology; central direction and support from private sector |
| Nature of problem | Run-down state of cities; 'pockets' of poverty |
| Explanation | Pathological behaviour of deviant groups; obsolescent but improving urban fabric |
| Aim of policy | Contradictory: correct pathological behaviour; continue improvements to urban fabric; modernise and redistribute |
| Mechanisms | UP, CDP; area improvement; clearance and decentralisation |
| Resourcing | Coming under pressure |
| Management | Mainly local and experimental |
| Political support | Largely consensual |
| Legislation | Little direct legislation; 1969 and 1974 Housing Acts |
| Monitoring | Limited feedback from CDPs; little from other initiatives |

scale residual social problems. In the UP and the early CDP they adhered to the assumption (outlined in Chapter 2) that full employment and the welfare state had eradicated primary poverty; later the failings of the welfare state were acknowledged. The preferred explanation for urban problems was initially social pathology. This 'blamed the victims' and was subsequently, though only slowly, rejected, in favour of a modified, non-Marxist form of structural explanation.

It is clear that all the early urban initiatives had a common aim: to provide opportunity for individuals and communities by encouraging self-help, mutual aid and a better targeting of local authority services. The chosen mechanism for the delivery of this aim was the area-based policy. However central departments and local authorities chose and defined areas and projects with little real theoretical or empirical justification. Funding was relatively small-scale and the CDPs, in particular, were badly managed and co-ordinated, although the UP generally also lacked any real sense of central or local direction. In the latter part of the period under study, rivalry occurred between the DoE and the Home Office. Little in the way of new legislation was passed perhaps because the problems were first considered to be small-scale and, latterly, recognised as being enormous.

There was undoubtedly political commitment to the initiatives with the exception of the CDP in its latter years. This commitment came about for a number of reasons. There was clearly a desire by the Wilson–Callaghan government, in a period of serious political crisis, to be seen to be doing something for its inner-city electorate. There was also an attempt to fulfil the positive side of race relations policy and a desire to ensure social peace in British cities and avoid the calamities which afflicted many United States cities during the 1960s. Although the UP and CDPs were so poorly conceived and badly carried out that it was unlikely that they would ever have rewarded this political commitment, it was perhaps more important that the government was seen to be doing something rather than actually achieving anything substantial.

In the case of the UP and CDPs there was almost no monitoring and evaluation, but this is not to say that there was no attempt to carry out these functions, particularly in the case of the CDPs. As we have seen, the sort of integrative framework necessary to combine and generalise results was never created. The majority of CDPs asserted their independence and set up their own co-ordinating system, which came into direct conflict with government. Because of this, and for ideological reasons, their work went largely without official evaluation although their conclusions undoubtedly influenced both the IASs and the CCPs. The more fragmentary UP was, in a sense, too *ad hoc* for formal evaluation. The CCPs and the IAS present a different picture. The former was dead almost before birth but benefited from the work of the Home Office Deprivation Unit. The latter incorporated a small action research auto-evaluation element but received effective evaluation in the 1977 White Paper, *Policy for Inner Cities*.

We can say that a number of academic careers were launched via the CDPs, but this hardly counts as a significant policy outcome. We could also argue that, again via the CDPs, some local communities developed a greater sense of community, self-organisation and ability to articulate demands for better local authority services and more resources. We could point out that numerous small projects and groups benefited from UP funding and that the IASs paved the way for the landmarkn 1977 White Paper. Against all this we could argue that nothing really changed; urban problems persisted and in a sense were legitimised by the ineffectiveness of the urban initiatives. For all the above reasons we cannot in any way term the initiatives reviewed so far a coherent 'policy' in the sense discussed in Chapter 1.

## Conclusion: the crisis of the mid-1970s

It may seem somewhat unusual to conclude the present chapter with a discussion of such a complex and wide-ranging issue as the 'crisis' of the 1970s. However, events which took place in the economic and political spheres over the period 1970–6 were to have profound ideological and political consequences.

There are numerous accounts of the crisis of the mid-1970s (e.g. Gutmann, 1976; Jessop, 1980). What can be stated with some degree of certainty is that, from about 1973, British capitalism entered into a period, then unique in the post-war era, of severe structural crisis, in which both unemployment and inflation were rising (something previously thought impossible) and the economy was either stagnant or actually experiencing 'negative-growth' – a situation known as 'stagflation' (Altvater, 1973).

The Heath administration attempted to use traditional Keynesian demand management techniques to counter the situation. However, this 'Barber boom' (named after the then Chancellor of the Exchequer, Anthony Barber) had only temporary impact and effectively made matters worse. When the new Labour government came to power in 1974 it inherited a desperate situation: it was to preside over a country in which unemployment would rise to over one million and inflation touch 25 per cent. Everything the state attempted seemed to make matters worse. Even Labour's pragmatic temporary conversion to what the then Chancellor, Denis Healey, described as 'practical monetarism' failed. By the end of 1976 the economic bedrock on which the post-war consensus rested was in severe difficulty.

The best accounts of this period is undoubtedly that of Middlemas (1991, part I, especially ch. 1). While largely written from the perspective of the political and business élite, it brilliantly captures the extent to which the foundations of the post-war Social Democratic settlement were shaken by the momentous events of the period. It shows how the crisis went beyond mere material factors to the very heart of the post-war settlement leading, first, to a questioning and then to a loss of faith in the established modes of thinking and practice in government.

This loss of faith created the context from which the New Right (see Chapters 1 and 5 for more details) emerged. Brittan (1975) challenged the very basis of post-war liberal democracy, arguing that the constant need of the two parties to appeal to and win the votes of a variety of diverse interests had produced a dangerous spiral in which more and more promises were being made by the parties to win elections which were proving increasingly difficult, if not impossible, to fulfil once elected. This threatened to undermine the authority of the state and create a *legitimacy crisis*. Concommitant with this was King's (1975) argument that this constant expansion of the state was producing *overloaded government*, which was taking on more and more commitments but becoming less and less able to fulfil them. Additionally, Bacon and Eltis (1976) argued that public expenditure was *crowding out*, in both financial and physical terms, the private sector, and thus undermining the motor which provided the resources for the whole of society.

Taken together, these ideas provided a sustained attack upon the post-war settlement, emphasising the virtues of a minimal state, individual liberty, choice, the free market and the entrepreneurial spirit. Most of all it was asserted that the unshackling of these forces would benefit society as a whole. The Institute for Economic Affairs (IEA) and, to a lesser extent, the Thatcher/Joseph Centre for Policy Studies (CPS) played an important role in spreading and popularising these ideas. Many were not new (arguably they dated back to Adam Smith's work and all had certainly been around since the 1950s) but it was the events of the mid-1970s which created the vacuum into which they could insert themselves. This, of course, was not an automatic process and required a political party, the Conservatives under Margaret Thatcher, to articulate them and bring them to bear on government.

It was into this cold climate that the lessons and results of the early urban initiatives emerged, and it was this climate that determined the limits and possibilities of action for any government which intended to act on the new structural diagnosis of urban problems. The 1977 White Paper, *A Policy for the Inner Cities*, bore the indelible imprint of this crisis; we will now go on to consider it in depth.

# 4 The Watershed? Urban Policy 1977–79

This chapter is primarily concerned with the 1977 White Paper *Policy for the Inner Cities* (HMSO, Cmnd 6845). We examine the context in which it was published, its implications for urban policy and the proposals which flowed from it via the Inner Urban Areas Act, 1978. We will:

- Outline the key background themes which were current at the time when the White Paper was being prepared.
- Discuss the White Paper itself and the proposals it contained.
- Examine the operation and effectiveness of the 'partnership authorities' which were created by the 1978 Act.
- Compare theoretical interpretations and assess policy coherence.

## The background to the White Paper

In Chapter 3 we outlined the social, political and economic state of Britain in the mid-1970s. We also identified the shortcomings of the then current urban initiatives. We shall not repeat that material here; we shall simply summarise the key issues which structured debate during the planning phase for the 1977 White Paper.

The publication of research by the CDPs and IASs undermined the prevailing social pathology approach to urban problems. As a result, the assumption that urban poverty was the result of the behaviourial patterns of individuals and communities and the way to deal with it was to change the behaviour of those in poverty, was challenged. The mythical power of the area approach was also questioned. It was clearly no longer adequate for policy-makers to assume that discrete pockets of urban poverty could easily be identified and that lines could be drawn around them on maps; both the CDPs and IASs challenged this view, pointing to the structural causes of urban poverty and its intimate link with wider issues of urban economic decline (CDP, 1977a, 1977b; Llewellyn-Davies and associates, 1977).

The second factor structuring debate on urban policy in the mid-1970s was the division of responsibilities between the Home Office and the Department of the Environment. As we have already pointed out, the former was responsible, among other things, for the UP, CDPs and Section 11 Grants under the Local Government Act, 1966. The latter had undertaken the IASs. Any review of approaches to urban problems would have to look at the extent to which this division of responsibilities generated competition between the two departments, hindered co-operation and led to an inefficient use of resources and less effective urban initiatives.

Third, we should remind the reader, briefly, of the wider politicoeconomic context in which planning for the White Paper was carried out. The British economy had entered a crisis by 1975 (see Middlemas, 1991; Jessop, 1980) and appeared to be in a state of terminal decline. At the same time, the state appeared unable to cope with these problems; its role was being questioned, with increasing doubt being cast upon the effectiveness of state intervention and in particular the value of public expenditure.

All in all, conditions were hardly sympathetic to the launching of a major and wide-ranging review of a problem which available research suggested was rooted deeply within the structures of a capitalist economy and which would require major investment to even begin to counter that decline. The situation was further complicated by the Labour government's political unpopularity and its need to retain, or win back, key sections of its electorate by doing something, or being seen to be doing something, to help them.

Planning for the White Paper was initiated by the new Secretary of State at the DoE, Peter Shore, who displayed a greater interest in urban decline and poverty than has his predecessor, Anthony Crosland. While Shore's appointment was an important catalytic element in the reassessment of urban policy, it would, however, be wrong to see the decision to review urban initiatives as solely a result of his appointment. As we have noted, the results of CDP reports had been available for some time and information from the IASs, established by a Conservative, Peter Walker (the then Secretary of State for the Environment), in 1972, were beginning to permeate government thinking during 1976. Indeed Higgins *et al.* (1983,

p. 121) note that the formal review process, begun in 1976, had its roots in a process which began in August 1975, before Shore's appointment.

The review considered both the causes of urban problems and the organisational and administrative arrangements best suited to remedy the problems and aid the victims. Higgins *et al.* (1983, pp. 117–18) have noted that this was something of a departure from previous practice, as it represented 'A systematic attempt . . . to set out policy objectives in advance of a new initiative. This was a sharp break with the previous approach by which such new initiatives were worked up and their objectives defined, if at all, in the privacy of Whitehall'.

## The White Paper: *Policy for the Inner Cities*

In our view, the 1977 White Paper represents the first serious attempt by a government in the post-war era, if not in this century, to understand the nature and causes of Britain's urban problems. Despite our suggestion that its proposals cannot be divorced from the Labour government's need to restore its electoral popularity and retain its electoral constituency, we believe the White Paper to have been a watershed event in the development of urban policy. Exactly what sort of watershed however, is open to dispute.

### The diagnosis

As we noted in Chapters 2 and 3, for most of the period between 1945 and 1968 there had been no urban policy as such. In policy terms, the period was dominated by a combination of the physical approach and the social pathology approach: both made extensive use of area-based policies. There was little official awareness of the urban–rural shift and its effects; indeed policy seems, to an extent, to have unconsciously reinforced this trend. Nor was much thought given to the possibility that Britain's cities were in a state of serious economic, social and physical decline caused by wider regional, national and international economic forces which, since at least 1945 and more likely the 1880s, had been undermining Britain's position within the world economy.

The crucial achievement of the 1977 White Paper was to go some distance towards rectifying these critical lacunae. In its second paragraph it noted that: 'too little attention has been paid to the economic well being and to the community life of the inner areas and the physical fabric in some parts is badly neglected or decayed' (HMSO, 1977, p. 1).

Furthermore, explicit acknowledgment of the effects of the urban–rural shift was also made, accompanied by an admission that government policies had actually contributed to this shift and thus needed to be reconsidered and in some cases modified, or even reversed. It was argued that the urban–rural shift and deindustrialisation had been accompanied by a widespread physical decline in the built environment within the inner cities, most notably with regard to the housing stock. This had been exacerbated by the disjunction between clearance and rebuilding (HMSO, 1977, paras 11–13) leading to a situation in which there were considerable expanses of vacant and derelict land. When added to a lack of investment in inner-city resources and community amenities, this created an environment that encouraged neither new industrial investment nor inward migration; indeed, it had the opposite effect. Thus a vicious spiral was created which, the White Paper declared, needed not only to be broken but also reversed. The strategy for the achievement of this end was to entail the analysis of how general forces interacted to produce a particular set of local problems (HMSO, 1977, para. 21).

The social dimension was also acknowledged, with the recognition that urban problem areas 'have a higher concentration of poor people' (HMSO, 1977, p. 3), reflecting both high levels of unemployment and low levels of pay. In addition, there was an indication, although only partial, that the government was aware that, while inner cities had lost population overall, the results of population movement were complex. As a result, although a much reduced population remained, new but different residents were being drawn in by the type of labour and housing markets left behind. These residents were discriminated against, not only in terms of community resources but also with regard to access to key resources such as mortgages. In particular, the White Paper openly acknowledged that, in some cities, race and racial discrimination was a key element in the urban 'problem' and that urban policy should take explicit account of the needs of ethnic minorities (see Chapter 10).

*The remedy*

Part III of the White Paper demonstrated an awareness of the multi-faceted nature of urban decline. The forces causing this decline were recognised to be of a number of types, operating at a variety of levels and thus requiring co-ordinated action at a variety of levels, from the national to the local. The general aims of the policies which were to address this new-found diagnosis were:

(1)   the need to seek economic improvement;
(2)   the need to improve the physical environment;
(3)   social improvement; and
(4)   a new balance between population and jobs.

Economic improvement was felt to require action on two fronts (HMSO, 1977, para. 27): retaining existing jobs and the encouragement of indigenous industrial growth, particularly via the cultivation of small businesses, job training and an improved transport infrastructure. This, it was declared, necessitated action by both public and private sectors. Physical improvement required improvement of the housing stock, better use of vacant land, and a general beautification of the local environment. Improvement of the social infrastructure of inner areas (HMSO, 1977, para. 29) was somewhat vaguely defined but seemed to refer to the immediate amelioration of the conditions of those living in inner areas, while economic and physical improvement work would have effects in the medium and long term. Together, these aims would, it was hoped, counter tendencies to decentralisation by retaining existing inhabitants/firms in the inner cities and attracting new ones (HMSO, 1977, para. 28). The need to secure a new balance between jobs and population was clearly a crucial aim, but one dependent upon the others, and particularly upon physical and economic improvement. The new balance needed to occur not just in the context of particular cities but also in relation to their wider regional contexts (HMSO, 1977, para. 30).

Part IV of the White Paper described the methods, agencies and organisations which would put into operation the above proposals. The primary agency in the regeneration process was to be the local authorities. The government stated that they 'are the natural agencies to tackle inner area problems' (HMSO, 1977, p. 8). This 'naturalness' was held to be a product of their closeness to the problems, experience of the relevant areas, local accountability and existing role as providers of many of the key services (e.g. social services, housing) which would play a major part in any renewal process.

Interestingly, despite this clear decision to go for a leading role for the local authorities, there is an equally clear indication that the Government gave serious attention to the possibility of taking responsibility for renewal out of the hands of local authorities and handing it over to quasi-governmental organisations, similar to New Town Development Corporations (see Chapter 2) and broadly the same as the Urban Development Corporations which the Conservative government would introduce in 1980 (see Chapter 7). Such organisations could, it was argued, 'bring to bear single-minded management, industrial promotion expertise and experience in carrying out development' (HMSO, 1977, p. 8). This option was rejected because of the White Paper's belief in the need to ensure the involvement of the local community in the rejuvenation process.

The commitment to the local authority role was tempered by a new realism which may have reflected the emerging New Right critique of the state. Local authorities were expected to become more 'entrepreneurial in attraction of industry and commerce' (HMSO, 1977, p. 8). They were not to be given *carte blanche* to develop idiosyncratic remedies to local problems; they were to work in *partnership* with other government agencies at both central and local level in order to overcome localism and departmentalism and allow a co-ordinated and comprehensive approach to the problems to be adopted, a development influenced by the CCPs. Moreover, wherever possible, voluntary organisations were also to be closely integrated into these organisational arrangements and into specific programmes, thus ensuring that the local community played a major role and that programmes reflected its aspirations and needs. As the White Paper noted: 'Self-help is important and so is community effort' (HMSO, 1977, p. 8). Finally, and perhaps most significantly, the *private sector* was to be fully involved. The White Paper stated:

> The absence of much spontaneous growth and regeneration is one of the hallmarks of the inner areas . . . Local authorities now need . . . to stimulate investment by the private sector . . . The resources and energies of small and medium size firms are

essential if real progress is to be made and the diversity and vitality, for so long a characteristic of inner cities, is to be restored. (HMSO, 1977, p. 9)

The public sector's role was thus to provide the conditions (infrastructure, a sympathetic planning regime, and so on.) in which the private sector could flourish. In a sense, local government, and other public sector bodies, were being asked to *facilitate* the development of the private sector, and in particular to address the needs of small and medium-sized firms. These were seen to be particularly important as it had frequently been alleged that the planning and redevelopment policies of local government had played a major role in forcing these types of firm either to close down completely or to relocate outside the inner city. This viewpoint was to receive greater emphasis on the return of the Conservative government in 1979, small and medium-sized firms then being seen, for a period at least, as the potential regenerators of the inner city (Nicholson *et al.*, 1981).

The White Paper also recognised that the encouragement of industrial growth involved an *inter-regional* aspect. As a result it was hoped that the Department of Industry (DoI) would use its regional development grant funds to support industrial growth in the inner areas of cities in the Assisted Areas. Additionally it was hoped that the DoI would use its Industrial Development Certificates and Office Development Permits flexibly and creatively to 'facilitate the growth of employment in inner areas' (HMSO, 1977, pp. 12–13). The government also acknowledged the need to enhance the pull of inner areas by providing a more sympathetic planning regime and ensuring that the local population had the necessary skills to attract firms. To the latter end, the Manpower Services Commission (MSC) was required to give its policies a distinct inner city dimension.

This rejigging of existing policies and reorientation of public sector activity to benefit the inner cities was common to all participating agencies. It provided a key means by which the '*unified approach*' to inner area problems was to be achieved and a piecemeal response avoided (HMSO, 1977, para. 59). Even existing urban initiatives were to be recast. The Urban Programme was shifted away from its major emphasis on community and social projects towards industrial, environmental and recreational programmes.

Decentralisation policies were to be recast and New Towns policy was effectively abandoned.

In a practical sense, the White Paper indicated that the government intended to establish *Partnership* arrangements, in which they would enter into 'partnership' with the selected local authorities and other agencies with the express aim of achieving a unified approach to urban decay. The Partnership Authorities would receive preference in the allocation of Urban Programme funds. In addition, further areas would be designated as *Programme Authorities*; they would receive second preference in the allocation of funds. A third tier of *Other Designated Areas* was also to be established. In Scotland the White Paper proposed a targeting of increased UP funds on the east end of Glasgow (McKay and Cox, 1979, p. 254; see Chapter 9 for more details).

The DoE, operating in Scotland and Wales through the relevant Development Agencies which had been set up in 1975, was to have overall charge of the new *inner area policy*, as it became known (Sills *et al.*, 1988). Locally, as we have stated, the lead role was to go to the local authorities. In order to drive the policy along lines which would enable the 'unified approach' the government laid great stress on the need for *corporate management*. To this end it signalled an intention to disseminate the results of the CCPs which, as we have already noted, were brought into the DoE from the Home Office and concerned with the application of corporate management to problems of deprivation and the allocation of resources within local authorities.

Obviously, the resourcing of the programme, especially one as ambitious as this, was to be absolutely crucial. The proposals in the White Paper included an increase in Urban Programme funding from £30 million to £125 million per annum by 1979/80. However, by far the greatest source for this finance was to be the Rate Support Grant (RSG) which in 1977 provided £6000 million to local government (HMSO, 1977, para. 47). There was, however, no intention of increasing the RSG to finance the programme. What was envisaged was a redirection of funds from the 'shire' counties to the urban areas. It was also assumed that considerable additional resources would come in 'hidden transfers' from other central government departments, such as the Department of Industry, as they recast their policies to favour the inner cities. Moreover, it was hoped, though never clearly stated, that all this government activity would encourage the private sector to invest in these areas. This in turn, it was hoped, would both create more financial resources for local and central government via taxes, and also create jobs and community resources for inner area inhabitants via 'trickle-down'. In other words, it was intended that a *multiplier effect* would come into operation, creating an upward spiral of resource generation which in turn could be reinvested in the chosen areas.

## Commentary

Undoubtedly one of the most important aspects of the White Paper was its recognition that urban decline and urban poverty had *structural causes located in economic, social and political relations which originated outside the areas concerned.* This represented the official acknowledgement of what the CDPs, IASs and academic researchers had already been saying (see Chapter 3). Given this, the White Paper clearly represents an important step forward, even a watershed, in the development of post-war urban policy. It rejected the previous piecemeal approach to urban problems and for the first time created the possibility that a genuinely integrated policy could be developed. There were, however, a number of problems.

## Finance

The very fact that the White Paper had acknowledged that the problems facing Britain's cities were deep-rooted and had their causes in the historically-created industrial structures of those areas, caused difficulties. The diagnosis implied that any action to counteract these forces would require *the commitment of very large financial resources over a considerable period of time* at a time when the wisdom of public expenditure was being questioned. By the standards of the time, such a commitment was expected to originate almost entirely from the public purse.

Quite naturally, the government (or more specifically the Treasury) was wary of making very substantial long-term resource commitments over which it had little or no control and little evaluative evidence on which to base an investment decision. The whole system of public expenditure control was primarily concerned to prevent, or at least to limit, the government's commitment to policies which implied a large, continuous and possibly expanding commitment of public resources (Heald, 1983, chs 1–3). Even at the height of the post-war consensus, governments had been wary of such commitments; by the time of the White Paper's launch the situation had changed considerably. Ideological doubts about public expenditure had taken root and there was a widespread, and growing, assumption that public expenditure was 'out of control' (Stewart, 1977; Heald, 1983). This did not augur well for the resourcing of the inner urban programme.

## The private sector

What was already an extremely inauspicious situation in which to launch a major new public policy was made even worse by the rise to prominence of ideas that state action was an inefficient, ineffective and uneconomic method of dealing with problems. 'The market', that is, private sector activity, was increasingly being put forward as a better solution. Indeed, for the political forces represented by Margaret Thatcher, by then leader of the Conservative party in opposition, the growth of the state during the post-war era was part of the problem. As she was later to argue, the boundaries of the state should be rolled back to enable private enterprise to step in.

The impact of these ideas can clearly be seen at work in the White Paper. We should note the emphasis on the private sector, the stress on creating an infrastructure conducive to private-sector-led growth, and on the need for local government to relax its planning controls and take a much more sympathetic view of the needs of business. Urban regeneration was to be a partnership between public and private sectors in a way that earlier approaches had never been. Yet, ironically, very little space was given to how the private sector might formally be integrated into the development and actualisation of policy. At best it seems that the government hoped its actions would create the context in which the private sector would decide to invest. In the middle of a global recession this perhaps reflected a little naïvety.

It is by no means clear whether the Labour government's change in attitude to the private sector represented a genuine conversion to free market economics. It may merely have been a tactical retreat in order to win and maintain the confidence of the international financial community. We would suggest that the apparent change was an attempt to appease the growing strength of the market lobby and secure the emergence of more favourable conditions in which it could ensure an election victory. This latter aspect is important; by

1976 unemployment had risen to around 1.5 million and many of the unemployed were part of Labour's essential bed-rock electoral support in the inner cities. The 1977 White Paper may be seen partially as a rather hurried element in the electoral strategy for retaining that support.

### Management

For all the stress which was placed on the increased role for the market, the organisational forms and methods advocated by the White Paper bore an extremely strong resemblance to those of corporate management as advocated in local government in the 1960s and 1970s (Bains, 1972; Greenwood and Stewart, 1974; for critical commentaries see Dearlove, 1979; and Clapham, 1985). In part the influence can be seen to come from the experience of the CCP experiments and their formal linkage to the White paper (see Chapter 3). In effect, the White Paper hoped that, by adopting these organisational and management techniques, the relevant bodies would prioritise urban problems, placing those identified by the White Paper at the top of the list, redirect their resources towards them and adopt integrative and co-ordinative management systems which would bind and focus all their energies on the problems identified. The clear hope was that not only local government but also central government departments would reassess their policies, giving them a specific inner-area dimension.

Corporate management was also expected to lead to greater efficiency. Its use, it was hoped, would mean that little in the way of new resources would be required. Indeed, in the House of Commons, the resources made available in the Inner Urban Areas Bill were described by the Conservative MP Michael Heseltine (then Opposition spokesperson on the Environment) and several other participants in the debate, as modest and, in more than one case, as 'chicken-feed'.

For Labour, the Secretary of State for the Environment (Peter Shore) stressed that: 'The Bill is only one part, albeit an important one, of our attack on the problems of urban deprivation' (Hansard. Vol. 943, col. 1686, 9.2.78). It was repeatedly asserted that major resources would be made available by central departments 'bending' their programmes to benefit inner areas. The reality of the situation was different; the envisaged resource bending did not occur. Higgins *et al.* (1983, p. 118) correctly suggest that the White Paper represented an administrative solution to the problem of minimising input and maximising output, and a misplaced belief that improved management methods can function as a panacea for all problems.

*A watershed?*

The causal analysis advocated by the White Paper clearly recognised that the area approach was totally inadequate. Yet despite this, such an approach remained central to the White Paper's proposals. This can partly be explained in the context of the shortage of resources: it was assumed to be better to concentrate on a few areas where the limited resources available might be expected to make a difference. However, it also reflects a failure to acknowledge fully the futility of drawing lines around areas on maps on the assumption that, by so doing, the forces leading to decline could be cornered, countered, and even reversed.

So was the 1977 White Paper really a watershed in post-war urban policy? It would seem that we have presented evidence that would cast doubt on our earlier claim. Yet this very much depends upon how the notion of a watershed is understood. It is very tempting to understand it as a clean and total break with the past. Unfortunately, this interpretation, while obviously attractive, is far too simplistic; breaks are never clean and total. Rather they consist of series of dislocations which, while introducing new elements, retain important, and often contradictory, elements of the past. Established patterns of thinking and understanding are simply not discarded in a moment, nor can established practices easily be abandoned.

While apparently dropping the social pathology approach and replacing it with a much more valid diagnosis of the problem, the government was unable to jettison key organisational elements and the area approach from its previous policies. This suggests elements of both continuity and discontinuity; the watershed notion is principally reflected in the causal diagnosis rather than in the organisational and management forms which were adopted.

## The Partnerships

In this section we will examine in detail the experience of the Partnerships in order to see to what extent they were able to realise the ambitions of the White Paper. We will place this examination in the wider context of the declared goal of the White Paper concerning co-operation between central and local government (detailed studies can be found in Higgins *et al.*, 1983, ch. 5; Lawless, 1980, 1986, ch. 4; Nabarro, 1980; Parkinson and Wilks, 1983, 1986; Sharman, 1979; and Tilley, 1979).

*Selection*

The Inner Urban Areas Act, 1978, created seven Partnerships, fifteen Programme Authorities and nineteen Designated Areas (Table 4.1). The seven Partnerships were located in Liverpool, Birmingham, Lambeth, the London Docklands, Manchester/ Salford, Newcastle/Gateshead and Hackney/Islington. It is noteworthy that, while all seven would usually be classified as 'deprived areas', it would be difficult to argue that they were any more deprived than a score of other inner-city areas.

The selection of three of the areas (Lambeth, Liverpool and Birmingham) may be linked to the fact that areas of the same cities had been chosen, for equally unclear reasons, as part of the IASs. Given the extent to which the Partnerships sought to build on that earlier initiative, we can see their selection in terms of continuity. It

**TABLE 4.1   Partnerships, programme areas and designated areas**

| | |
|---|---|
| **Partnerships** | Birmingham; Liverpool; Manchester and Salford; Newcastle and Gateshead; Lambeth; Hackney and Islington; London Docklands |
| **Programme areas** | Bolton; Bradford; Hammersmith; Hull; Leeds; Leicester; Middlesborough; North Tyneside; Nottingham: Oldham; Sheffield; South Tyneside; Sunderland; Wirral; Wolverhampton |
| **Designated areas** | Barnsley; Blackburn; Brent; Doncaster; Ealing; Harringey; Hartlepool; Rochdale; Rotherham; St Helens; Sandwell; Sefton; Wandsworth; Wigan; Blaenau Gwent; Cardiff; Newport; Rhondda; Swansea |

may be that the remaining four reflected the Labour government's desire to be seen to do something for its electorate but, as McKay and Cox (1979, p. 256) argue, it seems unlikely that this would be a prime reason for choosing locations, particularly locations where the safety of the Labour vote was not, to any significant extent, in doubt at the time. One is left with a sense that there was clearly a certain arbitrariness about the whole process.

## Structure

Each partnership had broadly the same basic structure (Lawless, 1986, ch. 4; Higgins *et al.*, 1983, ch. 5). In essence this had three tiers. On the top tier was the *Partnership Committee*. It was chaired by a central government minister and contained representatives from the central government departments which were deemed to have a role to play in the regeneration of inner areas. They were accompanied by senior representatives from local government (county and district), the health service and the police. The Partnership Committee's role was to act as a co-ordinating body and ensure that the multiplicity of organisations worked towards the same end; it was not an executive body.

At the second tier was the *Officer's Steering Group*. It was chaired by a regional director of the DoE and contained senior officers from other government departments, relevant personnel from the local authorities involved and other interested parties such as the Chief Constable and senior officials from the local health authority. Its primary responsibility was to develop a programme of action tailored to the local Partnership's needs and to ensure its realisation. The *Inner City Team* was to be found at the third, and lowest tier. It was made up of relevant officers from local government and local representatives of central government. Other interested parties such as voluntary groups were co-opted on to the team. In essence, this was where the majority of the day-to-day work was carried out and where plans drawn up at higher level and passed downwards had to be made a reality.

## Policy aims

The policy aims of the Partnerships were essentially dictated by the White Paper. The relevant committees were asked to draw up programmes of action which reflected problems, and propose solutions in a fashion consistent with the White Paper. While the Partnership Committee worked at a fairly general level, the Inner City Team was clearly and obviously charged with making a local reality of the policy. At the top of the list of policy aims was *economic regeneration* and it was hoped that there would, additionally, be a particular emphasis on retaining and attracting the *private sector*.

Local authorities were empowered to make loans to firms, and much was made of this during debate about the Act. However, the main issues identified in the Inner Urban Areas Act mirrored the White Paper and implied a straightforward emphasis on improving the road and housing infrastructure of the areas concerned and ensuring that the local population had the skills required by existing and prospective employers. Attention was additionally to be given to improving educational, recreational and community facilities in the selected areas and it was hoped that the voluntary sector could make a major contribution to such developments. Finally there was a hope that improved health services could be achieved. This was all to be underwritten by a process of general environmental improvements, which included the landscaping of vacant and derelict sites, and land reclamation.

*The Partnerships in operation*

The Partnerships had a certain elegant simplicity about their structures but, as with all such experiments in co-ordination and management, they contained a series of potentially explosive and unresolvable problems. Let us begin at the national level. As we noted earlier, government policy had played a part in encouraging the movement of population and industry out of cities. Indeed Massey and Meegan (1978) argue that, during the 1960s, the government-created Industrial Reorganisation Committee (IRC), through its role in encouraging mergers and rationalisation, actually hastened the closure of inner-city factories. It was this type of policy which had to be reversed and this required the relevant central departments to rethink their policies and give them a bias in favour of the inner city rather than against it.

This the Inner Areas Policy attempted to do. Lawless (1981), for example, notes that the initiatives flowing from the White Paper required the Department of Industry (DoI) to alter its policy on the allocation of various forms of regional aid, most notably regional development grants. This it steadfastly refused to do and the £700 million it had to spend in 1978/79 was largely directed *away* from inner areas. Although the Partnerships in London and Birmingham were in any case outside the area qualifying for regional aid, the main problem was that the DoE lacked the authority to force the DoI (or indeed any other department) to 'bend' its policies in the manner desired. The best it could do was to persuade.

Lawless (1981, pp. 5–6) notes that the DoE was relatively unsuccessful at such persuasion. Only the MSC made attempts to ensure that its initiatives had an inner-city dimension and even there the extent of commitment was debatable (Lawless, 1981, pp. 9–12). Lawless also suggests that the DoI's creation of the National Enterprise Board (NEB) in 1975 to assist the growth and development of internationally competitive industries, rather like the actions of the IRC, precluded other than minimal investment in the partnership areas, or urban areas in general. Given the commitment of the NEB to areas of high unemployment, he may be overstressing this point. However, elements of contradiction between the policies of government departments certainly persisted and the effect of the was one of 'spreading the icing on the cake too thinly'.

Also, at the national level lay a problem of funding. As we have noted, the vast majority of the additional funding required to resource the programme was to come from the redirection of the RSG from shire to urban areas. Shirley Williams, the then Secretary of State for Education, expressed considerable doubts about this tactic, as did the Home Office (Higgins *et al.*, 1983, pp. 125–6). Thus from the very beginning, and at the very highest level, there were very serious political, financial and administrative obstacles placed in the path of the new policy.

Things were no better at the Partnership level. Several of the Partnerships involved more than one local authority and this was, in some cases, to provide a recipe for conflict. In at least two cases the local authorities found it impossible to work together. Manchester/ Salford might as well have been two separate Partnerships; they were unable to draw up a joint plan for the area. They therefore formulated plans for their own areas and split the additional funding accordingly (Parkinson and Wilks, 1983, p. 31). In Liverpool there were strong conflicts between the district and county council

(Parkinson and Wilks, 1983, 1986). Liverpool also illustrates a second problem within local authorities: political instability and traditional competition between departments for dominance interrupted the development of the plan and funds were carved up on the basis of a departmental pecking order rather than on a generally agreed programme of action (Parkinson and Wilks, 1983, 1986).

Inter-agency conflict provided a third negative theme at the local level. Higgins *et al.* (1983, p. 145) note how, in the Lambeth Partnership, requests to the area health authority to give priority to the partnership area were rejected on the grounds that it only covered a part of the health authority's area and that it could not receive priority over other parts. In the Docklands Partnership, Sharman (1979) notes how each of the London Boroughs within the partnership area appointed their own Industrial Development Officers to attract industry to their particular borough, thus promoting competition between the authorities who made up the Partnership and hampering the development of a co-ordinated approach to the area's problems. Contrary to government hopes, the voluntary sector found itself largely marginalised from both policy-making and resource allocation (Lawless, 1986, pp. 83–4).

The essence of these problems has been ably summed up by Lawless (1980, p. 31): 'Evidence from the Partnerships suggests that effective coordination has been limited, and that some organisations view the arrangements as a threat to autonomous policy making'. The central element to these difficulties may well have been problems stemming from what Parkinson and Wilks (1986) have defined as the 'top-down' nature of the initiative. It was begun and, to a considerable extent, controlled and framed by central government. Obstacles emerged to confound the chosen 'administrative fix', in this instance corporate management. As elsewhere (see Dearlove, 1979; Clapham, 1985) corporate management failed to act as a unifying force and departments, at both central and local level, failed to subordinate their priorities to the wider goals of inner city regeneration and focus all their energies and resources on an agreed set of problems.

This situation was made worse by the fact that the Partnerships were launched in a rather hurried fashion during 1978 as an election loomed on the horizon. The Labour government clearly wanted the Partnerships to be up, running and having an effect before a possible autumn election. This meant that there was very little time to engage in the required strategic planning. As a result, in order to spend the money allocated, authorities found themselves spending it on projects already in the pipeline or projects shelved due to lack of funds. Thus there was a somewhat uncoordinated appearance to the first year of the Partnerships, and the hoped for stress on industrial/economic regeneration was lacking. Just into their second year of operation, they found themselves under the administration of a new and apparently radical free-market anti-state Conservative government.

**Assessment**

It may seem a little harsh to try and assess the policies flowing from the White Paper given the early ejection of the government which proposed them. We believe, however, that sufficient evidence exists to make a general assessment of their development during the period under consideration using the criteria we proposed in Chapter 1 (Table 4.2). We will return briefly to the Partnerships in the next chapter for an assessment of their eventual fate.

The conception of the urban became more coherent and the notion of urban decline was clearly acknowledged in the White Paper but it would be stretching belief to argue that a clearly defined notion of 'the urban' existed. The major step forward was the move from a social pathology to a structural approach, this allowed the government to acknowledge that urban decline had to be located in a wider context: urban problems were related to cities' long-term economic decline, the urban–rural shift, and deindustrialisation. However, while there is no doubt that the White Paper clearly identified the general nature of urban decline, a question mark must hang over the extent to which it correctly identified the *causes* of that decline. It took a rather cautious position, emphasising the long-term nature of the decline, pointing to the loss of people and jobs from cities, and highlighting the shortfall of private investment (HMSO, 1977, pp. 2–3). The resulting policy aims were, quite rightly, the reversal of these trends. However, the resulting policy mechanisms were a rather unhappy mixture of traditional post-war state intervention, corporate management techniques and market forces.

TABLE 4.2   Urban policy 1977–79

|  | Urban Policy |
| --- | --- |
| Conception of urban | Relatively coherent; urban decline given central position in 1977 White Paper |
| Theoretical approach | Structural; state-directed partnership with private and voluntary sectors |
| Nature of problem | Long-term economic and environmental decline; concentrated effects in cities |
| Explanation | Deindustrialisation affecting urban fabric; urban–rural shift |
| Aim of policy | Reverse industrial decline; stop urban–rural shift |
| Mechanisms | Partnerships; area-based policies with tenuous links to national policy; greater role for private sector |
| Resourcing | Small compared to acknowledged scale of problem |
| Management | Corporate management; co-operation between central and local government |
| Political Support | Largely consensual though role of state coming under question |
| Legislation | Inner Urban Areas Act, 1978 |
| Monitoring | Limited |

New Right critics would argue that the existing, and indeed resulting, problems were caused by the forms of state intervention which were retained. The time had come to allow a much more dominant role for market forces as the only realistic method of regenerating urban areas. Marxists (Rees and Lambert, 1985), on the other hand, would argue that decline has its origins in uneven development, which was an inevitable result of industrial capitalist processes on world, national and regional levels. From this perspective the problem, in part, has its causes at the international level way beyond the reach of individual national governments. A strict Marxist interpretation might suggest that any attempts to reverse the decline within the confines of capitalist society were doomed to failure or could succeed only at the expense of condemning other areas to a similar fate of decline. From this perspective the UP could be portrayed as being merely concerned with ameliorating the worst excesses of decline (Bridges, 1981/2).

The aim of the UP was clearly to regenerate urban areas. However, the inherent contradictions between a recognition of a structural process and the need for a recognisable local policy output, and between the need for public investment and the desire to encourage the private sector, were never clearly addressed. This is especially so for the role of the private sector. It could only be expected to participate if a profit could be guaranteed, but that was not the case. Furthermore, the potential for clashes between policies facilitating regeneration for local residents and those enabling regeneration which would benefit private capital were considerable. It would appear that the policy aim was by no means as clear as it might have been, and the potential for conflict over and amongst them was considerable.

The mechanisms for the achievement of the aim were also problematic owing, in part, to the failure of each of the Partnerships to draw up adequate plans of action for their areas. Nabarro (1980, pp. 35) pointed to 'the lack of any convincing discussion, in any of the documents, of the causes of the crisis in their particular locality . . . The Partnerships have not attempted to work out how they are affected by these forces [identified in the White Paper], or attempted to assess the strength of the trends working against them'. The use of what amounted to an area-based approach inadequately conceptualised and articulated to a structural explanation compounded this shortcoming and indicated that not only the aims and explanations, but also the remedies proposed in the IUP were contradictory.

We have already argued that the funding arrangements for the IUP were inadequate. We pointed to the problems involved in any significant reallocation of resources within the RSG and the low likelihood of central departments, and their local representatives, significantly reorientating their existing programmes towards the inner cities. It is this element in the analysis which is most susceptible to a pluralist assessment; the competition between interest groups within central and local government effectively undermined the proposed approach to funding. The funds eventually allocated to the Partnerships were clearly inadequate to the task of regenerating the chosen areas. In effect, they were what Nabarro (1980) described as 'pump priming' funds or, in more market-based terminology, 'seed corn'. Their failure to entice the private sector meant there must have been little understanding of its real needs and, as Nabarro (1980, p. 25) notes, IUP funds were largely used to undertake 'projects which fall outside the main programmes of central and local government, or for topping up what has been done in other ways'. Lawless (1986, pp. 80–1) also notes that the additional funds received by the Partnerships were frequently used to fill in gaps caused by funds lost in the post-1976 expenditure retrenchment.

The situation regarding the management of the IUP has been ably summarised in two astute and perceptive articles: Cox (1979) and Hambleton (1981). Like ourselves, Hambleton pointed to the failure of the new policy initiative to 'challenge three fundamental organising principles of urban government: uniformity of service provision, functional service management and formal political and departmental hierarchies of control' (Hambleton, 1981, p. 64).

While being aware of the 'symbolic' element of the policy, he believed that there was a wide range of individuals who were, consciously or unconsciously, committed to the IUP approach to inner-city regeneration (Hambleton, 1981, p. 68). With Cox, this was certainly not the case, as from the very outset he emphasised the 'cosmetic' nature of the policy. He argued (Cox, 1979, p. 2) that:

> the shape of inner urban policy has been determined to a large extent, by a desire to minimise administrative upheaval, while at the same time attempting to do something for the inner city, within the inevitable fiscal constraints imposed by the Treasury's economic policies aimed at reducing public expenditure. (Cox, 1979, p. 6)

In terms similar to those used by Hambleton and ourselves, he identified what he termed an 'administrative inertia' which prevented/blocked the development of a policy that would seriously tackle the problems of the inner city. For Hambleton (1981, p. 52):

> Inner city policy cannot be viewed as an alternative to wider social and economic policies to help deprived groups, nor can it be

expected to transform inner city living conditions in the short term. The policy can, however, ease the transition from one labour market structure to another and can help to compensate inner area residents for their relatively disadvantaged position.

As regards management arrangements, we have therefore once again shown that a policy which required considerable co-ordination and co-operation failed rather badly.

We have already considered the issue of political commitment. The IUP undoubtedly had an almost total support from the Labour Party, whether for electoral or other reasons. Its acknowledgement of the private sector might have been expected to appeal to Conservatives but, given the increasingly strident free-market lobby, was generally felt not to go far enough. At first sight the passing of the Inner Urban Areas Act, 1978, combined with existing powers, would also appear to have provided a legislative basis sufficient to the task. Yet the depth of the urban problem and the political instability of the times meant that the lifespan of any legislation could not be guaranteed and, although once again it is rather unfair to make judgements on one single year's experience, it would appear that the government failed to set up any initial evaluative machinery with which to assess the effectiveness of either the policy or the legislation.

**Conclusion**

We have noted a number of problems with the initiatives flowing from the White Paper and have discussed them at some length. What we have not discussed is the failure of those policies to address racial discrimination directly. Having opened the door by identifying racial discrimination as a serious part of the inner-city problem, the White Paper immediately shut the door again by devolving responsibility for it to the relatively peripheral Commission for Racial Equality (see Chapter 10). One of the most disappointing aspects of the 1977 initiatives was their failure to address this issue; there was a complete lack of even ritual exhortation that organisations should give their policies a dimension designed to counter racial discrimination.

Overall, we find ourselves reaching a series of apparently contradictory conclusions. On the one hand the White Paper and the policies which flowed from it represented an important break with previous practice. On the other, there were important elements of continuity with previous practice, not least with the area approach. Moreover, as we have also pointed out, despite the fine aspirations for a comprehensive and co-ordinated central and local approach to urban problems, old problems of competition, political infighting and departmentalism dogged the initiative. In this situation voluntary organisations found themselves sidelined with little or no influence over the development of policy and the allocation of resources, while the private sector seems to have been most noticeable by its absence. Finally, we have shown that the resources made available were quite small. This leads to us to agree in general terms with the comments on the Inner Urban Areas Bill by the Conservative Opposition's spokesperson on the Environment (Michael Heseltine). He argued:

My concern about the strategy is growing. I suspect that the strategy is more a description for a set of policies than a set of policies that will achieve results in the circumstances. I suspect that it is the illusion of a policy. (Hansard, Vol. 943, col. 1701, 9.2.78).

# 5 Urban Problems since 1979: The Conservative Approach

This chapter will focus on the general approach which post-1979 Conservative governments adopted towards urban regeneration. We will cover the following themes:

- The general ideas which informed urban policy during the premiership of Margaret Thatcher. This will entail a general discussion of *Thatcherism*.
- The state of Britain's cities in 1979 and the nature of urban problems as they evolved during the 1980s.
- The key themes which the Conservatives stressed in their attempt to translate theory into the practice of urban regeneration. In particular we will be concerned with how a 'free-market' approach affected the definition of urban regeneration and led to the prioritorisation of urban *economic* regeneration and the domination of a strategy of *property-led regeneration*.

## Thatcher and Thatcherism

As we argued in Chapter 1, Thatcherism was a contradictory articulation of neo-liberalism and neo-conservatism, reconciled, somewhat precariously, on a populist political platform and perhaps best encapsulated in the persona of Margaret Thatcher herself. While it achieved, and to an extent continues to exert, a degree of governmental and political dominance, its development was constrained by the political system, by pre-existing institutions and organisations, by world events, and particularly by the need to win elections. It was not a new and lasting consensus. Indeed, a number of authors have questioned whether it was even sufficiently coherent to merit the status of an 'ism' (Riddell, 1983; Keegan, 1984; Marsh and Rhodes, 1989). The political agenda was certainly changed, perhaps decisively, but as yet events are too recent for any definitive judgements.

Margaret Thatcher herself was the fulcrum around which the union of neo-liberalism and neo-conservatism moved. This process began when she successfully challenged Edward Heath in 1975 to become leader of the Conservative Party, and evolved over time (Ranelagh, 1991, ch. 7). She appealed to certain traditions which existed within the Conservative Party, and to particular popular sentiments among sections of the electorate. Hall (1983) summarises this style as *authoritarian populism*. She created what Bogdanor (1983, p. 17) has called 'a new electoral coalition'. This challenged the existing establishment, attempted to restructure British society, and internalised the contradictions between neo-liberalism and neo-conservatism. For much of the 1980s this process entailed a battle between innovation and radicalism on the economic front, and retrenchment and backward glances on the social front.

Thatcherism was also supremely pragmatic. The wilder urgings of more radical supporters and advisers were often ignored, and incremental approaches to reform favoured over root-and-branch revolution (Ranelagh, 1991, pp. 2–3). Both industrial policy and regional policy should have, on strict free-market terms, been abandoned; for political reasons both were retained in diluted form. As further evidence of this pragmatism, the Thatcher administrations seldom attempted to move forward on too many fronts at once; there was also a willingness to make tactical retreats in order to wait for more favourable conditions to emerge.

Many of Thatcherism's objectives required that the central state be strengthened. This would appear to contradict neo-liberal ideas on the state but posed no problems for neo-conservatives, who saw it as essential to restore the authority of the state. Neo-liberals were able to reconcile themselves to this by arguing that the obduracy of existing entrenched interests required that the government, in the short term, took more power in order to reduce government in the longer term. Elements of centralisation were also justified in classic liberal terms by arguing that what few things the state does it should do with authority. Thus privatisation (Marsh, 1991), a centrepiece of the government's strategy of freeing-up the economy and reducing the role of the state, required a considerable degree of centralisation for its objectives to be achieved.

*Thatcherite social policy*

Pragmatism can perhaps best be seen in relation to the welfare state. Here, despite constant urgings to dismantle the welfare state and replace it with a mixture of private insurance, friendly societies, charitable provision and workfare (Seldon, 1981; Green, 1982; Harris, 1988), Thatcherite social policy evolved rather cautiously. The sale of council housing represented perhaps the most striking attack upon the welfare state, yet the vast majority of council dwellings were not sold (Atkinson and Durden, 1990). Only towards the end of the 1980s were radical plans to reform education, the NHS and local government put into practice.

In an overall sense, Thatcherism attempted to restructure rather than dismantle the welfare state (McCarthy, 1989; Savage and Robins, 1990; Johnson, 1990). This restructuring sought essentially to shift the role of the state from that of provider to that of facilitator/enabler (Ridley, 1988). The intended effect was to move individuals away from dependence to independence. The then Secretary of State at the Department of Health and Social Security (DHSS), John Moore (1987, p. 5), argued:

We [the Conservatives] believe that dependence in the long run decreases human happiness and reduces human freedom. We believe the well-being of individuals is best protected and promoted when they are helped to be independent, to use their talents to take care of themselves and their families, and to achieve things on their own, which is one of the greatest satisfactions life can offer.

The emphasis was on responsible individuals and the family helping themselves, with the state only assisting those in real need, and then only for as short a period of time as was practicable, in order to break the *dependency culture* created by the welfare state (Baker, 1990; for a sustained critique of dependency culture see Dean and Taylor-Gooby, 1992). Responsibility for social problems was placed upon individuals, thereby absolving both state and society from responsibility.

*The Thatcher years*

It is clearly difficult to offer any objective assessment of the Thatcher years. Even central issues such as her governments' economic record are subject to great controversy. What can be said with some certainty is that Thatcherism dominated the political scene and exerted an influence into the 1990s. It reflected trends in operation since the 1950s: an increasing 'privatisation of life' involving the breakdown of wider communal values and their replacement by more individualised and instrumental values (Zweig, 1961), and, as a by-product, accentuated and intensified differences in terms of class, region, race and gender, and created a more anomic society.

This was the legacy which was left to John Major as Prime Minister in the early 1990s. While he continued and even intensified key reforms initiated by Margaret Thatcher, there was an attempt to move away from the more contentious elements of her legacy and establish an agenda which could be construed as being more compassionate (for a post-Thatcher Conservatism see Willetts, 1992). However, the abolition of National Economic Development Council (NEDC) in June 1992, indicated that there would be no return to the types of relationship between government and interest groups which prevailed in the 1960s and 1970s. It seemed that John Major might be more willing to consult and listen than Margaret Thatcher had been, but unlikely to stray too far from the positions which she established.

## Urban problems since 1979

The general economic, political and social context within which Thatcherism came to prominence and to power set considerable limitations upon the realities of policy formulation and implementation. We will now turn our attention to a consideration of the key contextual factors which constrained urban policy during the Thatcher era. As we have seen in earlier chapters, by the time the Conservatives came to power in 1979 the true nature and extent of urban decline was becoming abundantly clear. Three key issues were of particular relevance: deindustrialisation, the urban–rural shift, and the increasingly conspicuous nature of the North–South divide.

*Deindustrialisation*

By the end of the 1970s the world economy was in one of the most severe slumps in the post-Second World War era. The effects of this were to be of considerable significance for the already weakened British economy. The processes of deindustrialisation, already marked in areas dominated by nineteenth-century industries, began to spread into areas with industrial structures dominated by more modern, twentieth-century industries such as motor car assembly, electrical engineering and chemicals. This had serious implications for those areas, largely urban, in which such previously buoyant industries were located.

By the mid- to late 1970s deindustrialisation had spread to the heartland of twentieth-century manufacturing industry – the West Midlands (Healey and Clark, 1984, 1985a, 1985b; Flynn and Taylor, 1986a, 1986b). In the West Midlands county between 1978 and mid-1983 unemployment increased by 300 per cent, with manufacturing industry experiencing the greatest losses – 151 117 jobs between 1978 and 1981. This represented almost a quarter of all manufacturing jobs in the county (Flynn and Taylor, 1986a, pp. 872–3). In Coventry alone, between 1978 and 1982, 39 286 manufacturing jobs (39 per cent of the total) were lost (Healey and Clark, 1985a, p. 1354). By any standards these manufacturing losses were substantial. When they are aggregated with losses in other sectors, such as construction and services, the decline is quite simply astonishing. Martin and Rowthorn (1986) present similar evidence on more general developments in the British urban economy.

The causes of this decline can be traced back to decisions taken in the 1950s and 1960s and further aggravated by actions taken in the early 1970s (Massey, 1984). In the case of the West Midlands, the severity of the job losses were in part due to the highly integrated nature of a local economy, centred around metal and car industries which became subject during the 1960s and 1970s to intensive overseas competition. On the national scale, the economic policies of the early 1980s, which were strongly free market and anti-interventionist, did little to mitigate, and arguably exacerbated, the effects of recession and uncompetitiveness. The consequences were particularly marked for manufacturing industry and, as a result, national unemployment rose to between three and four million by 1985, depending upon how it was calculated, and the

United Kingdom lost 25.4 per cent of its industrial employment or over 2.3 million jobs (Jones and Wild, 1991, p. 3).

The process of deindustrialisation was to continue throughout the 1980s. Its impact, however, has to be seen in the context of the growth of service industries, particularly those concerned with the so-called 'producer services' such as finance and information (Daniels, 1987; Champion and Townsend, 1990, ch. 6). This growth was to lead to a downgrading of interest in the phenomenon of deindustrialisation as service growth appeared to be not only replacing lost manufacturing jobs but also offering a new way for the economy to develop. A significant restructuring of the economy appeared to be underway, not only in the obvious sense of the changing balance between manufacturing and services, but also in relation to the nature of the jobs (casual, part-time), the gender division of the workforce, and the economic geography of the United Kingdom. However, the beneficiaries of this growth were not generally the people who had previously worked in manufacturing industries (Jones and Wild, 1991, p. 27).

*The urban–rural shift*

In Chapter 4 we discussed the nature of the urban–rural population shift (Cross, 1990) and indicated its importance for long-term urban decline. Champion and Townsend (1990, p. 53) suggest that the urban–rural shift had reached its peak by the mid-1970s and by the early years of the first Thatcher administration had declined substantially. However, even during the 1980s:

> the more rural areas were still gaining population far more rapidly than the nation as a whole, and the more general process of deconcentration from the metropolitan counties and from the largest settlements in non-metropolitan counties was still continuing apace. (Champion and Townsend, 1990, p. 53)

Moreover, in the latter half of the 1980s, a second wave of non-metropolitan growth was underway with 'the remoter, mainly rural areas and resort, port and retirement areas . . . being the main beneficiaries' (Champion and Townsend, 1990, p. 54). Inner London, the locus of the chief growth of producer services, provided an important exception (Frost and Spence, 1991a,

1991b) but, generally speaking, the movement of people and jobs out of cities to suburbs and then to small free-standing towns and rural areas continued throughout the 1980s. Such areas benefited most from the services boom of the mid-1980s (see Champion and Green, 1987, 1992, for general surveys).

*The North–South divide*

Although both deindustrialisation and the urban–rural shift continued during the 1980s, it was, perhaps for political reasons, the North–South divide which attracted most attention during that decade. Smith (1989) provides a useful introduction and overview of the salient dimensions of the divide, while empirical studies include Champion and Townsend (1990) and Champion and Green (1987, 1992). In essence, throughout the 1980s, while the North of Britain continued to decline, the South, and most notably the South-East, was the country's major growth region and a process of considerable economic and social differentiation, reminiscent of the 1930s, emerged. This differentiation was not simply restricted to phenomena such as income, wealth and employment but also encompassed factors affecting lifestyle and life chances more generally (e.g. health and life expectancy).

Both deindustrialisation and the urban–rural shift interacted with and underpinned the North–South divide. By far the highest levels of job losses occurred in the Northern and Central regions of Britain north of a line drawn between the Wash and Bristol (Lever, 1987, p. 76). The highest levels occurred in the traditional industrial zones of peripheral regions such as Scotland, Wales, the North West and the Northern region. Needless to say these were the regions whose economies were based on declining nineteenth-century industries highly concentrated in urban areas. Thus in the early 1980s urban and regional economic decline combined to create a particular regional geography of high unemployment.

By the mid-1980s, the short-lived economic recovery linked the urban–rural shift and the North–South divide. The South-West and East Anglia, although traditionally peripheral regions, benefited significantly from their relative proximity to London and the more affluent South-East, not least because many large firms decentralised parts of their operation out of London into the rest of the South East and surrounding regions. This was particularly significant in the key growth areas of banking, insurance and finance, where both East Anglia and the South West experienced considerable employment expansion, although admittedly from a relatively low base (Champion and Townsend, 1990, p. 103). East Anglia also appeared to generate indigenous population and industrial growth throughout the 1980s (Champion and Townsend, 1990, pp. 51, 110–12, 123; Champion and Green, 1992).

In the early 1990s as the recession which began in 1988/89 intensified and the economy of the South-East and adjacent regions suffered severely, there was some indication of a narrowing of the North–South divide (*Guardian*: 4.1.93, 19.2.93). The worst effects of the recession were, for the first time in the post-war era, experienced by the service sector and the South-East was particularly hard hit. Between 1989–91 unemployment increased fastest in the South-East – from 3.9 per cent in 1989 to 7.0 per cent in 1991 (*Regional Trends* 1992, table 7.16). Firms did not fail to the same extent in the North, perhaps because most of the inefficient firms had been shaken out during the earlier recession of the late 1970s. Whether or not this convergence will continue is currently debatable. Given the superior infrastructure and better qualified workforce in the South, the gap will probably re-emerge.

*An increasingly complex geography?*

The three themes which we have briefly reviewed in the preceding paragraphs clearly interact and manifest themselves in a fluid and changing fashion. Neither the proximate causes of urban problems nor their geography are set in tablets of stone. For example, there is some evidence that, just as in the early 1980s the Midlands became part of 'the North' in terms of employment decline, by the latter part of the 1980s at least part of it (the East Midlands), along with parts of South Wales, had slipped back into 'the South' (Champion and Townsend, 1990, pp. 110–25). Furthermore, the crude regional scale of our analysis undoubtedly obscures the fine detail of the processes which were underway. Some towns in declining regions experienced booms, while other towns in growth regions declined. Indeed, a considerable amount of attention was given to the question of the extent to which specific *localities* contradicted overall regional trends (Cooke, 1989; Harloe *et al.*, 1990; Champion and Townsend, 1990). As a result of this research a much more complex view of urban and regional change and the nature of urban problems has emerged.

This complexity is evident in Champion's and Green's 1987 and 1992 studies of 'booming towns'. They indicate that the early years of the 1980s saw a 'massive widening of the North–South divide' (Champion and Green, 1992, p. 243) and that, overwhelmingly, booming towns were located in the South-East, tended to have populations of between 60 000 and 200 000 and had an industrial structure strongly biased towards finance, insurance, banking and related activities (Champion and Green, 1987, pp. 104–7). They point out that, as national economic growth picked up, the benefits may have been shared more widely throughout Britain. However, their final conclusion is that the North–South divide remained as strong as ever. What changed in the mid-1980s was that there appeared to have been some rearrangement of booming towns within the South East and an improvement of some towns in the North. Throughout the period it would appear that the position of the largest cities actually got worse.

This complex geography has been further complicated by the series of events which, although not necessarily connected, followed the stock market crash in 1987: the property market crisis and the more general world economic downturn which set in toward the end of the 1980s. In the early 1990s, with unemployment increasing rapidly and likely to top three million in 1993, many of the buoyant employment sectors of the mid-1980s were being placed under severe strain. As we discussed above, major instances of restructuring, rationalisation and job loss occurred in formerly affluent areas such as the South-East. Frost and Spence (1991b) cite the pressures impacting on Central London's economy in the early 1990s, problems which were not simply internal but, equally importantly, stemed from competition from other major financial centres, especially Frankfurt am Main. Were the City of London's standing as a global financial centre of the first rank to be threatened, serious problems would be posed not only for London but also for the rest of the South-East. Just as the South-East benefited from the overspill of the City's success in the mid-1980s, so it could lose out were there to be major cutbacks in response to competition from overseas financial centres.

In summary, the urban problems which faced the Conservatives in 1979, and which they continued to encounter through the 1980s and into the 1990s were those resulting from a persistent process of deindustrialisation coupled with demographic and industrial restructuring. There was a pronounced geography to these processes and their outcomes. It would not be fair to say that the period was one of unremitting gloom, but, on balance, the larger metropolitan areas fared consistently badly. We will now turn our attention to a critical examination of how the Conservatives sought to apply their New Right ideologies to these urban problems.

## Putting theory into practice

We can isolate three key features of the Conservatives' attempt to bring New Right and Thatcherite theories and polemics to bear on urban problems:

- a greatly enhanced role for the private sector;
- property-led regeneration; and
- the promotion of small businesses.

Michael Heseltine, then Secretary of State for the Environment, encapsulated this view in one of the few attempts by a government minister to outline a coherent approach to urban regeneration prior to the 1987 general election. He argued that:

> It is . . . our responsibility to devise policies to allocate the public sector resources that we have available, and to encourage to the maximum possible extent the investment of private sector finance in profitable ventures that relate to the areas of deprivation. (Heseltine, 1986, p. 3)

### The pre-eminence of the private sector

During the 1980s, and particularly after 1985, it became clear that the private sector would play a key role in urban regeneration. By 1989, the Audit Commission could note that 'There is now little argument about the proposition that private sector-led growth is the main long-term answer to urban deprivation' (Audit Commission, 1989, p. 1). One of the few semi-official attempts at justifying a such a strategy came from a Department of the Environment official writing in a private capacity (Solesbury, 1990, p. 187). He argued:

> There are three key characteristics to current national urban regeneration policy: it has an economic focus, concentrating on supply-side measures, with the leading role for the private sector . . . the economic changes are seen as central and the right point to break into the problems. Get the urban economy working again and social and environmental improvements will follow . . . the supply-side approach . . . is to stimulate growth . . . by improvements in the supply of land, labour, capital and entrepreneurship . . . Most of these measures are designed to stimulate the private sector . . . There is a particular difficulty in those areas where strong and capable private enterprise and agencies are thin on the ground – urban areas . . . Hence the increasing calls for the private sector not just to reinvest but to become again public leaders on the pattern of the Victorian city.

Despite such statements of faith, very little attention was given to exactly how market forces would bring about a rejuvenation of urban areas. The notion of the altruistic private sector was an important perspective which the Conservatives sought to promote. Pressure was exerted on private sector companies to take a more active, community-orientated role.

To publicise this altruism, a series of private sector-led initiatives were launched. *British Urban Development* (BUD) was set up by major construction firms with working capital of about £50 million to encourage development in inner cities – although the Confederation of British Industry (CBI) estimated that something like £50 billion was actually required simply to clear and prepare derelict sites in cities for redevelopment (CBI, 1988). Other longer-standing, initiatives included *Business in the Community* (BIC) and the *Phoenix Initiative*.

The CBI document *Initiatives Beyond Charity* (CBI, 1988) signalled that private sector philanthropy had its limits. While business had obligations to the community these in themselves would not be enough to regenerate rundown areas of cities. The report made an appeal to enlightened self-interest by pointing out the implications of urban decline for society in general, the taxpayer, and business in particular through 'less spending by city residents, wasted land development opportunities and problems in recruiting young people, particularly from ethnic minorities' (CBI, 1988, p. 9). However, the report noted the massive cost of reversing urban decay, and argued 'The resources needed to turn decline into growth in our major cities will . . . have to spring from sound economic development, driven by private investment decisions taken on the basis of the commercial returns available, not from a sense of charity'.

Business, it was suggested, could also help in other ways: by taking on a leadership role and using its experience at local level to create public–private partnerships or *growth coalitions* (Harding, 1991) to help encourage and plan growth in co-operation with community interests. According to Harvey (1989b) the increased role played in such partnerships by urban governments signalled a change in their role from managerialism to *urban entrepreneurialism*; he goes on to argue that in such partnerships 'the public sector assumes the risk and the private sector takes the benefits' (Harvey, 1989b, p. 7).

Partnership is an ambiguous concept. The tendency has been for it to be of a largely tokenistic and symbolic nature; there was little in the way of genuine empowerment of local communities. Investments were generally confined to profitable central city locations and any excursions outside such locations sought substantial public subsidy. It was simply assumed that the private-sector side of the partnership would bring within it values which would help galvanise and transform the public-sector side. By helping to create an enterprise culture, the values of people in partnership areas would be transformed. Thus moral regeneration would accompany physical and economic regeneration.

### Private sector pre-eminence: a case study
Perhaps the best instance of a private-sector-led partnership was Birmingham Heartlands. This initiative attempted to take a strategic approach to the regeneration of a rundown area covering 2350 acres (940 hectares) to the east of Birmingham city centre (Carley, 1991). The partnership included Birmingham City Council, the local Chamber of Industry and Commerce and five large development firms, but was led by Birmingham Heartlands Ltd, a private company with ownership resting 65 per cent in private hands and 35 per cent in public hands. The aims of the company were 'to provide

a strategic framework which coordinates activity within Heartlands, to market and promote the area, to aid the assembly of land and development packages, to promote new development projects and to support training and community development efforts' (Carley, 1991, p. 108).

Criticisms of Heartlands focused on the effectiveness of co-ordination within the project, the level of public funds made available, the lack of an integrated regional and national infrastructure investment policy, and the requirements placed upon the private sector (Carley, 1991, pp. 111–13). Serious doubts were also raised concerning the extent to which mechanisms existed to ensure that local people benefited from any developments which occurred. Salmon (1992, p. 36) noted that 'Four years into the life of this joint venture, there are, however, serious doubts about the extent to which the residents of Heartlands are going to benefit from the physical and economic restructuring of the area'.

Heartlands, like other public–private partnerships, also suffered from the effects of a sustained recession, which made it difficult for private companies to second employees to work in such organisations, dramatically reduced property prices and more generally reduced the opportunities for profitable investment (these problems are even more dramatically illustrated by the case of Canary Wharf, London – see Chapter 7). As a result of these problems, after discussion with the then Environment Secretary, an Urban Development Corporation with a projected five-year life was set up in early 1992 to cover the Heartlands area.

*Assessment*

Initially it seems to have been assumed that, if the national economy grew, then the private sector would benefit. As an automatic by-product, declining areas would benefit and, somehow, the residents in rundown inner cities would reap the benefits of economic growth through the trickle-down effect. The main role for the state in such situations was thus simply to help create the general conditions for national economic growth and the specific conditions for private-sector development.

Arguably, this approach succeeded in the mid-1980s, but by the end of the decade even Government ministers, for example Trippier (1989), were beginning to acknowledge that not every area or everyone had benefited from the 1980s 'economic miracle'. To a certain extent this continuing uneven development was actually due to the governments' unwillingness to compromise their promotion of the private sector and allow for local circumstances.

While no one would argue that the private sector has no role to play in urban regeneration, practice casts some doubt on the theories which present the private sector as a panacea for dealing with economic problems in general and urban decline in particular. Ultimately it is hard not to agree with Boyle's (1989, p. 19) view on public–private sector partnerships that 'The private sector selects the potential profit; the public sector provides the so-called "gap-finance" and uses a state agency to weaken the regulatory environment'.

*Property-led regeneration*

As we suggested earlier in this chapter, a key urban problem facing the Conservatives was the decline in manufacturing industry. However, growth during the 1980s, and hence profit opportunity for the private sector, was in the services sector. As a result, service industries assumed a pre-eminent role in the Conservative prescription for urban regeneration.

Within the service sector the central role in regenerating urban areas fell to the property industry. Much emphasis, drawing on US examples, was placed on *flagship projects* such as luxury housing, waterfront developments, high quality office complexes, retail centres, conference and hotel developments, and even concert halls. These developments facilitated *boosterism* or *place marketing* (see Hambleton, 1991a, 1991b) and aimed to generate the initial impetus to get regeneration going and create the right atmosphere for further investment.

The empirical studies of Morley *et al.* (1989), Key *et al.* (1990), Nabarro (1990), Richard Ellis (1990a, 1990b) and Debenham, Tewson and Chinnocks (1991) suggest that, in the United Kingdom at the beginning of the 1980s, the major investment institutions in the UK were also the major owners of commercial and industrial property. They played a key role in structuring property finance and sought predictable and stable long-term returns. During the 1980s, however, new entrepreneurially-based property companies emerged to occupy a more important market position. The partial withdrawal of the investment institutions from the property market more or less coincided with the deregulation of the financial system in the UK and its even closer integration with the international financial system.

This internationalisation of capital demanded a variety of new, international, commodities capable of being traded on world markets. One of the commodities which was increasingly used was property, and investment thus began to move into property capital. However, as property, especially in 'global cities', became increasingly internationalised, property markets in locations as distant as New York, London and Tokyo became increasingly interdependent and the chances of problems in one spilling over into others and creating a generalised crisis of global property markets increased. This is precisely what happened in the later 1980s and early 1990s (Hallsworth and Bobe, 1993).

It was assumed that the London building boom which followed the flow of investment money would inevitably create jobs for local people. In practice, the creation of mechanisms to ensure long-term benefits for local people was ignored, except for the provision of training schemes. Nor, as Turok (1992, p. 374) points out, did property investment necessarily make much difference to the wider regional economy. He argues that it encouraged a neglect of the strategic planning and co-ordination of development which undermined future investment when infrastructure deficiencies occurred, as they did at Canary Wharf and in the London Docklands more generally (see Chapter 7). Government faith in property-led development also ignored the fact that there might well be conflicts between private sector interests. Nor did it recognise the possibility of serious conflicts of interest between what developers wanted and what local people wanted. Overall, it gave an unambiguous primacy to property speculators, a strategy which Barnekov *et al.* (1989) and Boyle and Rich (1984) have described as *privatism*.

The greatest paradox of property-led regeneration was that it was dependent upon the state. The state was needed to intervene to help create the conditions for investment and ensure that returns were acceptable. It acted via subsidies, grants, infrastructure investments and the relaxation of planning regulations. As Tweedale (1988, p. 194) has rightly noted:

the public sector is massively subsidising the private sector's efforts . . . redevelopment does not, therefore, represent an

attempt to solve the inner city problem. Rather, it is an attempt to restructure the spatial form of the city in line with the restructuring of its economy, enabling new land uses to match the economic functions of the city.

This state-aided process of restructuring has been referred to by Miller (1978) as *recapitalisation*. As a result, the urban centres of the capitalist world underwent a process of internal and external restructuring during the 1980s (Thrift, 1987; Castells and Henderson, 1987; Fainstein, 1990; King, 1990). Needless to say, these two process were closely interrelated as cities competed with one another for their positions in the global economic hierarchy. Given the immense sums of money involved it was inevitable that national states would become involved in order to preserve or enhance the position of their cities within the world system.

*Property-led development: a case study*
In Britain, London was the locus of the vast majority of commercial property market activity. Within London, developments were concentrated in the City. London is no ordinary capital city; as a 'global city' it plays a key role in structuring the international financial system and the global economy (Pryke, 1991). This means that it has a pivotal position in the circulation of financial and commercial capital and, as a result, is at one and the same time spatially part of the UK space economy but separate from it. The buildings associated with global functions act as global investment opportunities; they become tradeable like stocks and shares and their value ceases to have any relationship to the actual costs of construction.

During the 1980s, before the onset of recession, a number of developments occurred in the London property market. Some lower level managerial functions were decentralised out of London but, more importantly, changing information technologies rendered existing City buildings unsuitable for future use, and growing overseas competition and the associated liberalisation of the financial markets generated pressure for change as London attempted to maintain its position as a global city in the international economy. Within London itself there was also intense competition as areas adjacent to the City attempted to develop office space to attract new (usually overseas) entrants into the financial markets (Lenon, 1987; Pryke, 1991). The demand for modern office space spilled over into the rest of the South-East and was accompanied by, and helped fuel, a consumer boom involving an increased demand for residential property and retailing and leisure outlets.

New and complex forms of finance were made available to the entrepreneurial property companies of the mid-1980s (Morley *et al.*, 1989, ch. 4; Nabarro, 1990). This new finance stemmed from loans from offshore banks, paper issues on the stockmarket or complex intercompany trading of paper 'rights'. It generated an overarching demand for high profits in order to meet the demand for high returns by investors. It appears that, in the atmosphere of heightened financial competition which prevailed during the period 1985–9, many lending institutions loaned money without investigating the nature of the investment or the market. As early as 1987, the Chairman of the Bank of England was warning banks about getting over-extended *vis-à-vis* loans to property companies. Arguably this over-investment created the conditions of instability which were later to lead to a crash in the property market. By 1992 the banks had made direct loans of over £40 billion to the property sector and loans to industry which were secured by property were estimated to be worth anything up to £100 billion (Debenham, Tewson and Chinnocks, 1991).

In response to the pressures for property in the mid-1980s, planning authorities relaxed their planning regulations to allow major, and previously unheralded, developments to occur. The apparently ever-increasing demand for property, constantly increasing property values and steeply rising rents appeared to offer excellent investment opportunities. However, the problem with the property market/industry, as Key *et al.* (1990, p. 20) note, is that it is 'subject to slow processes of adjustment and (runs) for most of the time, a long way from a stable equilibrium'. This is a polite way of saying that the market is subject to wild swings between boom and slump and that the link between supply and demand is somewhat tenuous – a situation heightened by the essentially speculative nature of much property development.

By the late 1980s it was clear that the boom was over. There was a massive oversupply of office space in and around central London. Plender (1992) notes that in 1992 there was 32.4 million square feet (c.3 million square metres) of empty office space in London, that is

18 per cent of the total London office floorspace. This vast oversupply, combined with an economic downturn and high interest rates, created major problems for property companies as rents fell and property values tumbled. One estimate noted that, in the year to the end of June 1992, rental values fell by 16 per cent, with a drop of almost 3 per cent occurring in June 1992 alone (Price, 1992). As a result, several major property companies found themselves in dire straits, which eventually led to bankruptcy and/or receivership (e.g. Heron, Mountleigh, Speyhawk, and Olympia and York). The state of the London property market by the end of 1992 was desperate. Property speculators were offering rent-free periods and/or free fitting to tempt new tenants into signing. Other deals included property firms agreeing to take over the existing property of the client. As a result of this latter development there was a great deal of secondhand office space being held vacant and waiting to come on to the market – producing a two-tier market (Daniels and Bobe, 1992). The situation of over-supply is thus likely to persist and the property market will probably remain in a state of slump well into the second half of the 1990s and perhaps beyond.

It might be argued that the crisis of the property industry was simply a problem confined to London but, because of London's dominant position in the British economy and its effects on the surrounding South-East, the country as a whole suffered as lending institutions which had made losses on property loans were forced to make major provision for bad debts and be more cautious over any new loans they made. Furthermore, the London situation was repeated in several, minor, forms throughout the country, with speculative developments occurring in many British cities. Success or failure very much depended upon the city's place in the regional economy. As a result some cities within a region prospered (e.g. Manchester and Newcastle) whilst other cities were largely by-passed by such developments (e.g. Liverpool and Sunderland).

*Assessment*

Ironically, a great many of the problems with property-led regeneration could have been avoided had government been prepared to look more critically at one of the key sources of inspiration for the strategy – the USA. A great deal of stress was placed on the property-led rebuilding of US cities such as Boston and Baltimore and the growth of other 'newer' cities such as Houston. It was frequently argued that these cities demonstrated just what the private sector could do.

Renewal in Baltimore focused on the Inner Harbour area (Law, 1988a; Hula, 1990; Bond, 1991), while in Boston the major downtown area was transformed (Parkinson, 1988b). A great many resources were put into selling these developments to encourage further investment in the respective cities. However, in much the same way as the later British case, the public sector played a major role in initiating and underwriting the projects. Without public-sector funds and support it is unlikely that either city would have seen the level of renewal apparent today. Additionally, the US experience suggests an apparent lack of benefit accruing to the poorer and more disadvantaged populations of both cities. There is little evidence that 'trickle-down' has occurred and attempts made to ensure that the poor benefited from renewal seem to have had a minimal effect. In some cases it would appear that social and spatial inequalities have actually been further entrenched and even exacerbated by the regeneration process. As Hambleton (1991b, p. 15) has pointed out: 'Whilst these policies have brought about startling, in some cases stunning, physical change in the downtown areas of numerous cities it is abundantly clear that they have contributed to a social and economic polarisation within American cities which is alarming'.

Of course, an ardent free-marketeer would maintain that the public-private co-operation evident in Boston and Baltimore constituted illegitimate interference with the market. S/he would prefer to point towards the example of cities such as Houston, where the free-market has been allowed to let rip. Although there is no doubt that Houston has experienced high levels of growth this century and especially since 1945, the social, environmental and economic costs of minimal levels of state planning have been high (Feagin, 1988, ch. 8; Kirby and Lynch, 1987). Feagin has shown particularly clearly that a private sector left to its own devices can create a series of social costs relating to toxic waste, sewage and garbage disposal, water supply, air pollution, traffic problems and a host of other services. Many of the problems have again most acutely affected the minority and low-income community. Moreover, it has been the residual public sector which has been expected to pick up the bill for dealing with them. This, combined with a slowdown in Houston's growth industries had by the early 1980s created something of a fiscal crisis for the city (Feagin, 1988, pp. 235–7).

Houston, Baltimore and Boston all show that the private sector cannot be relied upon to concern itself with the welfare needs of local populations; its objective is profit (Hambleton, 1990, ch. 10). This means that strategic leadership requires a substantial input from the public sector. Unfortunately, this runs against the trend of the past decade or so in Britain where a process of increasing centralisation of power and marginalisation of local government has been underway (see Chapter 9). Hambleton points to the importance of emphasising equity as a key factor in structuring both the planning of renewal projects and outcomes of any such projects (Hambleton, 1991a, p. 64). Unfortunately, as we noted earlier, equity is a notion which was declared a potential hinderance to human progress, economic growth and urban renewal during the 1980s (Joseph and Sumption, 1979).

## The role of small businesses

Since the 1970s there has been a growing emphasis in the UK on the contribution that small businesses make to economic growth. In general terms there has been an assumption that the strength of an economy is in some way related to the number of small businesses (the vitality of the Japanese economy is frequently linked to the large numbers of small businesses found there). As a result of this interest, governments of all parties have sought ways to encourage the formation and growth of small businesses. By the early 1980s even more stress was being placed on these enterprises; they were seen by New Right governments as embodying all that was best about the free-market: entrepreneurship in its highest form.

The work of Birch (1979) was interpreted as suggesting that, in the USA, small firms had been the major source of new job creation. British commentators quickly drew upon his work and argued for the government to take a more supportive approach to small businesses in order to encourage their growth (Brinks and Coyne, 1983; Bright *et al.*, 1988). In particular it was argued that the tax system should be modified to encourage the formation and growth of small businesses, that central and local government should pursue purchasing policies which favoured such enterprises, and that banks should take a more sympathetic and supportive attitude towards the needs of the small businessperson.

During the 1980s, a considerable number of government initiatives were launched to encourage the setting up of small businesses and then to support them once established (May and McHugh, 1991, pp. 4–13). Assessing the effects of this activity is very difficult because, as Froud (1985, p. 381) points out, support for small businesses was highly ideological. Furthermore, there are genuine disagreements over just how many jobs were created by small businesses, both absolutely and in relation to other types of enterprise (Storey and Johnson, 1989; Mason, 1987a). What is clear is that small businesses have very high 'death rates'; Lloyd and Mason (1984, p. 218) found, in their sample in Merseyside and Manchester, that 60 per cent failed to survive for ten years. Storey and Johnson (1989, p. 204) came to a similar conclusion:

> Out of every 100 manufacturing businesses which begin, 30 cease to trade within two to three years. A further 30 cease to trade over the next seven to eight years, so that after a decade only 40 businesses will survive. Of these 40 businesses, four will provide half the jobs.

One of the oft-voiced hopes for small businesses was that they would grow into giant high-technology firms, as happened with Texas Instruments in the USA. It was argued that, even if only a few small businesses grew into such technological giants, then all the effort would have been worthwhile. Unfortunately, there is very little evidence available to suggest that many small businesses are involved in high-technology sectors let alone that they will grow to become international giants in the next decade. One of the few pieces of research which has touched upon this issue (Lloyd and Mason, 1984) was less than encouraging: it found that very few of the small businesses in its sample were engaged in activities that could be classified even vaguely as 'high-tech'. More recent research (Storey and Strange, 1993) on Cleveland has noted that, while the number of new firms being created during the 1980s increased threefold compared to the 1970s, this did not lead to the creation of more new jobs because of the smaller size of new firms relative to old. More importantly, the authors noted that the types of firm being created would do nothing to improve the competitiveness of the UK economy and did not form the basis for long-term economic regeneration.

Equally disturbing, Lloyd and Mason (1984) suggested that there were marked regional variations in the number and type of small businesses being set up. They noted that regional economies dominated by large, externally-owned branch plants were less likely to possess the socioeconomic structures and skills necessary to encourage small businesses to set up and flourish; in essence this describes the economies of declining regions. New small businesses were often set up in response to redundancy and were related to, and dependent upon, the existing industrial structure. They were seldom innovatory. On the other hand, those regions which had a wider variety of company types, smaller enterprises, and traditions of research and development were more likely to incubate innovatory small businesses. These two distinctive experiences of small business development perpetuated existing national socioeconomic divides.

The plethora of initiatives set up by government to support small businesses on a national basis did little to counter this tendency. Mason and Harrison (1986, pp. 227–8) argue, with reference to national small businesses initiatives, that:

> take-up rates are likely to vary substantially among regions. Specifically, it seems probable that take-up rates will be highest in the South East, South West and East Anglia, which are economically prosperous areas with already well-developed small firms sectors, and lowest in the depressed regions of northern Britain where small business activity is poorly developed . . . the existence of such variations will serve to widen, rather than reduce, existing regional disparities in economic well-being in the United Kingdom.

This aggravation of existing inequalities would seem to suggest a need to target small business aid more carefully. In the 1980s such a strategy would, however, have contradicted the governments' general unwillingness to interfere with market forces.

It would be a mistake to see small businesses as a single undifferentiated category of firm. Storey and Johnson (1989), focusing on small manufacturing businesses argue that, while small businesses are generating jobs, they are not doing so in numbers sufficient to compensate for job losses from large manufacturing firms. Furthermore, they suggest that the increase in the birth-rate of small manufacturing firms has more to do with the poor economic performance of large firms than any desire by individuals to become entrepreneurs. Indeed, in many cases, the stimulus for small-business formation is a large firm restructuring its internal and external operations. In such instances the small business is highly dependent upon the large firm and its fortunes. Storey and Johnson offer a disturbing general conclusion:

> there is no intrinsic benefit to the UK economy from having more firms and particularly more small firms. The increase in the number of firms since 1980 is likely to be more a reflection of recession than a source of rejoicing. (Storey and Johnson, 1989, p. 186)

The work of Keeble *et al.* (1991) on business services offers a more optimistic analysis. There has been a significant number of births in this sector and, perhaps more importantly, despite a fairly high death-rate, many small firms have experienced rapid growth. However, the downside of this optimism is that the vast majority of growth has taken place in south-east England and, as a result, has further accentuated the North–South divide.

## Conclusion

In this chapter, building upon Chapter 1, we have outlined the general New Right ideas that have informed the activities of Conservative administrations since 1979 and the particular politico-ideological form in which they have been articulated – Thatcherism, pointing out the limitiations and pragmatism of the latter. We identified the urban problems facing the 1979 Conservatives as being deindustrialisation, the urban–rural shift, and the North–South divide. The general emphasis of the Conservative challenge to these problems stressed the primacy of the private sector, the pre-eminence of the property industry and the potential of small businesses. Each of these themes was ideologically justified, most clearly by reference to neo-liberalism.

The verdict on these general approaches is predominantly negative. On the whole, they failed to create sufficient service jobs to replace those lost in manufacturing. Furthermore, the types of job and the corresponding built environment required by service industries were very different from those of manufacturing industry; social and spatial inequalities were often accentuated. In addition, and perhaps most galling for the New Right, these general approaches were, to an extent, dependent upon state assistance.

# 6 Reshaping the Urban Policy Inheritance

A lot happened to urban initiatives during the Thatcher years. There is no easy way to divide these developments into manageable but distinct chapters. We will therefore make a basic distinction between the policies which the post-1979 Conservatives inherited and those they created. This is entirely a distinction of convenience; we recognise that there is no hard and fast distinction between the two sets of initiatives. As we shall see, even those programmes which the Conservatives inherited were often fundamentally restructured to reflect Thatcherite preoccupations. In this chapter we will examine the reshaping of the policy inheritance. We will consider five areas which each impacted, to a varying extent, on urban problems:

- Regional policy.
- The urban programme.
- Urban regeneration.
- Housing policy.
- Employment-related initiatives.

## Regional policy

The accepted aim of regional policy was to redistribute jobs more equitably within Britain and to prevent the employment-based inequalities between northern and southern Britain. During the early 1970s questions were voiced increasingly regarding its effectiveness. It appeared that, rather than addressing the fundamental causes of regional employment inequalities, it was simply an attempt to ameliorate differences (Parsons, 1986). Furthermore, its impact was challenged; Ashcroft and Taylor (1979, p. 43) concluded that: 'the success of the redistribution of industry component of regional policy has been very heavily dependent upon the rate of industrial expansion in the economy as a whole'.

111

At best it appeared that the incentives which formed the essence of regional policy encouraged the creation, in the declining regions, of branch plants of multinational companies. When the economic downturn of the 1970s came, this *branch plant economy* crumbled. The branch plants were the first to be closed down following decisions taken in corporate headquarters located elsewhere (Massey, 1984, pp. 100–7). Additionally, the mid-1970s saw the emergence of a generalised unemployment problem which tended to overshadow regional imbalances in job opportunities.

*Regional policy under Thatcher*

The shortcomings of regional policy were well recognised by the time the first Thatcher government was elected in 1979 (see Parsons, 1986; Smith, 1989, ch. 4; Prestwich and Taylor, 1990). Its position was made even more precarious by the election of a government that drew upon a neo-liberal prioritisation of the role of the market, defined state intervention as illegitimate and questioned not only the practical effectiveness of state intervention but in addition argued that it made matters worse by not creating 'real jobs'. As Smith (1989, p. 97) notes: 'regional policy did not fit in with the new Conservative philosophy'. It is hardly surprising that the death of an interventionist regional policy seemed imminent after the Conservative victory in 1979. What made it seem even more likely was the appointment of Sir Keith Joseph to the position of Secretary of State at the Department of Industry, the department responsible for regional policy.

However, there was no outright abolition of the system. Instead, a process of reform took place. This apparent preference for reform rather than revolution may be attributed to the element of pragmatism in Thatcherism that we identified in Chapter 5: throughout the 1980s there remained major regional disparities in unemployment levels (Table 6.1). Even when unemployment appeared to be falling (between 1986–9), it still finished the period almost twice as high in percentage terms in the North as in the South. Such differences implied a justification for some form of regional policy. Yet more pragmatically, to have abolished regional policy altogether would have meant that Britain would no longer have been able to apply for funds from the European Community's European Regional Development Fund (ERDF). This would have

**TABLE 6.1 Unemployment by region 1979–89**

| Region | Unemployment Rate | | | Change 1979/89 |
|---|---|---|---|---|
| | 1979 | 1986 | 1989 | |
| South-East | 2.6 | 8.4 | 4.0 | + 1.4 |
| East Anglia | 3.1 | 8.6 | 3.6 | + 0.5 |
| South-West | 4.0 | 9.5 | 4.7 | + 0.7 |
| E. Midlands | 3.3 | 10.1 | 5.7 | + 2.4 |
| **South** | 2.9 | 8.8 | 4.3 | + 1.4 |
| W. Midlands | 3.9 | 12.9 | 6.6 | + 2.7 |
| Yorks and Humberside | 4.0 | 12.7 | 7.6 | + 3.6 |
| North-West | 5.0 | 13.9 | 8.6 | + 3.6 |
| Northern | 6.4 | 15.5 | 10.0 | + 3.6 |
| Wales | 5.3 | 13.8 | 7.8 | + 2.5 |
| Scotland | 5.6 | 13.4 | 9.5 | + 3.9 |
| **North** | 4.9 | 13.6 | 8.3 | + 3.4 |
| Great Britain | 3.9 | 11.1 | 6.2 | + 2.3 |
| South–North difference | 2.0 | 4.8 | 4.0 | + 2.0 |

Source: After Champion and Townsend (1990) p. 131, table 7.2.

deprived declining regions of access to considerable European funding – in 1992–3 Britain's share of the ERDF was £958m (*Guardian*, 25.2.93).

Initial reforms involved reducing levels of financial assistance, abolishing office development control, and liberalising (and subsequently abolishing) Industrial Development Certificates (Prestwich and Taylor, 1990, pp. 150–3). The first major change, the White Paper *Regional Industrial Development* (HMSO, 1983), redrew the map of regional assistance, abolished Special Development Areas, made Regional Development Grants (RDGs) payable only in Development Areas, and reduced the scope of the Development Areas so that they covered only 15 per cent of the population. Although some service industries were made eligible for RDGs, and Intermediate Area status was extended to the West Midlands, the White Paper planned an overall reduction in the RDG of £300 million *per annum* by 1988. Prestwich and Taylor

(1990, p. 153) suggest that the cuts in areas qualifying for assistance might have been even greater had government not been concerned to maintain eligibility for the ERDF.

The next major change occurred in 1988 after Lord Young had taken over as Secretary of State at the merged Department of Trade and Industry (DTI). A new White Paper, *DTI – The Department for Enterprise* (HMSO, 1988a) put forward the abolition of automatic RDGs; firms in future had to apply for *Regional Selective Assistance*. This would only be payable to firms which could demonstrate to civil servants that a development would not take place without grant aid. In addition, a new range of grants to encourage the formation of small businesses and innovation was introduced. Prestwich and Taylor (1990, p. 157) argued that:

> The kernel of the DTI's revamping is to switch its role from one of intervening in existing big industries to one of encouraging the formation of new companies. This continues the central objective of the 1983 revised policy on regional industrial development, which was to encourage the development of indigenous potential within the AAs (assisted areas) with a long-term objective of self generating growth in these areas.

By the end of the 1980s, the reform of regional policy had brought about an effective marginalisation of traditional regional policy as greater selectivity in assistance was coupled with an emphasis on the role of market forces and new (small) businesses. As Darwin (1990, p. 1) has noted, the approach had become dominated by: 'market forces and the belief that economic prosperity will both "ripple out" from congested areas as relative costs of new development change, and "trickle down" from prosperous groups in the community to reach everyone'.

After the 1992 election, the purportedly more interventionist Michael Heseltine was appointed to the DTI. His initial pronouncements (DTI Press Notice P/92/440) stressed closer links to individual industrial sectors, better representation of industrial interests, research and development, and some attempt at 'picking winners'. Regional policy was noticeable for its absence from the DTI press notices; indeed it was allocated to the Regional and Small Firm section, whose responsibility also encompassed inward investment, small firms and the Enterprise Initiative. This new association offered the possibility of integrating regional policy with other DTI-led initiatives for economic regeneration. However, traditional regional policy hung on as the recession continued to bite. Indeed, in 1993, the DTI conducted the first re-examination of the boundaries of the Assisted Areas since 1984. High on its list of issues to address were the claims for assisted area status coming from the newly-impoverished South-East.

## The Urban Programme

The DoE remained the key government department concerned with urban problems after 1979. The plethora of programmes and initiatives which come under its control, and which we will review in this section, included the inherited *Partnerships and Programme Authorities*, and a related subsequent creation, *City Challenge*. Other programmes which we will cover in this section include *City Action Teams* (CATs) and the Department of Employment's *Task Forces*.

### Objectives

In general terms, the post-1979 Conservatives believed that the problems of British cities derived from the *flight of the private sector*. This, they felt, was largely caused by rigid local government bureaucracies and inflexible labour markets squeezing the private sector out. The central need was to encourage private investors to return.

This general view was not clearly spelt out in relationship to the UP. As late as May, 1985, Ministerial Guidelines for the UP (DoE, 1985a: 1) simply stated that:

> The Government's objectives . . . are: (i) to improve employment prospects in the inner cities, by increasing both job opportunities and the ability of those who live there to compete for them; (ii) to reduce the number of derelict sites and vacant buildings; (iii) to strengthen the social fabric of the inner city and encourage self-help; (iv) to reduce the number of people in acute housing stress.

However, the key element in achieving these objectives was clearly the private sector. It had to be encouraged to return to cities at all costs. Urban Development Corporations and Enterprise Zones (see Chapter 7) were major new tools by which this aim was to be achieved. The existing UP required restructuring. This took place gradually: like regional policy, there was a pragmatic reframing of the policy inheritance.

## The Urban Programme Review 1981

The Partnership and Programme Authorities were the central elements in the UP which the Conservatives inherited. The more long-standing traditional UP, which offered grants to support small-scale activities by local authorities and voluntary/community groups, also remained, but by 1979 already had lower priority.

Nevertheless, it was the traditional UP, with its largely social concerns, which came under immediate threat upon the election of the Thatcher administration and the instigation of the 1981 review of the UP. Somewhat surprisingly, given the views expressed in the section on Thatcherite Social Policy in Chapter 5, the review recommended retention of the entire UP, including the traditional elements. However, it stressed the importance of improving management in order to give better value for money. This was to be a constant theme of subsequent reviews of the UP. As Sills *et al.* (1988, p. 51) noted: 'These years marked a change in direction . . . Priority was given to restructuring the economy of the inner city, with economic and capital expenditure favoured over social consumption projects, such as in recreation, education or housing'.

The survival of the UP, and particularly its traditional elements, can probably be linked to the outbreaks of rioting in Britain's inner cities in 1980 and 1981 (Benyon and Solomos, 1988). In this context the UP, and indeed urban policy in general, provided for *territorial crisis management* (Pickvance, 1990). It had a high symbolic value (Edelman, 1977), giving the appearance of doing something about a very visible problem but failing to attack root causes.

Whether it was genuine or symbolic, the UP attracted considerable sums of government money (Table 6.2). It is noteworthy that, for the two financial years after the 1981 riots and in the run up to the 1983 election, spending on the UP increased in both absolute and relative terms. It only fell back, in relative terms, in the financial years after the 1983 election victory. The

TABLE 6.2   The Urban Programme 1979/80 to 1986/7 (£ millions)

| Year | Total | Total Adjusted |
|------|-------|----------------|
| 1979/80 | 175 | 210 |
| 1980/1 | 202 | 202 |
| 1981/2 | 215 | 193 |
| 1982/3 | 295 | 246 |
| 1983/4 | 310 | 246 |
| 1984/5 | 320 | 244 |
| 1985/6 | 317 | 228 |
| 1986/7 | 317 | 220 |

Source:   After Sills *et al.* (1988) p. 52, table 3.

Bristol riot of 1980 and those in, *inter alia*, Brixton and Toxteth in 1981, did therefore lead the government to direct some additional funds towards the inner cities.

*The Urban Programme Review 1985*

The 1980/1 riots delayed a more thoroughgoing reform of the UP. This eventually took place in 1985 and emphasised a specific need to focus spending on economic and, to a lesser extent, environmental projects rather than on social issues. The 1985 Guidelines noted: 'Ministers expect a continued presumption in favour of economic projects' (DoE, 1985a, p. 2). Table 6.3 illustrates the impact of this shift in emphasis.

The move of the UP towards economic projects was in line with the governmental emphasis on economic regeneration and took place within the context of a declining financial base as funds were increasingly directed away from the UP towards urban development corporations and other initiatives with less local authority input. Furthermore, local authorities were asked to contribute 25 per cent of the total cost of UP schemes at a time when, it is estimated, they lost some £22 billion in rate support grant (*Times*, 17.10.89). Hegarty (1988) has shown that, for Partnerships, funds received via the UP did not even make up for grant lost via the Rate Support Grant System.

**TABLE 6.3   Categories of expenditure in partnerships and programme authorities (percentages)**

|  | Partnerships | | Programme Authorities | |
|  | 1986/7 | 1989/90 | 1986/7 | 1989/90 |
| --- | --- | --- | --- | --- |
| Housing | 9 | 12 | 7 | 8 |
| Social | 39 | 23 | 37 | 22 |
| Environment | 20 | 17 | 16 | 19 |
| Economy | 32 | 48 | 40 | 51 |
| Total (£m) | 123 | 107.87 | 96.9 | 96.69 |

Note:   The number of partnerships remained the same while the number of programme authorities increased between the two dates.

Source:   Department of the Environment *Urban Programme Fact Sheets* 1986/87 and 1989/90.

## Managing the Urban Programme

The post-1979 Conservative governments placed an increasing emphasis on management. Developments in the UP were strongly influenced by the Financial Management Initiative (Pollitt, 1990). Two developments followed. In 1985 the DoE set up *City Action Teams* (CATs) and in 1986 the Department of Employment set up *Task Forces*. Neither had any significant funding of their own, but both aimed to achieve better management, co-ordination and use of funds, including UP funds.

CATs and Task Forces worked at the local level, building up links between local authorities, voluntary organisations, local communities and the private sector and, where necessary, overcoming inter- and intra-authority conflicts. As Kenneth Clarke (then Minister for Employment) argued, when announcing the setting up of Task Forces in 1986: 'This initiative is a further step to improve the targeting and enhance the benefit to local people of the money channelled through existing central Government programmes' (Hansard, 6.2.86, col. 447).

Both Task Forces and CATs represented a belief, previously articulated, albeit in a rather different form, by the failed CCPs (see Chapter 3), that, by adopting the right organisational form and management methods, limited funds can achieve objectives in excess of baseline expectations. For the post-1979 Conservatives this objective was the creation of conditions which would *lever-in* significant private-sector investment. While acknowledging the valuable contribution of CATs and Task Forces, and the difficulties they faced, the National Audit Office (NAO) review of inner city programmes noted the need for both to improve their working procedures and effectiveness (NAO, 1990, pp. 10–14).

A 1990 consultation paper addressed the effectiveness of the UP in general (DoE, 1990). It identified a need to streamline operations and 'achieve greater delegation of responsibility and better value for money from the system' (DoE, 1990, p. 1). The consultation paper bore the clear imprint of the Financial Management Initiative. It aimed to specify a distinct role for the UP, devolve greater responsibility from the centre to regional offices of the DoE and local authorities, and set up a one-year timetabled cycle for the submission and approval of bids.

*The reformed Urban Programme*

The ideas in the 1990 consultation document were incorporated into the Urban Programme Annual Programme Guidance issued by the DoE (DoE, 1991a, 1992a). The main elements of the reformed UP were (DoE, 1991a, p. 1):

1. A strategic approach to the economic renewal of tightly-targeted inner-city areas to secure long-term improvements to the quality of life of people in those areas and to the local environment.
2. An action statement setting clear goals that can be monitored.
3. Collaboration with local interests including the private and voluntary sectors in the strategy and the delivery of the programme.
4. Effective co-ordination of UP resources and other urban regeneration initiatives for the target areas.
5. Effective management, including adherence to the timetable.

The Guidance also stated that 'Roughly 50% of the content of programmes will be projects aimed at promoting economic regeneration (in most cases the percentage will be higher)' (DoE,

1991a, p. 6). Finally, it argued that 'Better value for money is likely to be obtained if resources are concentrated in a small number of areas at a time, and activities of different programmes are mutually reinforcing' (DoE, 1991a, p. 7).

These developments placed increased delegation of responsibility to local authorities within a clear framework of what the DoE would find acceptable. In order to be successful local authorities had to conform to centrally determined guidelines within a pre-determined timetable. They had to promote economic development projects, identify areas for special attention, and endeavour to concentrate their own and other funds on to the regeneration of those areas. The latter requirement was to prove particularly problematic: disjunctions could develop between a local authority's main programme spending intentions and local UP spending. Management reforms, aiming to overcome this problem, subordinated local priorities to central ones.

Another problem concerned the Government recommendation that:

> projects for UP support will be selected for maximum impact (including their impact collectively within a package), it is likely that the trend will be towards fewer projects in total, and a number of *highly visible* projects chosen for their wider benefits to the community as a whole. (DoE, 1991a, p. 6 – emphasis added)

Given the Government's overwhelming emphasis upon economic regeneration by the private sector, bids involving high-profile *flagship* private sector developments tended to be defined as beneficial to the community and thus secured approval. The sum effect of this and other constraints was to confirm that there were clear limits to the devolved management of UP funds. A successful UP bid might actually lead to greater central control on local actions or, at the very least, force the prioritisation of private-sector needs over social/community needs.

Continued pressure on public expenditure through 1992/3 placed the whole future of the Urban Programme in doubt. In November 1992, Michael Howard (Secretary of State for the Environment) announced that Urban Programme funding was to be cut drastically: by £61 million for the financial year 1993/4, by £85 million in the following year, and by a further £11 million in 1995/6 (*Financial Times*, 19.11.92, p. 10; *AMA News*, December 1992, p. 216). According to one report, up to 34 000 jobs were at risk because of these cutbacks, many in the voluntary sector (*Observer*, 7.3.93, p. 11). The DoE also began to scrutinise its list of fifty-seven urban programme authorities in the light of information emerging from the 1991 Census. Some authorities were likely to be excluded and new ones included.

The sole development was the release of an additional £20 million for inner-city capital projects via an *Urban Partnership Fund* launched in late 1992. Local authorities were expected to contribute some of their own capital receipts from council house sales in order to qualify for a share of the money, but the majority of the funds were to come from the private sector. Just forty-six authorities shared the £20 million (*Independent*, 13.2.93).

*City Challenge*

City Challenge appears to have developed out of a general review of the DoE's urban initiatives in the wake of Michael Heseltine's return to the DoE in 1990. It represents a continuation of the themes outlined in the 1991 Urban Programme review referred to in the previous section and for that reason we will consider it in this chapter.

Upon his appointment to the DoE, Michael Heseltine went on a tour of urban areas in order to:

> find out the scale of achievement, and to assess the most effective way of encouraging progress. The best way to do that is to talk to the people who live and work in those areas, and to those who share my commitment to bringing even more investment. (DoE Press Notice 102, 25.2.91)

By early March 1991 he had decided upon a competitive bidding approach as being the most effective way of encouraging progress. He announced his decision in a speech to Manchester Chamber of Commerce and Industry (Heseltine, 1991a) in which he stressed the importance of partnership between local government, community, private sector and voluntary sector. He argued:

when I speak of the need for a sense of partnership in our modern cities, it is today's equivalent of that Victorian sense of competitive drive linked with social obligation. Success and responsibility go hand in hand today just as surely as they did a hundred years ago. (Heseltine, 1991a, p. 9)

Heseltine placed particular emphasis upon the need to encourage 'local creativity'. He saw competition as essential in unleashing that creativity, arguing that: 'competition is the vital catalyst for the new approach' (Heseltine, 1991a, p. 7). Importantly, he also took this idea further: 'Men and women will compete with one another and give of their best. People will set the pace and exercise their discretion' (Heseltine, 1991a, p. 9; see also DoE Press Notice 138, 11.3.91). This approach has remarkable resonances with the notion of active citizenship that found an outlet in Conservative circles at the end of the 1980s (Hurd, 1988, but see Issac, 1990 for astute criticisms). In a second speech, in May 1991 (DoE Press Notice 335, 23.5.91), he fleshed out his ideas, acknowledging that individual ministers and CATS, as well as citizens, each had important roles to play in urban regeneration.

In mid-1991, the outcome of these statements, the *City Challenge*, was formally launched. Fifteen of the fifty-seven UP.Authorities were invited to submit competitive bids, for which ten of them would win additional funding (DoE Press Notice 335, 23.5.91). Later, a further six UP Authorities were allowed to bid. The bidders were to 'enter into five year agreements with the Department of the Environment to tackle some of our worst social conditions' (DoE Press Notice 474, 31.7.91).

In the first year eleven of the twenty-one bids were successful (DoE Press Notice 474, 31.7.91). They shared £82.5 million per annum over a five-year period, with each receiving an average of £7.5 million per annum. In February 1992 a second round of City Challenge was launched, in which fifty-four of the fifty-seven UP Authorities took part in a competition to gain a share of £750 million over a five year period. The twenty winners were announced in July 1992. The complete list of beneficiaries from City Challenge is set out in Table 6.4.

It should be noted that City Challenge funds were not additional funds. They were top-sliced from other programmes (DoE, 1992a, p. 1). Furthermore, the expectation was that City Challenge funds

**TABLE 6.4   City Challenge winners by rounds and deprivation ranking**

| Authority | Deprivation Ranking | Successful Round |
|---|---|---|
| Hackney | (1) | 2 |
| Newham | (2) | 2 |
| Tower Hamlets | (3) | 1 |
| Lambeth | (4) | 2 |
| Brent | (8) | 2 |
| Manchester | (11) | 1 |
| Leicester | (12) | 2 |
| Wolverhampton | (13) | 1 |
| Lewisham | (16) | 1 |
| Birmingham | (14) | 2 |
| Liverpool | (14) | 1 |
| Kensington and Chelsea | (17) | 2 |
| Sandwell | (19) | 2 |
| Nottingham | (20) | 1 |
| Blackburn | (21) | 2 |
| Middlesborough | (23) | 1 |
| Bradford | (26) | 1 |
| Kirklees | (31) | 2 |
| Walsall | (34) | 2 |
| Hartlepool | (35) | 2 |
| Bolton | (36) | 2 |
| Newcastle | (37) | 1 |
| Sunderland | (38) | 2 |
| Derby | (41) | 2 |
| Stockton | (46) | 2 |
| Wirral | (48) | 1 |
| Sefton | (50) | 2 |
| Wigan | (53) | 2 |
| North Tyneside | (54) | 2 |
| Barnsley | (55) | 2 |
| Dearne Valley | (*) | 1 |

* indicates a joint bid by three UP Authorities – Rotherham (55) Barnsley (56) and Doncaster (51).

Source: Department of the Environment Press Notices 474, 31.7.91; and 497, 16.7.92.

should be supplemented by additional resources drawn from other sources and, of course, the private sector (DoE, 1992b). The government aimed to facilitate effective use of these resources 'by simplifying and streamlining grant procedures to enable project packages to be assembled' (DoE, 1991b, p. 5). It was anticipated that CATs would exert a co-ordinating role and, at the same launch as round two of City Challenge, the DTI Minister responsible for Task Forces, Edward Leigh, announced that up to four new Task Forces could open to assist successful bidders, thus helping 'ensure a concentration and co-ordination of central Government programmes in areas of greatest need' (DTI Press Notice, P/92/97, 18.2.92).

*City Challenge: assessment*

The competitive approach embodied in City Challenge had a number of implications. First, it gave central government even greater control over what the UP authorities spent on resources. Second, via CATs and Task Forces, it enhanced central control over how the programmes were actually carried out. Third, it led to increased inter-authority rivalry as each UP Authority attempted to produce bids which conformed with the dictates of the centre.

Oddly, there was no apparent relationship between the success of a bid and a bidder's place in the DoE's own ranking of multiple deprivation. All authorities, regardless of the problems they faced, received identical sums of money. As De Groot (1992, p. 197) has commented, City Challenge: 'requires councils to obtain money for inner city regeneration on the basis of a highly politicised competitive bidding process which has no objective relationship to levels of need or even ability to deliver'.

There were also problems with the objectives of City Challenge. The DoE's guidelines (DoE, 1992b) to authorities taking part in the bidding process stress that 'City Challenge is about local initiative.' (DoE, 1992b, p. 1) and that any economic transformation should benefit local residents. The initiative was intended to take account of local circumstances: 'objectives will depend on the area selected . . . they should tackle the problems which are perceived by the residents of the area and by potential investors as being crucial to its regeneration' (DoE, 1992b, p. 5). This clear intention begged the question of the extent to which the objectives of local residents and potential investors would coincide. Local concerns about low-cost housing, jobs and the general appearance of the area as a residential area might well conflict with investors' concerns with profit and the general transformation of an area in such a manner as to ensure that any investment is maximised. Both residents and investors might wish to see investment in infrastructure, but possible of different types: 'flagship' projects to help raise the area's investment profile are by no means guaranteed to benefit local people. As Kamis (1992, p. 7) has noted: 'It is difficult not to conclude that competitive bidding is a way of being seen to allocate "fairly" what are diminishing resources for urban regeneration with decisions based on market principle, rather than on the assessment of need.'

The area basis of City Challenge provided a third general problem. The initiative focused on small areas or 'needle points' (Hambleton, 1991b) but it was usually the wider local labour market which required transformation. While the guidance notes stressed the need to identify how a project fitted into the wider local economy, the absence of local and regional strategies and planning mechanisms made such hopes largely rhetorical. Ultimately the success of a bid depended upon the strength of the local, regional and national economy and it is likely that the success or failure of projects will be determined by forces outside the area.

The DoE's summary of the first successful bids reveals that all included the participation of the private sector and most were either in or adjacent to central city areas; they focused overwhelmingly upon infrastructure, and environmental works and site preparation for the private sector. Other initiatives included local training and improvements to housing conditions. Overall the primary aim was clearly to attract additional private investment in the hope of creating new jobs. The chances of this strategy succeeding in creating permanent new jobs during the depths of a recession were low. A pessimistic analysis would suggest that local authorities will finish up competing ever more fiercely for a diminishing supply of new jobs and the redistribution of the existing, diminishing, job supply.

City Challenge funds were top-sliced from seven DoE inner city and housing programmes (DoE, 1992b, p. 9). They deprived UP Authorities of funds they might well have received in any case, and redirected money towards a preferred few (Kamis, 1992). According to Labour Party figures, UP spending was to be cut in 1992/3 by £14.3 million and Housing Investment by £48.5 million in order to fund City Challenge. The successful local authorities were also expected to bend their own programmes to bring additional funds to bear on the City Challenge areas; this might mean that other deprived areas within the local authority could lose funds.

Some commentators are more sympathetic towards City Challenge than we have been. Colenutt (1992, p. 13) argues that it integrates physical development with social issues. Bentley (1992, p. 2) contends that it represents new thinking by the government and that it attempts to:

> address the failure of the property-led trickle-down approach of Urban Development Corporations, to benefit local communities, particularly those disadvantaged in the housing and labour markets. Though an area based initiative. . .It is also a comprehensive rather than piecemeal approach.

De Groot (1992, p. 205), whilst generally critical of City Challenge, also points out that there are positive aspects, notably 'the requirement for broad based partnership linked to the strategy for the area. For the first time government funding of urban regeneration activity has been associated with a comprehensive and integrated approach to development'. Another potentially valuable aspect is the participation of the local community in the development of the strategy.

As yet there have been no detailed evaluations of City Challenge. However, in late 1992, it was reported that the new Secretary of State for the Environment, Michael Howard, was less than enthusiastic about its effectiveness. In the context of increasing pressures to control and reduce further public expenditure, the initiative may be scrapped (Gosling, 1992). There will be no third round in 1993/4 and the DoE is unwilling to commit itself to restarting the initiative in 1994/5. By mid-1993 it appeared that City Challenge was being sidelined and perhaps forgotten.

**Urban regeneration**

The 1979 Conservative Government inherited the *Derelict Land Grant*, a measure designed to defray the high costs of bringing derelict land on to the market. The Conservatives subsequently developed two further grants with broadly similar objectives: the *Urban Regeneration Grant* and the *Urban Development Grant*. These latter initiatives were consolidated into the *City Grant* in 1988.

Because of their common ancestry we will review each initiative in this section although, strictly, the majority were Conservative creations rather than inherited measures. We will also review the rather more *ad hoc*, but still related, notion of *Garden Festival*.

### Derelict Land Grants

This initiative had its origins in a response to the Aberfan disaster of 1966, following which the Local Government Act, 1966, made funds available to local authorities to reclaim land in rural areas. In the 1980s the Conservatives reorientated the grant to benefit urban areas and, under the Local Government, Planning and Land Act, 1980, opened it up to the private sector to assist industrial, commercial and housing developments.

Between 1979–80 and 1987–8 the amount of Derelict Land Grant funding directed to inner city areas increased from around £5 million to just over £30 million per annum (DoE, 1988a, p. 33, fig. 13; and p. 1 fig. 1). During the financial years 1992/3 – 1994/5 funding will be £71 million per annum. This will rise to £83 million in 1995/6 (*Financial Times*, 19.10.92, p. 10).

Derelict land grants are paid as a proportion of the costs of bringing land back to its natural state. They aim to reduce the gap in cost between redeveloping previously used land and developing green-field sites (DoE, 1988a, p. 2). Their objective is that sites previously considered unprofitable or of marginal profitability will be brought back into use. Local authorities qualify for 100 per cent grant if they are located in Assisted Areas or Derelict Land Clearance Areas; 75 per cent in National Parks; and 50 per cent elsewhere. The private sector receives 80 per cent grant in Assisted Areas and Derelict Land Clearance Areas and 50 per cent elsewhere (DoE, 1988a, 1991c).

Derelict Land Grants can be seen as not only a strategy for land reclamation and return to usage, but also part of a wider attempt to rejuvenate the urban land market, particularly in areas where land has been rendered unusable by previous industrial usage and the costs of reclamation are high. To achieve this second goal, the grant gives 'preference . . . to reclamation schemes which would not go ahead without the aid of grant' (DoE, 1991d, p. 1). The theme of public–private partnership is clearly evident in the grant; a Derelict Land Grant General Note (DoE, 1991c) suggests that priority will be given to private schemes which complement local authority ones.

*Urban Development Grant*

The Urban Development Grant was the product of the *Financial Institutions Group* (FIG) which was set up by Michael Heseltine in the wake of the Merseyside riots of 1981 (Hornsby, 1982). The FIG was impressed by attempts to regenerate the cities of the USA and particularly by the USA's Federal Urban Development Action Grant (Rose, 1986). The Urban Development Grant appears to have been modelled on this initiative and was launched on an experimental basis in 1982.

Eligibility was at first limited to areas covered by the Inner Urban Areas Act, 1978, but was later extended to include Enterprise Zones (see Chapter 7). The aim of the grant was to assist commercial, industrial or housing developments which would not proceed without public subsidy. Public funding was to be kept to the absolute minimum and it was intended that the Urban Development Grant should be the grant of last resort. In the first instance a developer had to approach the local authority, which was then supposed to assess the viability of the development before passing it on to the DoE for a final assessment. Needless to say, this could be a time consuming process and much depended on the attitude of the local authority.

An excellent assessment of the Urban Development Grant was carried out by Aston University's Public Sector Management Research Unit for the DoE (see Johnson, 1988 for a summary). While this is by now a somewhat dated study, it does cover four of the grant's six years of life before it was merged into the City Grant in 1988. According to the report, by 1986, £78 million of public money had been spent on 177 projects which had brought in over £350 million of private investment.

This apparent success hid a rather more complex picture. It is difficult to assess the actual numbers of jobs created by the Urban Development Grant but the report suggested that project submissions overestimated by 62 per cent the number of jobs which would be created; two-thirds of the jobs created had previously existed, so only about a third were new. Only 18 per cent of jobs went to people who were previously unemployed. However, each new job was estimated to cost a relatively reasonable £9200 to £19 200.

Urban Development Grants certainly helped stimulate land transactions and increase land values, but the primary beneficiaries appear to have been landowners. Their impact on the jobs market was less clear. While being generally favourable in its assessment the Aston report notes that the grants, on their own, could do little to stimulate wider-scale regeneration in urban areas and would have been better employed as part of a broader strategic plan for city regeneration.

### Urban Regeneration Grants

Urban Regeneration Grants represent one of the shortest-lived grants ever created. Like the Derelict Land Grant, they aimed to 'subsidise the costs of reclamation, refurbishment and new build projects' (Wray, 1987, p. 17). The specification of a private-sector clientele was the distinguishing factor. Furthermore, as Martin (1990, pp. 45–6) notes: '[it] marked an important change in the direction of inner city policy: namely that like subsequent programmes. . .there was no formal local authority involvement in the . . . process'.

Urban Regeneration Grants aimed to turn non-viable projects into viable ones; the definition of a project's viability was negotiated by civil servants in partnership with the developers. The grant lasted for little more than a year before it was merged with the Urban Development Grant to create the City Grant, and it would seem that its life-span was dominated by confusion and red tape. The first grant took ten months to approve (Wray, 1987).

### City Grants

As we have noted, City Grants were created as a result of merging Urban Development Grants and Urban Regeneration Grants. In fact, as we will see in the next chapter, the City Grant represents just about the only new initiative contained in the major urban policy statement of the late 1980s, *Action for Cities*.

The City Grant is close to the model of the Urban Regeneration Grant. Private companies apply directly to the DoE for assistance, bypassing local government. This was justified as a way of speeding up the process. The grant was intended, like its predecessors, to 'provide support to private sector capital projects which benefit rundown urban areas and which cannot proceed without assistance' (DoE, 1988b, p. 1). This view has been refined somewhat during the life of the grant and by 1992 City Grant Guidance Notes (DoE, 1992d, p. 13) were stating:

City Grant is not offered to compensate for extravagant costings, over-pessimistic valuations, excessive profit allowances, or low rents/high interest rates arising from the state of the wider market. It is offered to offset specific effects of the inner city site and location on the project's commercial viability.

A cynical reading of this statement might lead one to speculate that, by ruling out a series of things that City Grants are not supposed to 'compensate for', the Government was covertly acknowledging that the City Grant had paid for them in the past. More straightforwardly, in the context of the economic slump of the early 1990s and, indeed, the known ways in which markets work, it is rather unreasonable to suggest that specific inner city property markets can be seen in isolation from wider factors, notably interest rates.

*Garden Festivals*
Garden Festivals (Robson, 1988, p. 111) were presented as a means of publicising land where urban regeneration schemes were in operation. They were intended to demonstrate to the private sector that land was available and had been brought into a state fit for sale. The first was held in Liverpool in 1984 and reflected personal interest by the then Secretary of State for the Environment following riots in part of that city (see Chapter 9). It made an initial profit but subsequently had a chequered history, including being sold to a private company which went bankrupt. Although later festivals fared rather better and attracted housing and landscaping developments, Garden Festivals were largely ineffective as flagship demonstrations of urban regeneration. The take-up of reclaimed land was, in practice, determined by the general health of the economy.

*Assessment*
The pattern of expenditure on Derelict Land Grants and City Grants has been one of steady actual and planned expansion (Table 6.5). In effect this indicates increasing state intervention, aiming to underwrite developments which the market would not otherwise take on; a crude form of public–private partnership. The urban regeneration grants thus offend against strict neo-liberal ideology. On other grounds, however, they are more compatible with Thatcherism. In particular, through the 1980s, they assisted in the steady reduction of the role of the local authorities (see Chapter 9).

TABLE 6.5   **Expenditure on regeneration grants 1988–9 to 1994 (£m)**

|            | 1988–9 | 1989–90 | 1990–91 | 1991–2 | 1992–3 | 1993–4 |
|------------|--------|---------|---------|--------|--------|--------|
| DLG        | 67.8   | 54.0    | 61.7    | 75.6   | 95.4   | 99.1   |
| City Grant | 27.8   | 39.1    | 45.4    | 55.5   | 71.0   | 77.6   |

Note:   Figures to 1990–1 are outturn, 1991–2 estimated outturn; others plans only.
Source:   HMSO (1992) p. 59, figure 60.

They have also been clearly and forcefully reorientated to the needs of the private sector. They are perhaps best viewed as elements in the emerging facilitative state, helping to revive the market in inner city areas.

## Housing initiatives

Up to this point we have been concerned with what might be strictly defined as urban initiatives. We will now turn to an area, housing, which, though not solely an 'urban issue', has a serious and direct impact on the lives of people living in urban areas.

Post-1979 Conservative housing policy has had four basic aims (Atkinson and Durden, 1990):

- to encourage the growth of owner-occupation;
- to minimise local authority housing provision;
- to target resources on those in need in order to achieve better value for money; and
- to revitalise the private rented sector.

Owner-occupation appealed to the Conservatives because it epitomised a spirit of independence and self-reliance. The New Right saw it as the opposite of the dependency culture which they took local authority housing to represent. Furthermore, home-owners 'paid their own way', thus reducing public expenditure. Local authority tenants were seen as supporters of the Labour Party and recipients of state support which they did not necessarily need. Providing local authority housing for *general needs* was seen as unwarranted and uneconomic state activity which deprived those in *genuine need.* The private rented sector was lauded as a free enterprise response to housing need.

## Local authority housing

A key characteristic of Conservative housing policy was a sustained attack on local authority housing, with a clear switch of resources away from the public sector to owner-occupation. Public expenditure on local authority housing fell from £4.5 billion per annum in 1980/1 to £1.4 billion in 1991/2, while the cost of mortgage interest tax relief rose from £2.19 billion per annum to £7.8 billion (Inquiry into British Housing, 1991). At the same time councils virtually ceased to build houses and sold over 1 million dwellings. The evidence available would suggest that sales were highest in southern England and lowest in Scotland (Dunn *et al.*, 1987). Some 5 million dwellings were still in the local authority sector at the end of the 1980s and the government attempted to break this residual state involvement by allowing tenants to opt out of local authority control into a tenancy arrangement with some other organisation such as a housing association or tenants' co-operative. By mid-1991 this strategy had achieved only minimal success with less than 80 000 units having transferred out of local authority control (Inquiry into British Housing, 1991, p. 67).

Increasingly, local authority housing became the tenure of the very poor. This concentration of people in poverty reflected wider processes of marginalisation and residualisation (Forest and Murie, 1983, 1986) and, while not a phenomenon purely of the 1980s, was considerably accelerated by Conservative policies. In urban and suburban areas it produced very high concentrations of social malaise (Syms, 1984; Pacione, 1989). Furthermore, there is significant evidence that the way in which the remaining local authority housing is allocated exacerbates existing inequalities within the deprived population creating *problem estates* from which there is little chance of escape.

## Owner-occupation

The unsuitability of owner-occupation for many people, particularly those living on low incomes in the inner city, has been clear for some time (Karn, 1979; Karn *et al.*, 1985). In essence, the problem is that the types of houses that low-income people can afford to buy are usually those in the worst condition in the most run-down areas. It may be difficult and expensive to raise the finance to purchase such properties and the properties are likely to be in need of considerable and costly maintenance which low-income purchasers, with high outgoings relative to their income, are unable to afford. In the boom of the mid-1980s, poorer people were able to trade into this potential trap.

In the stagnant residential property market of the 1990s poorer inner-city home-owners were unable to trade up and out by taking advantage of rising house prices. Furthermore, the impact of recession on employment brought a dramatic increase in mortgage repossession from 3480 in 1980 to 43 890 in 1990 (Inquiry into British Housing, 1991, p. 16). Over the same period mortgages in arrears of between 6–12 months increased from 15 530 to 123 110. Recent figures (Ford, 1992) suggest that while the number of loans two months or more in arrears had declined slightly to 773 240 by the end of March 1992, there had been a quite dramatic increase (38 per cent) in the numbers that were six months or more in arrears.

By the early 1990s mortgage arrears and repossessions were spreading out from the inner cities to affect the Conservative Party's middle-class support. Various attempts were made to ameliorate the crisis. The government's 'rents to mortgages' scheme reputedly helped fewer than twelve owners, according to one report (*Observer Housing Report*, 5.7.92, p. 2) and less than fifty according to another (*Guardian*, 30.7.92). State intervention appeared ineffective and many owner-occupiers found themselves saddled with properties whose resale price was less than the original purchase cost (a situation known as *negative equity*).

The threat to owner-occupation, particularly owner-occupation in the inner cities, should not be underestimated. Although inner-city housing may well move first when the continually anticipated upturn in the housing market arrives, it seems unlikely that owners will experience the sort of price gains that were common for most of the period up to 1989. Moreover, the building industry, which was buoyant until 1988, has slumped dramatically.

*Housing conditions*

Not only was there a dramatic reduction in house building in the late 1980s; disrepair also dramatically increased, with some local authority dwellings and even estates deteriorating to such an extent that it was deemed to be better and more economic to demolish them. Throughout the 1980s problems of disrepair were also increasing in the owner-occupied sector. By 1992 the number of unfit dwellings had risen to 1.3 million, the vast majority of which were in the private sector (*Independent*, 1.8.92).

Little seems to have been done to help low-income inner-city owner-occupiers whose properties are continuing to deteriorate at an alarming rate. To do so would, of course, require the government to acknowledge that owner-occupation is not some universal panacea and might in fact not be a terribly good thing for people on low incomes; it would also require state intervention.

Various attempts have been made to tackle run-down inner city and peripheral council housing estates. One attempt at Stockbridge Village on Merseyside in the early 1980s actually involved the private sector taking over a run-down council estate to revive it as a showpiece of what the private sector could do. The project eventually collapsed and the local authority was forced to intervene (Brindley *et al.*, 1989, ch. 8). Since this failure most attempts at regeneration have involved central government taking estates out of the control of local authorities and placing them in the hands of quangos. The most notable examples of this are *Housing Action Trusts* (HATs) and *Estates Action*.

HATs were launched by the Housing Act,1988 and were aimed at estates with problems so severe that a radical approach was demanded. Estates Action attempts to deal with estates suffering from less severe problems. HATs were created to enable areas of local authority housing to be prepared for sale to private or quasi-private (Housing Association) landlords. Tenants were to be given a choice in this matter, with ballots being set up to vote on choices of landlord. Rents were to be set by reference to the market. This further distanced the local authorities from involvement in housing provision and confirmed their role of dealing with emergency cases of extreme housing deprivation. In inner city areas and Labour-controlled peripheral local authority housing estates, opposition by councils, and indeed tenants, initially limited the impact of HATs and landlord-choice legislation. As a result, very few were set up and the government found itself forced to modify its stance on the issue of transfer out of council tenure after improvement.

Both Estates Action and HATs are linked in DoE guidelines (DoE, 1991b, para. 50) to City Challenge. As the guidelines point out: 'Urban programme authorities who successfully link estate regeneration proposals with other housing and inner city programmes will be in a good position to win extra resources for their area through City Challenge.' Like City Challenge, HATs monies are not additional funding. They are drawn from the existing housing budget. The shortcoming of this approach is clear: it may divert resources from other equally run-down areas in the locality. Furthermore, the success of a HAT will depend upon councils' ability to involve tenants and private companies in the schemes (*Guardian*, 1.8.91).

### Employment-related initiatives

Another theme not specific to urban areas, but with considerable relevance to such areas, is employment. We have already made numerous references to the fact that urban areas have been losing employment since the 1950s and that most employment growth is taking place in southern regions and in smaller, free-standing towns away from traditional industrial areas. Green's work (1986) points to wide variations in unemployment rates and the length of time spent unemployed, but essentially confirms the existence of a North–South divide and the problems of urban areas whose traditional manufacturing base has disappeared (see also Begg *et al.*, 1986).

Buck and Gordon (1987, p. 77) note that:

it would appear that inner city residents experience continuing disadvantage in the allocation of employment largely as a reflection of personal characteristics – of age, race, marital status, social class, skill or employment experience – which affect evaluations of their employability.

What is more disturbing is their suggestion that:

localized job creation policies in the inner city are unlikely to have much effect on the employment prospects of the disadvantaged

unless either the conditions of employment are too unattractive
for others to be interested in or recruitment is organised in a
manner which counters the normal selection criteria of the
market. (Buck and Gordon, 1987, p. 112)

Notwithstanding this pessimism, a variety of organisations and
schemes attempted, during the 1980s, to provide the unemployed,
and those likely to be unemployed upon leaving school, with the
skills demanded by new growth industries. Some, often run by the
Manpower Services Commission (MSC), were aimed at solving the
skills problem for those unemployed after leaving school. Others,
such as the *Training and Vocational Education Initiative* (TVEI) and
*Compact* were aimed at those still at school in order to prepare them
to compete in the new job markets of the 1980s.

These developments culminated in 1988 with the launching of one
overarching post-school initiative: *Employment Training*. This was
followed by a further initiative which signalled, through its name, its
intention to place a greater emphasis on the role of the private sector
– *Training and Enterprise Councils* (TECs). These would be set up at
local level and run by local business people to ensure that training
and local labour market needs matched one another (for general
overviews see Meacher, 1989; Atkinson and Lupton, 1990).

One of the most glaring gaps in employment training for much of
the 1980s was a lack of programmes specifically directed at inner
cities or targeted at the most vulnerable groups within the inner
cities such as black youths. Inner-city initiatives, with their emphasis
on property-led regeneration and automatic trickle-down, largely
neglected the issue of whether employment creation benefited
residents in inner areas. Davies and Mason (1986) pointed to the
way in which recruitment practices and negative stereotyping
excluded inner city residents from many jobs. Haughton (1990,
p. 185) noted that: 'As few as 17 per cent of jobs created under
initiatives in the inner cities are said to go to inner-city residents, the
remainder being taken up by in-commuting workers'. He went on to
note the failure of policy to address why certain groups of people
(often concentrated in inner areas or on peripheral council estates)
are systematically discriminated against in the job allocation
process.

By the end of the 1980s serious criticisms were levelled at this
failure to address discrimination. The Confederation of British

Industry's *Initiatives Beyond Charity* (CBI, 1988) stressed that, with existing skill shortages, it was in the private sector's own interests to take a more active role in ensuring that people in deprived inner areas received the right type of training. The *Employment Gazette* frequently carried reports on how employment initiatives directed towards the inner cities were assisting unemployed residents and people at school (e.g. Opie, 1991). Despite such optimism, Turok and Wannop (1990, p. 21) suggest that:

In general . . . the level of training provided by the projects is fairly basic and much of the work experience is non-skill specific . . . If directed clearly it might also help to alleviate skill shortages appearing in selected occupations and sectors. In addition it would help reduce the possibility that training projects are simply redistributing existing low level jobs among the target population.

Legally enforceable local labour market clauses, requiring the employment of local people, might allow such shortcomings to be addressed. Such a move was rejected in 1988 by Margaret Thatcher and her then Environment Secretary, Nicholas Ridley, as interfering with the market. At best, non-binding agreements are signed at local level and their implementation largely left to developers/employers. In some cases public subsidies have been used to encourage projects to employ local people but there still remains the problem of preventing discrimination in recruitment, especially with regard to ethnic minorities (see Chapter 10). City Challenge attempted to address the issue, but stopped short of setting legally enforceable employment targets for local people. Some TECs also took on an 'inner city dimension' (Christie and Rolfe, 1992), although it has to be questioned whether they have either the resources or the power to co-ordinate concerted action against employment discrimination.

Robinson (1989) suggests that a lack of co-ordination between the many organisations involved with promoting employment is one cause of the continuing problem of urban unemployment. More importantly, however, are questions concerning the type of development which takes place and the quality of the jobs created. As Colenutt (1992, p. 46) has noted, 'industry versus the service sector – goes to the heart of the debate about "market-led development". Is it to be a strategy for jobs defined by what the property market believes is most profitable at a particular point in time, or is it to be based upon a longer-term view of city employment and economic development needs?'

The government has largely avoided answering or even asking such questions and has left the market, supported and encouraged by government grants and subsidies, to take the property-led route to job creation. The alternative would require considerable intervention in the activities and recruiting behaviour of firms, something which the government since 1979 has been unwilling to do. So, despite some of the sophisticated job targeting recommendations made to the DoE (Turok and Wannop, 1990), positive proactive action in the inner cities seems unlikely to be forthcoming.

**Conclusion**

In the course of this chapter we have considered a number of initiatives and policy areas loosely linked by the fact that they, or their recognisable predecessors, were inherited by the incoming Conservative government of 1979. All were transformed in the ensuing decade. Generally they were freed from local government control, exposed to competitive pressures, opened up to the private sector and, with the exception of inner-city employment initiatives, targeted on to specific areas – often areas which also qualified for other grants.

By the early 1990s the growing scale and increasing visibility of inner-city problems forced the government to attempt to deal with some of the worst examples of urban decay, particularly on run-down council estates, by more direct, centrally controlled, methods. Estates Action, HATs, the City Grant and City Challenge, in combination with the use of CATs and Task Forces, could be seen as examples of this new co-ordinated approach to urban poverty and deprivation. However, these attempts frequently lacked any reference to the wider local, let alone regional and national, problems which created and intensified the very problems they were intended to address. Even in the key areas of housing and employment, there is little evidence that either general policies or specific initiatives achieved any success in reversing urban decline.

# 7 Urban Initiatives since 1979: Innovation, Consolidation and Assessment

In the previous chapters we provided an overview of Conservative thinking on urban regeneration and examined a series of inherited initiatives. This present chapter comprises three parts:

- A discussion of the innovatory initiatives which had the specific purpose of facilitating free-market, and more specifically property-led, forms of urban regeneration. These initiatives were Enterprise Zones (EZs), Urban Development Corporations (UDCs) and Free Ports (FPs).
- A analysis of the attempt by the third Thatcher government and the subsequent Major governments to consolidate and co-ordinate the Conservative approach to urban regeneration.
- An assessment of the practical contribution which the post-1979 governments have made to urban policy.

## Innovation in urban policy

### Enterprise Zones

Enterprise Zones were announced by the then Chancellor of the Exchequer, Geoffrey Howe, in his Budget speech of 1980 and given legislative approval in the Local Government Planning and Land Act, 1980 (Purton and Douglas, 1982). Their origins lay in the thinking of a geographer, Peter Hall (Hall, 1977) who, in 1977, argued that the situation in Britain's inner cities had reached crisis proportions and that conventional attempts to reverse this decline had failed to have any effect. He advocated a radical free-market strategy based upon the conditions which he argued existed in the rapidly-growing economies of the Far East. Zones should be created in Britain's inner cities where planning, employment, welfare, pollution, health and safety, and taxation legislation was significantly relaxed. This, he argued, would create a climate which would encourage the development of entrepreneurial talents, enterprise and innovation; such areas would act as *seed beds* for the small firms which were to be the motors of economic growth and job creation (see Chapter 5). Not only would this approach rejuvenate the inner city areas; it would also have *spillover* and *multiplier* effects on the surrounding local and regional economies. These growth points could thus play a major role in Britain's overall economic rejuvenation.

In the climate of the second half of the 1970s Hall's ideas were soon picked up by the then Conservative Opposition, in particular by the Shadow Chancellor, Geoffrey Howe. Howe made it clear that he saw such zones as a way of allowing people 'to earn and keep significant reward for the investment and effort we wish them to put into our urban deserts' (Howe, 1979, p. 10). He also saw the proposed EZs fulfilling another, equally important, function: 'the idea would be to set up test market areas or laboratories in which to enable fresh policies to prime the pump of prosperity and to establish their potential for doing so elsewhere' (Howe, 1979, p. 11). So not only were EZs originally seen as a way of turning around run-down urban areas, they were also a test of free-market ideas which, if they proved successful in inner cities, could be generalised throughout the United Kingdom.

By the time EZs were actually introduced, Hall's original ideas had been considerably watered down by the pressures of government and the forces of pragmatism. They bore little resemblance to Hall's notion of free-market enclaves. There was no major removal of UK legal and procedural regulation. The advantages were time-limited to ten years from the date of declaration and were limited to:

(i)    exemption from Development Land Tax . . . ;
(ii)   exemption from rates on industrial and commercial property;
(iii)  100 per cent allowances for Corporation and Income Tax purposes for capital expenditure on industrial and commercial buildings;

(iv) applications from firms in Enterprise Zones for certain customs facilities are processed as a matter of priority and certain criteria relaxed;

(v) exemption from industrial training levies and from the requirements to supply information to Industrial Training Boards;

(vi) a greatly simplified planning regime: developments that conform to the adopted scheme for each zone do not require express planning permission;

(vii) speedier administration of those controls remaining in force; and

(viii) reduced government requests for statistical information. (Roger Tym and Partners, 1984, p. 1)

Between 1981 and 1985, twenty-five zones were designated. More recently, a further two have been created, on Clydeside and Wearside, to deal with the closure of key local industries and, in April 1993, three were scheduled in response to the run-down of the coal industry. Most of the initial zones were located in or near long-standing run-down urban areas or, in cases such as Corby, in towns where the staple industry had closed down, so creating massive unemployment almost overnight.

*EZs: an assessment*
According to a review carried out by PA Cambridge (1987) for the DoE, between 1981 and 1986 63 000 jobs were located in the twenty-three EZs studied. Of these, about 35 000 were the direct result of Enterprise Zone policy. The consultants estimated the cost per job to the Exchequer at between £23 000 and £30 000 depending upon the assumptions used in the calculation. In 1990, the National Audit Office (NAO, 1990) noted that, up to the end of March 1987, the zones had cost the Exchequer £431 million. They suggested that the number of permanent jobs created was only 10 500, with an additional 2500 temporary jobs. The real cost per job to the Exchequer was estimated at approximately £30 000 (NAO, 1990, 23–4). It was doubtless these high costs per job which led the then Secretary of State for the Environment, Nicholas Ridley, to announce in 1987 that no new EZs would be declared except in exceptional circumstances.

There is some difficulty in assessing exactly what effects EZs have had. Like debates over the cost–benefit rate, the issue of *additionality* (the extent to which developments have occurred solely as a result of Enterprise Zone designation) involves a series of complex and disputable methodological issues (PA Cambridge, 1987). Most studies agree that the most attractive incentive offered by EZs for incoming firms, and the one most widely known and mentioned by them, was rates relief. The danger with this incentive was that it offered incoming firms an advantage over local competitors. Several studies (Massey, 1982; Talbot, 1988) have argued that, as a partial consequence of the rates incentive, the major effect of EZs has simply been to redistribute jobs within the local economy and reinforce existing industrial trends within the area. Several authors have gone further and argued that the real beneficiaries of the incentives available in EZs have been land owners receiving higher rents or land values as a result of developments within the zones (Cadman, 1982; Erickson and Syms, 1986; PA Cambridge, 1987).

Ironically, the zones which have been most successful appear to be those in which the public sector owned a high percentage of the land prior to designation. Thus not only have state subsidies/interventions played a major role in stimulating general development, but so too has the significant presence of a public-sector landowner. Location has been another potent factor in determining success or failure. PA Cambridge (1987) have suggested that the successful EZs created in southern England (especially the one in the Isle of Dogs in London's Docklands) were actually unnecessary as there was already a healthy demand in the local and regional economies; the subsidies were little more than additional profits for land-owners and developers. In contrast, in depressed areas the subsidies may have led weak firms to relocate into zones in order to take advantage of the protection offered by subsidies; Talbot's (1988) study of the Tyneside Enterprise Zone suggests that the zone may actually have sheltered some firms from the need to innovate and cushioned their profit margins.

Overall it is clear that EZs are not true experiments in the free market. They constitute and engender state intervention. The fact that their characteristics have not, except to a limited extent though simplified planning zones (see Chapter 8), been generalised to areas outside EZs, as was originally envisaged, is a tacit acceptance by the government of their cost and relative failure. Where they have been successful, within the context of Conservative ideology, has been in reducing local-government intervention in the affairs of firms. Many of the advantages associated with EZs involved less local-government interference, most notably the reduced requirements regarding planning legislation.

## Urban Development Corporations

Until the mid-1980s it is fair to say that EZs were, both in terms of expenditure and profile, more important than UDCs. However, by 1988, the government could argue that 'Urban Development Corporations. . .are the most important attack ever made on urban decay. They are already transforming inner cities' (HMSO, 1988, p. 12). UDCs are, or perhaps more accurately *were*, the jewels in the crown of Conservative urban 'policy'. From the two originally declared in 1981, their number increased to thirteen by the end of 1992, with the expansion taking place after 1987 (for excellent overviews see Lawless, 1988b, 1988c; Stoker, 1989; Colenutt and Tansley, 1990; Colenutt, 1992). We will devote substantial attention to this major initiative.

### Objectives and powers

In strict terms, a UDC is the organisation given the task of regenerating a designated Urban Development Area; we will follow convention and use the term UDC in a general sense to cover both meanings. UDCs are declared under Part XI of the Local Government, Planning and Land Act, 1980 (LGPLA), and derive their powers from that Act. In essence, a UDC may be declared if 'the Secretary of State is of the opinion that it is expedient in the national interest to do so' (LGPLA, S. 134). The issue of 'the national interest' is of some importance because it is this which effectively justifies taking the areas out of the control of local authorities and placing them in the hands of a non-elected body – the UDC.

The object of the UDC is 'to secure the regeneration of its area' (LGPLA: S.136) by 'bringing land and buildings into effective use, encouraging the development of existing and new industry and commerce, creating an attractive environment and ensuring that housing and social facilities are available to encourage people to live and work in the area' (LGPLA, S. 136). The Act contains no clear definition of regeneration and questions regarding the distribution of the benefits of regeneration are not addressed. The emphasis, however, has been on property-led regeneration and the enablement of private-sector activity.

UDCs have a variety of powers, the most important of which concern compulsory purchase to aid in land assembly and site preparation. The UDC also effectively becomes the planning and highways authority, although not the housing authority, for its area, thus usurping a series of key local government functions and powers. Much of the original covert justification for these extensive powers was the post-1979 Conservative view that local government in urban areas, which was often Labour-controlled, was part of the problem of urban decline. It was overly bureaucratic and characterised by a rigid planning system and high rates which discouraged enterprise. Moreover, it was also subject to the play of conflicting local interests which could effectively create a situation of perpetual inertia in which nothing was done while the area continued to decline. The Conservatives did not trust local government to play the lead role in regenerating run-down urban areas of national importance.

*Operation and finance*

As Table 7.1 illustrates, thirteen UDCs had been created in England and Wales by 1992. The London Docklands and Merseyside development corporations may be seen as the first generation, with a second generation being declared in 1987. A third generation of *mini-UDCs* with shorter life-spans, provisionally five years, and lower budgets, around £50 million, were declared in 1988, and a fourth generation, which may also be described as mini-UDCs, came into existence in 1992.

The London Docklands UDC (LDDC) has received by far the largest grant-in-aid of all the UDCs (Table 7.2). According to the National Audit Office, the LDDC spent a total of £380 million between 1981 and 1987; £315 million of this sum was grant aid and £60 million came from sales of property (NAO, 1988, p. 10). Over the same period, Merseyside UDC (MDC) spent £169 million. Since the declaration of the second and third generations, UDCs have absorbed by far the largest share of the DoE's urban expenditures (NAO, 1990, p. 15). This share has been rising and the LDDC has received an increasing share.

**TABLE 7.1**    **Urban development corporations**

| Name | Date of Designation | Size (hectares) |
|---|---|---|
| London Docklands | 1981 | 2226 |
| Merseyside | 1981 (expanded 1988) | 450 (1500) |
| Black Country | 1987 (expanded 1988) | 2598 |
| Cardiff Bay | 1987 | 1089 |
| Teeside | 1987 | 4858 |
| Trafford Park | 1987 | 1267 |
| Tyne & Wear | 1987 | 2375 |
| Bristol | 1988 | 360 |
| Central Manchester | 1988 | 187 |
| Leeds | 1988 | 540 |
| Sheffield | 1988 | 900 |
| Birmingham Heartlands | 1992 | 1000 |
| Plymouth | 1992 | n/a |

Source:   Colenutt and Tansley (1990) and DoE regional offices.

**TABLE 7.2**    **UDC expenditure 1989–92 (£ million)**

| Name | 1989/90 | 1990/1 | 1991/2 | 1992/3 |
|---|---|---|---|---|
| Docklands | 256 | 332 | 225 | 179.9 |
| Merseyside | 23 | 24 | 25 | 39.6 |
| Black Country | 31 | 32 | 33 | 46.2 |
| Cardiff Bay | 29 | 31 | 34 | n/a |
| Teeside | 36 | 38 | 36 | 55.2 |
| Trafford Park | 17 | 29 | 30 | 37.7 |
| Tyne and Wear | 36 | 38 | 36 | 49.1 |
| Bristol | 5 | 10 | 7 | 10.3 |
| Central Manchester | 11 | 14 | 16 | 27.2 |
| Leeds | 8 | 14 | 8 | 8.0 |
| Sheffield | 10 | 19 | 13 | 20.6 |
| **Total** | 462 | 581 | 463 | 473.8 |

Note:   Grand total for 1992/3 excludes Cardiff Bay; Plymouth UDC, launched in 1992, will spend £45m over a five-year period and Birmingham Heartlands UDC, launched in 1992, will spend £50m over a five year period.

Sources:   Colenutt and Tansley (1990) p. 35: HMSO (1992) p. 68; (1989/90–1991/2 figures for grant aid; 1992/3 figures include planned receipts from land sales and are NOT comparable with earlier years.)

*The London Docklands Urban Development Corporation: a case study*
LDDC, of all the UDCs, has received by far the most research
attention and it is this UDC which we too shall look at in most depth.
Not only, as we have just seen, has it had more financial assistance
from governments, it has also attracted far more private investment
than all the other UDCs put together – £8420 million out of a UDC-
wide total of £10 606 million (HMSO, 1992, p. 69, fig. 75); it is the
best example of what we, in Chapter 5, termed property-led development. It has additionally had the most quarrelsome relationship with
the local authorities it displaced and the worst relations with its local
population; both have complained bitterly about the lack of
consultation and benefits for the indigenous population.

The area which LDDC took over in 1982 had an economic and
social structure largely dependent upon dock-related industries
which had been in decline since the 1930s. There had been a series of
plans to reverse this decline, none of which had achieved a great deal
(DJC, 1980; Goodwin, 1986; Brownill, 1990a, ch. 2). The
Conservative government argued that by the early 1980s a situation
of deadlock had been reached while the decline of the area continued
unabated. They asserted that the local authorities in the area lacked
the will, finances and ability to reverse the decline and thus the
imposition of a single-minded UDC was justified.

From the very beginning there was strong local opposition to the
imposition of a UDC but the government pushed through the
legislation and quickly established the necessary basis for action: a
streamlined organisational structure, rapid decision-making, and
leaders from the private sector. LDDC, perhaps more than any
other UDC, encapsulated the government's belief in the power of
the private sector, market forces and property-led development. Reg
Ward, LDDC's first Chief Executive, argued:

> The LDDC sees its role as catalytic, not authoritative. It is not a
> development agency which imposes statutory controls and
> restraints upon the area. It is a resource centre which can
> identify and initiate action . . . We start off from the principle of
> being demand led . . . We look at the market, generate
> enthusiasm among potential investors . . . (Ward, 1982, p. 11)

The LDDC thus sought to stress land reclamation, site
preparation and the marketing of the Docklands in such a way as

to create a climate conducive to private investment. The LDDC was willing to listen sympathetically to any proposed investment and, if it accepted it, to expedite its implementation. The market took centre-stage; Ward disposed of the notion that there might be a Docklands community with interests that had to be taken into account by arguing that there were a series of Docklands communities, each having different 'traditions, cultures, attitudes and needs' (Ward, 1982, p. 11). The policy was one of fragmenting any opposition and employing statutory powers to develop a property-led approach to urban regeneration.

The LDDC's 1992 Corporate Plan lists some of its key achievements:

> £161 million investment in land acquisition; 600 hectares of derelict land reclaimed; £715 million investment in new or improved transport infrastructure; £1350 million public sector investment; £9100 million private sector investment; 41,000 jobs – 17,000 new and 24,000 relocated; total employment doubled from 27,000 in 1981 to 53,000 in 1991; a 56% increase in population from 39,400 to 61,000; 16,100 new homes completed; home ownership increased from 5% to 44%; £151 million invested in new housing for local residents; £76 million invested in education, training, support for industry, health and community programmes. (Taken from LDDC Corporate Plan, 1992)

By any standards these are major achievements and we do not seek to contest that a quite dramatic process of economic, physical and social restructuring was unleashed by LDDC, as any visitor to the area can quickly appreciate. Brownill (1990a), among others, has noted that LDDC's strategy can be divided basically into three phases:

1. **1981–5**. In this first phase LDDC's 'plan' was to clean up the Docklands, both physically and in marketing terms, and attract new *sunrise industries*. This frequently involved displacing longstanding, unsightly local employers and reclaiming land. At the same time, a great deal of emphasis was placed on the building of high quality/high cost owner-occupied properties for those who wished to return to the inner city and live close to their work.

2. **1985–1988/9**. By 1985 it was becoming clear that the initial 'industrial' strategy was not working. LDDC began to turn its attention towards the City of London a few miles upriver. With the era of financial deregulation ushered in by the Conservatives it was argued that the anticipated massive expansion of banks, dealing houses and other financial services associated with the City would lead to an enormous growth in demand for new, high-quality office space as the City strove to maintain its position in the global financial markets. The Docklands sought to play its part in this process and develop into a major new financial centre. Thus the LDDC's strategy in its second phase became one of office development and associated high-quality housing development, and its fate became inextricably bound up with the fortunes of the property industry and the flagship development of Canary Wharf.

3. **1988/9–the present**. Unfortunately, the boom in demand for office space in the Docklands soon came under severe pressure. As we saw in Chapter 5, the property-led boom of the mid-1980s came to an end. The Docklands felt the cold hand of recession acutely and there were a series of dramatic property company crashes culminating in the flagship centrepiece of the Docklands, Canary Wharf, going into receivership as the apparently untouchable world-wide property empire of its owners, Olympia & York, began to collapse. The third phase of the LDDC saw a recognition that it could no longer safely ignore the indigenous community's demands. At the same time, the local community and its elected representatives began to reassess the extent to which it could afford to continue to pursue a strategy of noncooperation with the LDDC. As a result a series of co-operative agreements were signed whereby LDDC provided funds and land for local building, refurbishment and training.

It would appear that the LDDC now favours a less confrontational and more co-operative style. This may simply be an attempt to smooth the way for new development and stifle local criticism – to make the Docklands more marketable and remove the image of an area beset by internal conflicts (DCC, 1990). It could, however, also represent a belated attempt to provide the social infrastructure required by a population which has doubled in just over ten years. Most probably it represents a recognition on LDDC's part, at the behest of private developers, that successful long-term development requires community support and a coherent relationship between the development of infrastructure and the pace of development (Brownill, 1990a). Early in 1993 the DoE indicated that it did not anticipate further large-scale office development in the Docklands. The remaining undeveloped sites, most notably the Victoria, Albert and George V docks, would be developed as urban villages with a mixture of housing tenures and forms of development (*Guardian*, 25.1.93).

A critique of the LDDC would point to the mid-1980s as a key problem period. First, there was an over-reliance on the general strategy of property-led development and the specific flagship Canary Wharf project. Second, inadequate attention was given to the development of a transport infrastructure to move the office-based workforce into the Docklands (Church, 1990). The Docklands Light Railway was quite inadequate for the task and the proposed eastward extension of the Jubilee Underground line was overly bound up with the fortunes of the collapsing property developers Olympia & York. Third, the massive building programme had surprisingly little impact on the local employment market. Only 9 per cent of the construction workers on Canary Wharf were from the local Borough of Tower Hamlets (DCC, 1992, pp. 13–14) and an unpublished evaluation of LDDC training schemes 'clearly shows that the LDDC's approach to education, training and unemployment has been very limited, poorly monitored and not at all successful' (HCEC, 1988, p. xv). Fourth, rapid house-price inflation in 1984–8 made it very difficult for local young people to afford to remain in the area. Finally, processes of consultation were limited; in evidence to the House of Commons Employment Committee 'the LDDC admitted that they were unable to find their own records relating to the draft code of consultation' (HCEC, 1988, p. xiv).

On the positive side, attention can be drawn to the figures concerning the major governmental tool for assessing the economic impact of the LDDC: the *gearing ratio* or amount of private-sector investment attracted for a given amount of public-sector money. According to the House of Commons Public Accounts Committee in 1987, £380 million of public funds had attracted, or *levered*, private investment of over £2 billion; a gearing ratio of 1:5.26. The LDDC itself was claiming in the late 1980s that gearing ratios were as high as 1:10 or even 1:12 but by 1992 this had fallen to 1:6.74

(LDDC, 1992). These calculations are controversial. Opponents of LDDC claim that published gearing ratios have failed to take into account the full range of public expenditure in the Docklands, ignoring expenditure by the Department of Transport, capital allowances and rate-free periods in the Isle of Dogs EZ, and money spent on site preparation and infill before the declaration of LDDC (DCC, 1990, ch. 3; ALA/DCC, 1991, pp. 2–4). According to these critics, £2.5 billion of public-sector funding went into the Docklands between 1981 and 1991 and the total figure will reach £5.4 billion by 1995 (ALA/DCC, 1991, p. 3). If we take the ALA/DCC figure of £2.5 billion up to 1991 and use LDDC's figure of £9.1 billion total private investment to the end of March 1992, a year later than the ALA/DCC period, the gearing ratio falls to 1:3.6.

The dependence of LDDC on public investment has been clearly illustrated in the sums spent on transport infrastructure. In March 1993 these were increased by the final announcement for the go-ahead of the £1.7 billion Jubilee Line extension. At the same time road schemes in and around the Docklands totalling £764 million were announced (*Guardian*, 25.3.93). These schemes are seen as essential to the Docklands' survival even as a secondary office centre and once again emphasise the key role of the public sector in underwriting private development.

There are therefore both positive and negative sides to the operation of the LDDC. In the end an adequate assessment is unlikely to be possible before the end of the century and even then much will depend upon the London, regional national and international economy. It seems unlikely that the Docklands will ever become a genuine second London financial centre. At best it will be used for the location of backroom financial services or by firms wishing to relocate and restructure, as the print industry did during the 1980s. Were London's position as a global financial centre of the first rank to be lost, the consequences for the Docklands could be dire, as the already low demand for office space would almost certainly collapse further, leaving millions of square feet of unwanted space in the Docklands.

### UDCs outside London

We have concentrated on the LDDC because it has been at the centre of discussions about UDCs and urban initiatives more generally. However, a brief overview of the experience of the other UDCs is relevant, particularly as the successes and failures of the LDDC relate to the peculiar circumstances of a UDC in a world city and may not be generalisable to other situations.

Of the other UDCs, Merseyside Development Corporation (MDC) has received the most detailed treatment (see Adcock, 1984; Parkinson, 1988a; Dawson and Parkinson, 1991). All studies agree that there is little or no comparison between LDDC and MDC. MDC was located in a virtually unpopulated run-down area of a city located in a declining region. Initially MDC intended to follow a strategy of industrial renewal. In the mid-1980s this proved unworkable and it switched to an emphasis on tourism and leisure services. This created considerable controversy among its board members and one, the leading free market economist Patrick Minford, resigned on the grounds that MDC had turned to a strategy inappropriate to Merseyside's labour market.

In addition to the obvious differences in size, MDC has differed from LDDC in two other important respects. First, MDC has not attracted large amounts of private investment; its gearing ratios, even when favourably calculated, are low. Given the weakness of the local and regional economy in and around Merseyside, this should come as no surprise. The key question which hangs over MDC is: even if it can regenerate its area, will it be able, as is expected of UDCs, to have an impact on its surrounding area and the region as a whole? MDC, with its emphasis on riverside tourism in downtown Liverpool, does not appear to have an appropriate strategy to achieve regional aims. Indeed, with two UDCs located in Manchester, it is highly likely that regional growth will become polarised as the three UDCs compete with one another for the location/redistribution of investment. Second, MDC has had reasonable relations with the surrounding local authorities. This may partly be a consequence of its lack of population on declaration, but it also reflects greater co-operation. It does not, however, mean that MDC has had a wholly beneficial impact on its area. According to the Gifford Report (1989) MDC's strategy has completely ignored the black population in nearby Toxteth and no attempts have been to direct programmes towards the black population or to monitor the effects of UDC activities on the black population. Moreover, while MDC has seen its income from central government increase, surrounding local authorities have experienced decreases throughout the 1980s. As Parkinson and Evans (1990, p. 81) have noted: 'The MDC may be improving the city's front door. The risk is that Government cuts may lead the rest of the house to crumble'.

Information about other UDCs is much more sparse. Bristol UDC was the subject of strong objections from Bristol City Council who challenged it in the House of Lords and succeeded in having part of it detached and returned to council control (Parker and Oatley, 1989). The Cardiff UDC has been even more controversial. Its proposal to build a barrage in Cardiff Bay has generated considerable opposition from local people and environmentalists (Brookes, 1989). Generally, however, the later UDCs appear to have learnt from the LDDC's mistakes; in particular their relations with local authorities are usually more cordial. Indeed, local government appears to have negotiated the Birmingham Heartlands UDC with the then Secretary of State at the DoE, Michael Heseltine, and the Plymouth UDC specifically aims to work in collaboration with the local authority. Personal communications with UDC officers suggest that, in some cases, this cordiality may be more apparent than real, reflecting attempts by both sides to reconcile their differences, at least publicly. Nevertheless,. considerable attention is now focusing on the development of consultation procedures.

The most recently declared UDCs are also different in that they were set up to counter specific problems. Birmingham Heartlands UDC represents an attempt to rescue a public–private partnership between Birmingham City Council and the private sector which had run into problems as a result of falling property prices, a general lack of resources and the difficulty of assembling sufficiently large land packages without compulsory purchase powers. The Plymouth UDC was set up primarily to deal with the run-down of military bases in the area and a particularly high local growth rate in male unemployment; much of its area will use land released by the Ministry of Defence (MoD) and it will be financed by both the MoD and the DoE to the tune of some £45 million.

### Assessment

There are no clear criteria by which the activities of UDCs may be assessed. The NAO (1988, p. 5) pointed out that there was no assessment of the first two UDCs by the DoE before the second and third generations were established. Much of the assessment which does exist has come from academic commentators, the NAO and House of Commons Committees such as the Employment Committee (HCEC, 1988) and the Public Accounts Committee (HCPAC, 1989). The absence of (published) assessments by the DoE may seem rather strange for a government which has constantly stressed the need to demonstrate value for money. It may well indicate the political importance and contentiousness of UDCs, the government's absolute belief in their ability to regenerate run-down urban areas, and an unwillingness to subject these public bodies to direct scrutiny. To do so would run the risk of exposing UDCs to a wider political debate about the way in which they operate and spend public funds. Certainly during the Thatcher years such debates were not welcomed.

A general assessment is, however, possible. So long as UDCs prioritise property-led development, they will inevitably focus primarily on narrow physical regeneration strategies revolving around flagship schemes, they will not contain mechanisms for ensuring that local people benefit, and their appropriateness will be questionable. Where, as in the case of LDDC and Olympia & York, a UDC's fortunes are largely dependent upon a major property developer who is exposed to the vagaries of the international property market, a further element of unpredictability and instability will be added.

Such problems will be aggravated by the continued lack of any national and regional strategic urban framework within which to locate the efforts of UDCs. This problem is most clearly illustrated in the North-West region where there are three UDCs (one in Merseyside and two in Manchester) and six City Challenge projects, but no mechanisms for co-ordinating activities for the benefit of the region as a whole; Adam Smith's 'invisible hand' appears to be the only legitimate means of co-ordination. It should also be clear that UDCs are not simply areas in which the market is allowed to operate in an unhindered fashion. They are public-sector bodies and involve considerable levels of state funding. Where they differ from previously existing locally-based organisations is in their relationship with the local population. As Batley (1989, p. 180) has noted: 'The conflict has been about what sort of intervention, under whose control and for what ends'.

*Free Ports*

In chronological terms, the last of the new initiatives developed by the post-1979 Conservatives was the Free Port. In 1984 six freeports (FPs) were set up, located in Southampton, Cardiff, Liverpool, Prestwich, Birmingham and Belfast. The first three were located in port areas and the other three in or near airports.

According to the organisation which has responsibility for them, Her Majesty's Customs and Excise (HMCE):

> A free zone or freeport is an enclosed area into which you may move goods without payment of customs duty and similar import charges, including value added tax charged at importation. You pay duty and the VAT charged on imports only if you consume them within the zones. You pay duty (not VAT) if you process the goods other than for export outside the European Community. (HMCE, 1984, p. 2)

In essence, Free Ports were therefore little more than giant bonded warehouses. They represented an experimental attempt to operationalise the Customs and Excise ideas underlying EZs and UDCs without exempting large areas from UK laws and regulations. Lloyd and McDougall (1984, p. 50) saw them being 'utilized by foreign entrepreneurs as a form of entreport, acting as distribution centres with storage of goods and components for trans-shipment'.

Very little research has been undertaken on Free Ports and they appear to have had little impact; the one in-depth study describes them as 'an almost unrelieved failure' (Davies and Butler, 1986, p. 1) and criticises the Treasury and HMCE for not doing enough to relax the burden of taxation and regulation in comparison with other European Free Ports (on Free Ports more generally see Butler and Pirie, 1983). Davies and Butler go on to note that Free Ports were used by the Government as part of an attempt to help areas of high unemployment, but 'when we look at freeports throughout the world it becomes clear that they stand the greatest chance of success in areas that are already prosperous, and in sites that are already popular stopping points on the trade routes of the world' (Davies and Butler, 1986, p. 33). All the UK Free Ports except Southampton were located in declining areas and none were particularly accessible to European trading partners. They may well have hoped to assist firms from outside the EC to establish a base within the Community from which to operate but, overall, the locations seem a little strange.

The public bodies which operated Free Ports lacked the powers/ inducements found in EZs and UDCs to attract businesses. Given this and their locations it is perhaps not surprising that they seem to have had little impact. Balasubramanyam and Rothschild (1985) argue that this failure stemmed from a lack of clarity regarding the objectives which the initiative was expected to achieve. It would be helpful if the government would allow an adequate research base to develop on what looks like becoming a minor footnote in the history of urban policy. When we contacted HMCE for information we received a very polite telephone call informing us that 'Mrs Thatcher had decreed [that] no information on FPs was to be released'.

## Consolidation in urban policy: action for cities

In the wake of her 1987 election victory Margaret Thatcher was widely quoted in the national press as having stated that 'Something must be done about Britain's Inner Cities'. What exactly was meant by this is debatable. A naïve analyst might assume that it suggested that something should be done about the poverty, unemployment and poor living conditions to be found in the inner cities. A cynical analyst would contend that she meant that the inner cities were the next area to be captured politically by the Thatcher revolution. Parkinson (1988a, p. 109) has noted how an anonymous DoE official pithily commented that 'Mrs Thatcher woke up on the morning after the election, saw little red city dots on the blue map of the country and decided we needed an inner city policy'.

### Action for Cities

Initially there was talk of a White Paper being published to bring together the disparate urban initiatives of the time. Finally, however, in March 1988, after several delays, a glossy brochure called *Action for Cities* (HMSO, 1988b) was launched in a blaze of publicity by Mrs Thatcher and a covey of ministers. It was followed by a series of 'businessmen's [sic] breakfasts' around the country aimed at trying to persuade the private sector to invest in Britain's cities. Margaret Thatcher, in her introduction to *Action for Cities*, claimed 'This booklet shows you that the government has a comprehensive approach to inner cities renewal' (HMSO, 1988b, p. 2). It is an important document for what it reveals and confirms about the nature of that 'policy'.

In line with prevailing Conservative philosophy, *Action for Cities* made it abundantly clear that the government could not be expected to, and would not, play the lead role in the regeneration of urban areas: 'The spark of regeneration must come from within the inner cities themselves.'(HMSO, 1988, p. 5). The state's role was presented as that of facilitator, helping create the right conditions for the private sector via investments in infrastructure, training, education and environmental improvements. The real stress was on the need for inner city residents to help themselves – to change their behaviour; it was largely a matter of unleashing the entrepreneurial talents which post-war bureaucratic forms of socialism had suffocated.

Interestingly, little or nothing was said that was new. As we saw in Chapter 6, Urban Development Grants and Urban Regeneration Grants were merged to form the *City Grant*, and *Housing Action Trusts* were created. The document also saw the launch of *City Technology Colleges*, an attempt by a department other than the DoE (the Department of Education and Science) to 'bend' its programmes towards urban areas and an initiative which had actually been announced two years earlier (Dale, 1989). The rest of the document included a list of measures, such as the Enterprise Allowance Scheme, the Loan Guarantee Scheme and the PICKUP Programme, which were not specifically aimed at urban areas and which also required the departments responsible to 'bend' towards the inner cities. McLaren (1989a, p. 18) estimates that new funding amounted to no more than £88.5 million in 1988/9 and a significant proportion of this was on new roads.

The desirability of concentrating funding from several government departments on to inner city problems was a major argument of *Action for Cities*: these efforts 'need to be pulled together more effectively, and brought to bear in the same place at the same time' (HMSO, 1988b, p. 4). According to Margaret Thatcher, total government spending on inner cities amounted to some £3 billion per annum (HMSO, 1988b, p. 2). The accounting which generated this figure has never been produced and all indications are that it could only be achieved by the creative addition of any governmental expenditure with a vague association with inner cities. It certainly far exceeds the 1979–87 eight-year expenditure total of the DoE on inner cities which amounted to £3350 million (*Hansard*, 16.3.87, vol. 1411, col. 397).

What is perhaps most important about *Action for Cities* is that it placed the emphasis unambiguously upon the leading role of the private sector and the need to do whatever was necessary to encourage its participation and the prioritisation of economic developments over social regeneration. This was clearly spelt out in an Urban Programme letter by David Trippier, one of the Ministers at the DoE, written in August 1988 (five months after the launch of *Action for Cities*). On priorities for 1989/90, he argued:

> We believe that the essential first step in the regeneration of run down inner city areas is the creation of a healthy local economy, and the Government's efforts are directed towards creating the conditions in which enterprise and businesses are able to flourish. This is why Ministers expect to see a presumption in favour of economic projects in inner area programmes. (Trippier, 1989)

The role of local authorities in the process of urban regeneration was barely mentioned.

*Action for Cities'* major stress was on increased efficiency and effectiveness via better co-ordination of policy at local and national level. We have already noted the role of CATs and Task Forces in this capacity at a local level. At a national level a Cabinet Committee was established in 1988 to co-ordinate the activities of central departments and a *Minister for Inner Cities* was created to ensure that co-ordination proceeded smoothly (Hennessy, 1989, p. 705). This was clearly an important commitment. However, there is no evidence to suggest that the Minister ever had sufficient power or resources to ensure that all the implicated departments used their funds effectively to benefit inner areas. As we have already noted in Chapter 4 in connection with earlier initiatives, the operating criteria and spending priorities of some departments could actually work against cities; this situation continued. Furthermore, the incumbents of the Ministry have rarely held their position for more than a few months and have usually also had other responsibilities, a situation hardly likely to encourage continuity and stability.

The successor documents to *Action for Cities*, *Progress in Cities* (HMSO, 1989) and *People in Cities* (HMSO, 1990) were very much in the same vein and echoed the triumphalist view that an economic miracle had occurred in the UK during the Thatcher years. However, the later documents give a more prominent role to local authorities, perhaps in response to the Audit Commission's criticisms of central government's deliberate exclusion of local government (Audit Commission, 1989). In 1990 David Hunt (then Minister for Inner Cities) acknowledged this shift of emphasis, noting the important role local authorities had to play in the regeneration process and specifically mentioning the role of Birmingham City Council in setting up Birmingham Heartlands in collaboration with the private sector (Hunt, 1990).

## New Life for Urban Scotland

Unlike the situation south of the border, the Scottish Office has overall control of development and the Scottish Development Agency (SDA – now merged with the Training Agency in Scotland to form Scottish Enterprise) existed to act as an interventionist agency seeking to bring about industrial and urban renewal. In 1988 *New Life for Urban Scotland* (Scottish Office, 1988) was published. While echoing many of the themes to be found in *Action for Cities*, particularly on the role of the private sector, it was, in the Scottish tradition, less hostile to local authorities. It also displayed more flexibility regarding social investment and placed a great deal of emphasis on the role of the community in regeneration. Indeed, in its successor *Urban Scotland into the 90s* (Scottish Office, 1990), the role of the community and that of the private sector were given more or less equal prominence.

The ability of the Scottish Office to focus a number of different initiatives on particular areas and the role of the SDA would appear to have created a more effective means to ameliorate the problems of inner cities and peripheral public-sector housing estates (McCrone, 1991). Additionally, the ongoing experience of the Glasgow Eastern Area Renewal Project (see Chapter 9) may have helped establish a better working relationship between the Scottish Office and local government, as well as providing experience of a long-term attempt to rejuvenate a run-down area using inter-agency co-ordination on a scale never achieved in the English Partnerships. The political hostility of the Scottish electorate to Thatcherism also led to further pragmatism on the part of the Conservatives; the Thatcher project was moderated and the Secretary of State ran things on more traditional pre-Thatcher lines.

Whatever the causes, it would appear that the new urban policy in Scotland is better directed, more consultative and more effective than its English counterpart. However, Maclennan (1990) notes that it is not without problems. He cites a lack of causal analysis and a failure to deal with the plight of those thrown out of work by long-term industrial decline. While acknowledging some improvement in this situation by 1990, he also argues that, outside targeted areas, the partnership between the Scottish Office and local communities is largely fictional. Boyle (1989) focuses on the dangers of too cosy a relationship with the private sector. He argues that *New Life for Urban Scotland* redefines all the programmes aimed at urban areas 'as a partnership between the state and private organisations' (Boyle, 1989, p. 21). Moore (1990, p. 67) echoes this theme in a critique of the SDA:

> The SDA is concerned about unemployment, but locally sees its overriding objective as supporting viable, that is commercial, businesses or locations where private investment is likely to be attracted, for example city centre sites. The Agency has never sought to challenge market criteria or private control of capital. It facilitates, subsidizes and works with business.The Agency may modify the market through its intervention but it does not usurp it.

So, despite advantages over the English situation, it would seem that, in Scotland, the same priorities dominate action and many of the same problems are reappearing, not least the question of the extent to which property-led development in particular and the private sector in general can meet the needs of those displaced by de-industrialisation (see Pacione, 1989; for a more sympathetic assessment see McCrone, 1991).

*The Urban Regeneration Agency*

Co-ordination between government departments was a key theme of *Action for Cities*. A report by the House of Commons Public Accounts Committee (HCPAC, 1990) on inner city regeneration also stressed this theme. It noted that, notwithstanding the Minister for Inner Cities, no single department had overall responsibility for inner cities. Moreover, while acknowledging that attempts have been made to create a broad frameworks for co-operation, it noted that such arrangements 'do not provide a systematic basis for assessing need and co-ordinating and monitoring implementation of relevant department programmes' (HCPAC, 1990, p. vi). Departments constantly claimed to the Committee that their own co-operation with other departments was improving, but there was little concrete evidence of effective steps to improve inter-departmental co-ordination of programmes:

> we are not convinced that there is sufficient liaison between departments at national level . . . we remain of the view that the multiplicity of bodies and initiatives involved is potentially a recipe for confusion and overlap. (HCPAC 216, 1990, p. ix)

The possibility of a body being set up to co-ordinate urban initiatives was announced by Michael Heseltine during the 1992 General Election campaign. An Urban Regeneration Agency (URA), headed by Peter Walker, the former Secretary of State for the Environment in the Heath Government and commissioner of the Inner Area Studies, would be created. To it 'will be transferred much of the responsibility for the urban policy of the Department of the Environment' (Conservative Party Press Release 649/92, 28.3.92). It appears that Heseltine saw the agency having considerable powers and acting as an 'English Development Agency' in a manner similar to the SDA. At one stage it was even thought possible that the URA would take over responsibility for the UDCs and EZs.

Michael Heseltine successor at the DoE after the 1992 election, Michael Howard, however, was less well disposed to a pro-active role for government in industrial regeneration and closer to an orthodox free-market position. Howard was not prepared to lose control over a major portion of his department's responsibility, and in a consultation paper (DoE, 1992c) launched in July 1992, a much-reduced role was mapped out for the URA. It is to be run by a board of six or more members and their overall strategy will have to be approved by both Heseltine (DTI) and Howard (DoE). It will take over responsibility for Derelict Land Grants, City Grants and English Estates (DoE, 1992c, p. 1; *Hansard* 3.11.92, col. 162) and its annual budget will be £268 million in the financial year 1993/4

(Morse, 1993). Any additional funds will depend upon negotiations between the DoE and the Treasury.

The Housing and Urban Development Bill, 1992, contained the legislative basis of the URA. Debates over the Bill revealed a primary expectation that the URA will focus on the 150 000 acres of vacant and derelict land in English cities (*Hansard* 3.11.92, col. 161) although it will have authority to work anywhere. Its powers will include compulsory purchase and the facility to override local authorities, and it will operate through partnerships with the private sector (DoE, 1992c, pp. 2–3). It may enter into co-operative relationships with UDCs and it will also co-operate with local authorities and Training and Enterprise Councils (TECs); public participation is to be limited. Very little has been said about the mechanisms for co-operation and critics suggest that its powers are reminiscent of the discredited approaches to urban regeneration pursued by UDCs in the mid-1980s (Morse, 1993).

Heseltine's original vision was for the URA to act as an English Development Agency, akin to the SDA. Howard's opposition has pulled it back from this ideal and, far from providing the necessary co-ordinating body, has created another 'semi-coordinator' which has perhaps been best described by John Redwood, Minister for the Environment: 'a roving development corporation . . . with the flexibility to go to parts of the country where there is a need' (Morse, 1993). Walker, in an interview in late 1992 (Lewis, 1992), still felt able to talk of the Agency taking a 'total approach' to urban problems. Yet given the limited stress on vacant-land reclamation, the limited resources and the known difficulty of persuading other government bodies to 'bend' their programmes, it seems as if the URA will largely be dependent on levering private sector investment. Until the private sector begins to recover from the effects of recession such a strategy is likely to develop very slowly, if at all. Nor can the state be expected to step in, given the pressures on public expenditure. Thus it seems likely that the URA will have, at best, only a minor impact. The need for an English Development Agency remains.

**Assessment**

The past three chapters have presented an in-depth analysis of urban policy in the 1980s and early 1990s. We will now draw together the general points of our analysis. First, we will see whether the different theoretical perspectives which we outlined in Chapter 1 can shed any light on our understanding of the processes behind the post-1979 urban initiatives. Second, we will use the framework for policy analysis set out in Chapter 1 to assess the coherence of the initiatives. Finally, we will offer a more critical perspective on the strategy and its results.

*Theoretical perspectives*

In terms of the theoretical perspectives outlined in Chapter 1, the period since 1979 is very interesting. The government in power explicitly asserted its New Right credentials; did its actions measure up to the ideas we outlined in Chapters 1 and 5? Can a Marxist explanation be sustained? Is a pluralist perspective tenable, given the hegemony of the private sector?

*The New Right*

In strict neo-liberal terms it is highly doubtful whether urban initiatives should have continued given that they interfered with market processes. It would have been much better to allow markets to allocate resources in an unhindered fashion without the state intervening to modify these processes via grants and subsidies. In this analysis, the crises of the early 1980s and late 1980s/1990s would be seen as perfectly natural and acceptable. They created a situation in which uncompetitive firms closed down and others were forced to restructure and become more efficient. This created a leaner, fitter economy.

State intervention should thus have been limited to actions facilitating the market's operation. This would not have ruled out assistance for those in genuine need, particularly in the hiatus created during restructuring before investors returned to urban areas. Supply-side measures, such as training, clearly counted as legitimate state activities. Other initiatives were questioned. For instance, with regard to regional policy, the Adam Smith Institute argued that 'A far more cost effective approach would be to remove barriers to entrepreneurship and labour mobility' (Butler *et al.*, 1985, p. 9). They also suggested that the UP 'is more likely to be part of the [urban] problem rather than the solution' (Butler *et al.*, 1985,

p. 91). Thus most of the initiatives in the last three chapters were, at least in part, deemed to be illegitimate by neo-liberals.

However, as we have already suggested on several occasions, post-1979 Conservative governments have been both pragmatic and constrained by events; something had to be done, sometimes for electoral reasons, sometimes to combat highly visible problems such as urban unrest. Furthermore, they were also constrained by the neo-conservative element in their own ideology. This, being more concerned about preserving social order and authority, would be prepared to countenance actions (such as the urban programme) which offended against market principles. Thus, in many ways, post-1979 developments in urban policy have been an uneasy, and changing, mixture of neo-liberalism, neo-conservativism and pragmatism.

*Marxism*

For Marxists, the post-1979 developments would clearly confirm that urban problems have their origins in the capitalist mode of production. They would point out that capitalism goes through regular periods of crisis and restructuring (Fine and Harris, 1979, pp. 133–4). In the 1980s, the major role of the state was to assist in this process of restructuring, encouraging the capitalist body to purge itself of unhealthy elements, and leaving behind a more resilient capitalism.

As part of this process cities were forced to come to terms with the changing global economy in order to survive (Rees and Lambert, 1985). The urban initiatives covered earlier in this chapter sought specifically to underwrite this restructuring. Less obviously, urban areas found themselves engaged in a competitive process in which they attempted to market their location and resources in order to attract inward investment from *footloose* capital, a process which Harvey (1989b) terms *urban entrepreneurship*. The state's crucial function was to ensure the conditions for the reproduction of the capitalist system; to ensure that the workforce would accept whatever jobs and wages were available and would take responsibility for its own situation.

*Pluralism*

Pluralists may find the 1980s and 1990s somewhat difficult to explain. The consensus which characterised most of the post-1945 era collapsed and 'single party government' ensued. This removed one of the central planks of pluralism: effective party politics. The unwillingness of Margaret Thatcher to acknowledge the legitimacy of opposition to her rule, along with restrictions on civil liberties, created a situation in which many interests found themselves permanently excluded. A separation occurred between privileged in-groups (central government, the private sector, the property industry) and excluded out-groups (local government, the trade unions, the 'underclass').

Notwithstanding the difficulties for classic pluralist analysis, neo-pluralist theory has made major contributions to the understanding of the post-1979 period via the notion of *policy networks*. The privileged groups of the previous paragraph are linked in a policy network which contemporary pluralists see as essential to any understanding of policy-making. Rhodes (1988, pp. 343–64) has used the concept of networks to analyse inner city policy. The conclusion he arrives at is that the government failed to build effective networks. UP initiatives, for example, were:

> an attempt to create an issue network which failed because they did not have a distinct domain, were isolated from key policy networks and could not integrate the disparate interests involved. (Rhodes, 1988, p. 361).

Such an analysis is clearly supportable. Recall that central departments and local organisations frequently refused to bend their programmes to benefit deprived urban areas, thus undermining an attempt to direct concerted action at areas identified as multiply-deprived.

Additional support for pluralism comes from the fact that groups such as property developers and builders did not have things entirely their own way. Even during the height of Thatcherism in the period 1984–8, a plurality of organisations and interests were always involved in urban regeneration initiatives – although there was clearly considerable common ground between these groups. By the early 1990s, as the recession bit and property-led development began to collapse, attempts, arguably more symbolic than real, were made to open this closed circle. Residents' groups and others were formally incorporated into the consultation processes surrounding regeneration schemes such as City Challenge. Whether or not this presaged a rebirth of pluralism as an outcome of Prime Minister John Major's commitment to consumerism was unclear.

*Policy coherence*

Table 7.3 summarises the application of our framework for policy analysis to the post-1979 period. What emerges is a picture of considerable incoherence and contradiction. As with previous governments, there was no specific attempt to define the focus of activity. 'Urban' was equated with the inner city and operated as a metaphor for a variety of issues – dereliction, unrest, an underclass – generally suggestive of some threat to the perceived normal order of society.

The theoretical approach was, as suggested in Chapter 5, a mixture of neo-liberalism and neo-conservatism, although most emphasis was placed on the former. The market was a key theoretical construct. However, as we have clearly shown, it was underwritten by state intervention and subsidies of both a direct (grants/loans) and indirect (infrastructure investments) nature. Thus, while the market was favoured, state intervention was necessary to persuade it to take otherwise uneconomic decisions.

On one level, a structural analysis of urban decline was accepted which suggested that powerful economic forces had undermined the position of cities in the second half of the twentieth century, yet at the same time area-based initiatives were retained and remained central to urban policy. There was also a constant presence, sometimes covert, sometimes overt, of individual based accounts, most notably through the use of the notion of the 'responsible individual'. This allowed certain groups to be stigmatised as inadequate or maladjusted. They, along with interventionist government, caused the flight of capital and (responsible) populations from the cities.

Given this diagnosis it should come as no surprise that the stated objective was to attract investment and population back to the cities by allowing markets to operate in as unhindered a fashion as possible. Economic and physical regeneration was the aim, with social aspects either being ignored or significantly downgraded. Thus the role of the state was to create a climate and conditions favourable to investment. The private sector was initially seen as the prime mover and property-led development as the main mechanism for rejuvenation. Later in the 1980s the public–private partnership

**TABLE 7.3   Conservative urban policy post-1979: an assessment**

| | Conservative Urban Policy |
|---|---|
| Conception of 'urban' | Vague; area of dereliction; locus of market activity; locus of unrest; political issue |
| Theoretical approach | Neo-liberalism underwritten by state intervention; subsidy to private sector through infrastructural investments |
| Nature of problem | Physical and social dereliction; 'maladjusted' population; spatial concentration in inner city locations |
| Explanation | Flight of capital and population; too much state intervention |
| Aim of policy | Attract return of capital; create favourable investment climate; control unrest; reduce role of state (especially local government) |
| Mechanisms | Private sector lead role; later emphasis on public–private partnerships; public sector as underwriter/facilitator; central role of property-led development in 1980s |
| Resourcing | Variable; relatively good for LDDC; poor and unplanned for UP |
| Management | Emphasis on co-ordination and targeting of existing resources; little strategic management |
| Political support | Varied: important after urban unrest and 1987 general election; affected by central–local conflicts and differences over explanation of poverty |
| Legislation | Local Government, Planning and Land Act, 1980; much use of Circulars to enact minor changes/different interpretations |
| Monitoring | Considerable but mainly limited to value-for-money questions; ignores strategic overview and social impact |

come to occupy a much more prominent position, especially in the period after 1988 as a full-blown recession established itself.

Resourcing was never generous. Certain initiatives, such as LDDC, were very generously financed, often for political reasons. Other initiatives, such as the UP, operated almost on a year-to-year basis, with finance often being determined by wider events – improved in the wake of the 1981 urban unrest and cut back in the recessionary 1990s. Given the lack of resources and the Government's often-expressed belief that the public sector was inherently wasteful, it should come as no surprise that considerable stress was placed on the development of effective management regimes and targets. Yet the Audit Commission (1989) and the National Audit Office (1990) described urban initiatives as lacking clear direction and co-ordination with no sense of strategic direction. As a result, programmes and initiatives frequently operated in isolation from (or competed with) one another.

Political support was never great, essentially because the Conservative party had little to gain, electorally speaking, in the run-down areas of Britain's cities. Only specific events, such as outbreaks of urban unrest or Margaret Thatcher's fleeting personal interest in the inner cities after the 1987 election, attracted political support. For Conservatives, urban areas were the location of the 'other', 'the enemy within'. Consequently, there was little overt directed legislation. Very little that was passed could be described as specifically urban. Bodies such as UDCs and the URA had their legislative origins in wide-ranging acts which stitched together a number of disparate subjects. There was, however, a considerable increase in the monitoring of programmes. This was to be expected from a government which constantly stressed value for money. Equally expected was the form of the monitoring: an emphasis on internal audit and financial scrutiny and politically motivated wish-fulfilment using dubious statistics.

*Critical perspectives*

One of the most obvious facts about the period since 1979 is that a wide variety of programmes have come to be defined as urban. In addition to specifically urban initiatives there was an even larger number of policies and programmes which, while not specifically directed at urban areas, had implications for them. When viewed together as an overall policy package they constituted what the Audit Commission (1989, p. 1) described as a 'patchwork quilt' at both national and local level.

The post-1979 Conservatives took nine years to attempt a remedy to this lack of coherence. In *Action for Cities*, despite the DoE's leading role, the setting up of an Inner Cities Cabinet Committee and the creation of a Minister for the Inner Cities there was little evidence of any marked improvement. In 1990, both the NAO (1990) and the House of Commons Public Accounts Committee (HCPAC, 1990) again criticised the 'patchwork quilt' for its unclear definition of departmental roles and its failure to integrate the activities of the various organisations involved.

It would appear that government attention in the 1980s focused on the internal management of individual programmes. While this may have done a great deal to improve the internal running, impact and evaluation of programmes, it did not address the causal roots of urban problems or ensure that those most in need of help received it. Indeed, Stewart (1990) has argued that this stress on management was used to defend programmes from other departments rather than ensure that the causes of problems are tackled.

Ideas about the causes of urban problems changed during the 1980s. Political ideology played a key role in this process and the problem was defined in such a way as to make it congruent with the Thatcherite project. This, of course, was not a sudden change; 'urban policy' had evolved in this way throughout the period covered by this book. Thus, as both Cox (1979) and Hambleton (1981) have suggested, the British state has never been required fundamentally to restructure its mode of operation in order to tackle the inner city problem. During the 1980s, the focus was on 'the central city and the development prospects of redundant space or derelict land and buildings' (Stewart, 1990, p. 53). At the same time, however, the notion of the responsible individual (Baker, 1990) allowed an almost covert resurgence of individual-based explanations of urban poverty and decline.

MacGregor and Pimlott (1990) point out how these developments limited poverty to particular spatial locations and to 'deviant' communities. The notion emerged of an *urban underclass*. While consensual pre-1979 attitudes might have viewed such an underclass as a key target for welfare assistance, the New Right were less accommodating. The underclass were feckless, irresponsible authors of their own fate; they could be abandoned. As Keith and Rogers (1991, p. 21) have argued:

> in the political language of the right in the 1980s it [the inner city] is outside in the sense of being cast as alien, normally via the stigmata of race or socialism, the locus of criminal delinquency, the site of disorder. The conception of the inner city as internal demands a policy response; external conceptions provide a rationale, even an excuse, for inactivity, a justification of neglect and hostility.

The inner city 'problem' was therefore reconstructed in a variety of overlapping ways: as a collectivist-created nightmare; as a supply-side blockage; as a 'those who have missed out on the boom' problem; as a law and order problem; as a problem of individual inadequacy; as a race problem; as an underclass problem; and as a lack-of-entrepreneurial-spirit problem. All of these definitions tended to overlap in terms of time and space, different problems being constituted and utilised where and when appropriate. Urban 'policy' was only required because of political expediency. As Pickvance (1990, p. 20) notes:

> 'inner city' refers not only to a particular location but also to its symbolic connotations: poverty, housing stress, unemployment and racial tension. These perceptions are present in the public mind and explain why no British government can afford not to have an inner cities policy of some kind.

What had been so potentially radical and threatening about the 1977 White Paper was that it seemed to say that those experiencing urban deprivation were the victims of wider national and international forces and were not to blame for their own plight (Sills *et al.*, 1988, p. 24). After 1979 this perspective was rolled back and people were once again held responsible, albeit alongside the 'nanny state' and welfare dependency. This new position was entirely consistent with New Right demonology and the politico-ideological nature of its problem construction. It also legitimated leaving things to the market: it was not the state's responsibility to solve the inner city problem. State intervention was part of the problem; only the market and the individual could provide lasting solutions. When linked with ineffective organisational structures, poor co-ordination with wider policy areas, inadequate resourcing and a reliance upon speculative development and trickle down, the conclusion that post-1979 urban policy was merely a symbolic attempt to deal with urban decline is compelling.

Had it not been for the riotous activities of black and white youths in British cities during the early 1980s and the persistently high levels of urban unemployment and decay throughout the 1980s there would probably have been less activity directed at run-down areas of our cities and even less of an attempt to give the appearance of doing something. It is only when such problems become highly visible, when cities burn and force urban problems on to the TV screens, that they receive attention and stir consciences to demand visible action. Conscience is less important, however, than self-interest. The deep-seated and lengthy recession which started in the late 1980s reached into the Conservatives' southern electoral heartland. Paradoxically, this could lead to a more sympathetic analysis of economic decline. Pessimistically, the problems of urban areas may well slip into the background and be further confined to spatially discrete areas where the underclass live.

More positive assessments see the Conservative approach to urban areas as part of a wider, more coherent, strategy. Thus, Parkinson and Judd (1988, p. 1) argue that 'The Conservatives' urban policy has been one component of a comprehensive strategy to regenerate Britain's ailing economy by creating an enterprise culture'. During the early 1980s, as Britain experienced a major economic downturn, a swathe was cut through its manufacturing industry and the country experienced persistent high unemployment. The Thatcher governments constantly explained that the policies they pursued and the pain they created in terms of industrial closures and high unemployment were a price worth paying for the bright new tomorrow which was just around the corner and which their policies would produce. For a while in the mid-1980s there appeared to be, for some at least, a grain of truth in this argument. Yet at the time of writing the British economy is in the worst recession since the Second World War and looks unlikely to recover before the second half of the 1990s. It is clear that the wider strategy was never comprehensive because it was never able (or prepared) to tackle the fundamental structural weaknesses of the British economy. 'Urban policy' as such may, at a very general level, have been consistent with this overall strategy but, given the fatal flaws and the contradictory nature of the wider strategy, it was never likely to do anything other than ameliorate and contain the fall out from the wider strategy.

This wider strategy may be described as one of *privatism*. According to Barnekov *et al.* (1989, p. 1) 'Privatism stresses the social as well as economic importance of private initiative and competition, and it legitimises the public consequences of private action'. Moreover, it assumes that:

> the private sector is inherently dynamic, productive and dependable . . . that private institutions are intrinsically superior to public institutions for the delivery of goods and services; and a confidence that market efficiency is the appropriate criterion of social performance in virtually all spheres of community activity.

With specific reference to British 'urban policy', Geoffrey Howe, then Shadow Chancellor, summed up this approach in 1979 when he argued: 'Unless people are able to earn and keep significant reward for the investment and effort we wish them to put into our urban deserts, they are just not going to be interested' (Howe, 1979, p. 10).

In other words, self-interest operating through a free market should be the leading and motivating force in the rejuvenation of British cities. Of course, this emphasis on the market ignores the fact that:

> The market will not, and cannot, match provision to need or demand. The jobs it creates will be the ones that meet its needs, not those of the inner cities. It must be an imperfect response therefore and one that leaves the public sector in the position of having to service the market, or at least bridge some of the gap between the needs of the inner cities, and what the market provides. (Edwards, 1989, p. 82)

Thus, even at the height of the consumer and property boom in the mid-1980s, the state was forced to underwrite developments in many inner areas (even when they were likely to be profitable). With the fall in property values, this spectral image of a vigorous and thriving market place was savagely ripped away to reveal a situation in which, although small parts of our cities have experienced flagship style developments, the vast majority of run down areas, and the people living in them, have not benefited.

By the end of the 1980s a discernible shift was taking place as the government began to recognise the follies of the ostensibly pure market solution. City Challenge and the relaunched HATs sought to integrate public and private efforts at urban regeneration and included mechanisms, however inadequate, which attempted to ensure that local residents derived some benefit from developments. As the OECD (1987, p. 22) noted, 'Market mechanisms alone may be unable to ensure an effective and efficient allocation of investment and employment opportunities'.

**Conclusion**

We have covered the development of urban initiatives by the post-1979 Conservative governments in the course of three chapters. In our view one cannot talk of a Conservative urban policy. It does, however, seem possible to talk of an urban strategy: an advance on the previous unconnected urban initiatives. The key elements of the strategy appear to have been:

1.  To privatise the city in line with wider attempts to market all aspects of life and create conditions for new forms of capital accumulation;
2.  To bypass or marginalise local government, thus increasing central control;
3.  To restructure, politically and socially, the inner urban areas by fragmenting and diluting traditional Labour strongholds;
4.  Territorial crisis management; and
5.  To give the appearance of doing something to help those in inner areas – provided that the other elements of the strategy were satisfied.

Symbolism has been central to this strategy, as indeed it was to the earlier initiatives. Undoubtedly there were some successes. However, by constructing a strategy which abstracted its object of analysis from its context, the strategy was doomed to failure. The emphasis on privatism, the stress on property-led development, the progressive targeting of grants and attempts to introduce competition into urban regeneration were all crucially constrained by the operation of the national and, indeed, world economy. The free market experiment did not work for the inner cities. As Spencer (1987, p. 9) has stated: 'There is . . . no national urban policy in any meaningful sense – there are individual programmes, but no overarching policy framework'.

# 8 Urban Planning under Conservatism

In Chapter 2 we briefly described the role of urban planning legislation as an instrument for the promotion of urban containment. We indicated the importance of the Town and Country Planning Act, 1947, to the establishment of a post-Second World War urban planning system based on the preparation of land-use plans and the regulation of urban change through development control legislation. The impact of this system extended beyond its role in fostering containment. It provided, and, to a considerable extent, continues to provide, the guiding day-to-day framework which regulated development in British cities. If the approaches, initiatives and, latterly, policies, which we have examined in the preceding chapters constituted the emerging grand designs of governments for dealing with urban problems, then urban planning legislation provided the less spectacular everyday means by which much of the change was managed.

In this chapter we therefore return to the subject of urban planning. The material which we confront is considerable; our discussion is consequently focused on issues central to this present text: on the role of urban planning in the regeneration and containment of urban areas. Readers seeking a fuller account of the evolution of the British urban planning system should consult one of the numerous texts on the topic; a comprehensive recent account is Rydin (1993). Here we briefly examine:

- The shortcomings of the 1947 Town and Country Planning system and the various modifications which were made to it in the period up to 1979.
- The impact of the post-1979 Conservative governments on urban planning and the extent to which they managed to incorporate New Right or Thatcherite notions into the planning system.
- The role of planning legislation in the regeneration of inner cities and the containment of urban growth; our attention focuses on

the period after 1979 and on an updating of Ambrose's (1986) analysis to take account of modifications in the Conservative position in the early 1990s.

## The 1947 town and country planning system

As we indicated in Chapter 2, the Town and Country Planning Act, 1947 was essentially an element in the physical approach to urban problems; it provided the legislative framework through which the unconstrained growth of cities was to be limited. It also, we should now note, set in place many of the mechanisms by which inner urban areas were cleared and redeveloped during the 1950s, 1960s and, in part, the 1970s. Additionally, although it is beyond the scope of this text, the Act contained legislation on the preservation of buildings of historic interest. It was introduced with broad support from all political parties and represented an acceptable compromise position for many diverse interest groups (Cullingworth, 1985; Donnison and de Soto, 1980). Like other contemporary initiatives, its successful entry on to the statute books was in no small way a reflection of the continuation of a wartime ethos of co-operation and collective endeavour.

The 1947 Act introduced, for the first time, a comprehensive obligation on all developers to seek permission for their developments from the local planning authority. Decisions regarding developments were made by reference to three key instruments. The *General Development Order* (GDO) automatically granted permission to certain categories of development, while the *Use Classes Order* set out a typology of land use categories, implied that uses should be concentrated and stated that changes to an existing use would normally require permission. The *Development Plan* for the county or county borough gave a general twenty-year projection of future changes in land use with detail in urban areas being provided by the Town Map and, in clearance areas (Ravetz, 1980), the Comprehensive Development Area Map. In short, the Act identified what could be built where and the processes by which permission for the development might be obtained.

The content of the Act reflected a mixture of comprehensive regulatory power symptomatic of the 1945 Labour government and the interpretive, flexible administrative tradition of British administration (Healey *et al.*, 1988, p. 18). It also exhibited the socialist aspirations of the time in that it nationalised the development rights of private landowners, gave local government extensive powers of compulsory purchase at existing use value, and instituted a 100 per cent betterment tax on profits made by speculative land use change. These latter measures were designed to enable the assembly of land parcels in urban areas and facilitate comprehensive redevelopment by the public sector (Cullingworth, 1980), although the immediate justification was a desire to limit land speculation. There was a clear presumption that the public sector was to be the lead agency in the planning and redevelopment of British cities.

This indication was, perhaps, acceptable in the immediate aftermath of the Second World War. However, it was not acceptable to the incoming Conservative government in 1951. Ambrose (1986, p. 47) notes how it conflicted with traditions of private enterprise and the *laissez-faire* development regimes of the recent, inter-war, past. While in the immediate post-war period legislation for compulsory purchase at existing use prices and the betterment levy may have been acceptable instruments for reconstructing cities, they were never popular. The levy was repealed in 1952 and, in 1959, the provision for public-sector purchase of land at existing use value was also discontinued. In part these decisions were a reaction to state-led regulatory powers having an impact on both individual freedoms and on market forces. However, the levy had also been relatively unsuccessful. It was never integrated into the wider economic planning framework and, although it had been designed to enable councils to buy land to reconstruct cities, they had been unable, in a period of financial constraint on public investment, to afford even the artificially low costs of a favourably engineered land market. Furthermore, the measure actually caused stagnation in the land market and, to an extent, actually inhibited reconstruction because owners who were unable to make a profit hung on to their land and waited for a price rise. Post-war population growth fuelling the demand for housing, the return of the Conservatives to power and the recovery of the property industry from the wartime slump all combined to make it inevitable that the levy would go, and with it any presumption that the public sector would lead the process of urban change (Thornley, 1991, p. 24).

The 1947 Act exhibited a number of other problems (McKay, 1982). Of these, the most important were, first, the lack of integration between the town and country planning system and the processes operating in other, closely related areas. 'Planning' was the concern of the Ministry of Housing and Local Government; more specifically it was the concern of the local government wing of that ministry. Areas which could severely affect or constrain the efficiency of urban planning operations were functionally distant. For example, questions surrounding industrial change were largely debated in a separate department (industry) with town and country planning matters being restricted to the decision to grant planning permission and the assessment of the extent to which proposed developments corresponded with the development plan. In fact, the Ministry of Housing and Local Government sought, but failed to gain, a co-ordinating role regarding all the areas which had an impact upon town and country planning (Cullingworth, 1975). The role of planning activity was thus limited to questions of land use; social and economic engineering was excluded. This situation was to curtail the effectiveness of planning legislation and also provided a running basis for future debate within central government as the proponents of planning sought to extend its role and achieve a unified and coherent system.

The second problem area was the issue of co-ordination, or lack of it, between the development control activities of local councils and the broader-brush land-use planning work of the county councils. Though this difficulty was avoided in the unitary county boroughs, it presaged another debate which has continued to the present time: to what extent should relatively remote authorities seek to constrain the development of a locality? In the late 1940s, as in the 1990s, there were some doubts as to whether local government possessed staff with the required levels of expertise. There were also suggestions that certain local governments might abuse any powers they were given by opposing or subverting the policy directions which the then Labour government had chosen.

With the exception of the betterment issue, the 1947 planning system remained in place for much of the 1950s and 1960s. It thus provided the context for the mass expansion of the British urban space and the basis for the clearance and redevelopment of slum areas and the attempted containment of urban growth; it also operated alongside the early urban initiatives outlined in Chapter 2.

Characteristic of much of this period was a gradual retreat from the strongly public-sector perspectives evident in the 1947 Act. As we have already noted, the repeal of the 1947 betterment measures signified the commencement of this process, which was, in any case, in tune with the needs and aspirations of the consumerist, private-sector-orientated, middle-class beneficiaries of the 1950s and 1960s economic boom.

In 1962, Taylor Woodrow and Hallmark Securities were commissioned to investigate the extent to which regeneration could be carried out by the private sector. They concluded that it would be unprofitable unless there was substantial reform of the planning system. In light of the prevailing consensus politics this reform was not possible and what emerged was a clear notion that town and country planning should entail a partnership between the public and private sectors. The Ministry of Housing and Local Government argued that town centre redevelopment and renewal 'cannot be undertaken without public support and it cannot be carried through without private enterprise' (MHLG, 1962b, p. 6). The socialist vision of post-Second World War planning was steadily replaced by circulars and statutory instruments promoting negotiation with the private sector and the facilitation of enterprise. Although some positive powers for public-sector reconstruction remained in place, as did negative powers of control, it was gradually recognised that the 'heroic planning' involved in modernisation and clearance required significant private-sector involvement to succeed.

At the same time some of the deficiencies evident soon after the enactment of the 1947 Act, began, by the early 1960s, to become more significant. The Planning Advisory Group, set up in 1963 to investigate these problems and recommend changes in the town and country planning system, confirmed, for example, that local plans were tending to be isolated from the county and regional context (MHLG, 1965). The lack of concordance between development pressures and the indications of development plans was also becoming increasingly evident; the system was inadequate for contemporary needs. Furthermore, contemporary pressures flowing from the mission to modernise British cities were also causing problems for town and country planning. In particular, the large-scale urban motorway construction projects and clearance schemes (see Chapter 2) required advance planning and the compulsory purchase of inner-city housing and land. This frequently caused *planning blight* whereby whole neighbourhoods within British cities became derelict or were abandoned for significant periods prior to demolition. The 1947 legislation offered little scope for public involvement in or discussion of these land-use conflicts (Dennis, 1972). Such a situation was, in many ways, a direct consequence of the confinement of town and country planning to questions of land use; clearance and redevelopment were seen in purely physical terms and social factors were given little consideration.

*Structure planning*

The Planning Advisory Group's deliberations on these dilemmas also included thoughts on the extent to which local development could be conducted in isolation from strategic county, regional or central planning (MHLG, 1965). The recommendations which were put forward involved an increased element of central direction but also a retention of local discretion; they led directly to the passing of the Town and Country Planning Act, 1968, and the institution of the *structure planning* system as a replacement for the Development Plan concept. The development control function retained its basic 1947 framework.

Structure plans were the first major change in town and country planning for twenty years, with the exception of the betterment debate. They had three characteristics. First, they addressed the need for integrated planning: consideration was to be given to economic, transport and housing questions as well as land-use issues; social factors were also to be taken into account. Second, they were to be vertically integrated: the county-level structure plan was to be the framework on to which 'local' (town), 'action area' (major localised land-use change) and 'subject' (e.g. leisure, housing, etc.) plans were to be grafted at a later date. Third, in keeping with the move towards partnership with the private sector, they were to pursue a role of general guidance, in contrast to the rather more prescriptive ethos which characterised Development Plans and limited the scope for debate and negotiation by developers (Short, 1984, p. 167).

The goal of the structure planning system was therefore a somewhat hopeful one: integration with liberalisation. It was in tune with the contemporary ethos of corporate planning. There was also, at the same time, an attempt to counter the demonologising of the town and country planner by opening up planning to public scrutiny. In 1969 the Skeffington Report addressed the issue of public participation:

one cannot leave all the problems to one's representatives. They need some help in reaching the right decision, and opportunity should be provided for discussions with all those involved. (MHLG, 1969, p. 5).

This development, though welcome, can be subjected to a critical interpretation; participation was, at best, to be managed by the 'planocracy'. The mythical person in the street was given opportunities, but the most likely beneficiary was the development company with the well-briefed corporate planning lawyer (Simmie, 1974). The planners were to retain a paternalist role in which they presented their activities as value-free and ignored the impact of the values and constraints under which both they and the system operated.

The developments of the late 1960s, including measures, which we have not discussed, in the area of townscape conservation which were to be an important basis to the gentrification of inner cities in later years, were consolidated in the Town and Country Planning Act, 1971. It was hoped at the time that the local government reforms, then underway, would result in a local government system in which structure planning, local planning and development control would be brought together under a single unitary authority. In the event, the Local Government Act, 1972 (1973 in Scotland) did not enable this goal, and control and planning remained separate with the unclear distinction between local and structure plans being retained (Healey *et al.*, 1988, p. 23). The consolidated system did, however, offer town and country planning a role which extended beyond simple land-use questions and incorporated a focus on economic regeneration which was to draw increasing attention through the 1970s.

Before we conclude this brief history of town and country planning prior to the 1979 Conservative government we must return briefly to the betterment issue. After the repeal of the 1947 betterment legislation, local authorities became increasingly dependent on developers to assemble the land required to satisfy development needs. As a consequence, individuals, and indeed development companies, were able to make substantial profits when they purchased land parcels which, in the fullness of time, became essential to the completion of planned developments. Considerable fortunes could be made by purchasing land at an agricultural use value and then gaining planning permission for development. Such a speculators' charter was, of course, not appreciated by the Labour governments of the 1960s and mid-1970s. In 1967 the *Land Commission* was established with a brief to set up a land bank for public-sector development, and a 40 per cent betterment levy on development gain was instituted. This attempt to revitalise the role of the public sector foundered, as had the 1947 system, in the face of a stagnating land market, with owners refusing to release land on which adequate profit could not be made (Cox, 1984). It was scrapped by the Conservative government in 1971. When Labour was returned in 1974 it renewed its attack on windfall profits and enacted the *Community Land Act*, 1975. This measure, described by Ambrose (1986, p. 63) as 'a foolhardy and ill-thought-out advance that rapidly turned into a rout', entailed the purchase of development land just prior to development at its developed use value but minus a development land tax specifically focused on the profits from land speculation. The public expenditure needed to fund this venture was extensive and, at the time of the IMF crisis and a much-troubled minority Labour government, such support was not forthcoming. Indeed, its resourcing was halved soon after its institution and, not surprisingly, it was among the first town and country planning measures to be repealed by the incoming Conservative government of 1979.

Ambrose (1976), writing towards the end of the pre-Thatcher era, offered a critique of the 1947 system from the left: planning, he argued, did not conserve the city; did not exhibit social responsibility; offered only constrained opportunities for participation; was seldom politically neutral; and fostered exploitation by those who controlled the land and had power. The consequences of this for the inner city were marked; planning fostered rising land prices. Yet at the same time the New Right critique, outlined in Chapters 1 and 5, was equally applicable. Despite its move towards the needs of the developer, planning remained a monolithic local state bureaucracy characterised by sloth, consensus, redistributive tendencies, high expenditure and a disregard for the needs of wealth creators. It was unlikely to escape challenge following the election of the 1979 Conservative government.

We may summarise the history of town and country planning prior to 1979 as a process of gradual retreat from the quasi-socialist ideal put forward in 1947. Elements of the ideal were retained, and even advanced in the structure planning system, but essentially the process was one of gradual reorientation away from state planning and towards partnership with the private sector. The fact that much of the planning mechanism remained essentially unchanged throughout this period, even allowing for the change to the structure planning system, is an indication of the considerable flexibility of the 1947 system and its ability to adjust to changing circumstances (Healey, 1992).

## Planning under Thatcher

In this section we review the ways in which three successive Conservative governments sought, in the years following 1979, to change and refashion the town and country planning system to match their ideological position. Our discussion will follow closely the outstanding account by Thornley (1991) of this process and explore the antecedents to change and attempts to bypass, simplify and modify the pre-existing system. Interested readers requiring further detail on town and country planning under Thatcherism are strongly recommended to read Thornley's assessment.

Just as one explanation for the introduction of the early British urban initiatives (see Chapter 2) and later urban policy measures (see Chapter 6) was a process of copying and borrowing from North American experience, so the post-1979 changes to the British town and country planning system can also be traced to transatlantic influences. Of particular importance appear to have been arguments that dynamic, economically-successful cities operated weak planning systems offering a *laissez-faire* approach to land-use and avoiding strict zoning ordinances (Jacobs, 1965; Banfield, 1974). Houston was held up as an exemplar of this approach, in which the market was sovereign and the development of the city was freed from state regulation (Siegan, 1972; but see Feagin (1988) for a more critical assessment). These ideas were on general offer to a wide British audience as early as 1969 through the pages of the now defunct weekly *New Society* (Banham *et al.*, 1969). Walters *et al.* (1974), writing under the imprimatur of the influential conservative think-tank, the Institute for Economic Affairs, provide a deeper but less objective statement.

The theoretical position underpinning these contributions was a belief in the advantages of competitive markets and a distrust of local state planning bureaucracies. Although, as Klosterman (1985) argues, town and country planning originally aimed to mitigate the deficiencies of the market, this pro-planning view was not in the ascendant in 1979, as was made clear by the then Secretary of State for the Environment in his address to the Summer School of the Royal Town planning Institute:

> This country cannot afford the manpower involved in a [planning] system which in some parts can be negative and unresponsive. But above all we cannot afford the economic process of delayed investment, whether commercial, domestic or industrial. (Heseltine, 1979).

Position papers from the British Right clarified this position soon after the election of the first Thatcher government. Denman (1980, p. 37) for example, argued that town and country planning 'is a machine whose parts and assemblage were in large measure forged in wartime. It has served some purpose and is now creaky with age'. While Denman's views represented the position of the politically influential Centre for Policy Studies, Sorenson and Day (1981) reached an audience of planning educators with their exposition of libertarian planning in the pages of *Town Planning Review*. They argued a Hayekian perspective: that town and country planning should limit its attention to development control and specifically to the control of the negative externality effects of development upon adjacent properties (see Hayek, 1960, ch. 22). Steen (1981), writing for the pressure group of conservative industrialists, Aims of Industry, presented the case for the entrepreneurial city, orientated away from redistribution and towards wealth creation. His case rested strongly on an opposition to zoning policies and their mild British variant, the structure and local plan framework.

By far the most trenchant critique of planning came from the Adam Smith Institute (Jones, 1982; Adam Smith Institute, 1983). Five themes can be identified in their analyses. First, town and country planning employed what they felt to be a spurious 'sociological' notion of community; not only was sociology frowned upon, so was anything which suggested any social units other than the individual, the family and the firm. Second, planning was élitist; it imposed planners' values and offended the populist Thatcherite project. Third, it gave undue discretion to local government, which the Conservatives wished to curb (see Chapter 9). Fourth, its subjective nature and its checks and balances caused delay and cost to the private-sector entrepreneurial wealth creators. Finally, although it went against the grain of New Right analysis, there was an implicit suspicion that urban riots and the state of British cities in the early 1980s were in some way a consequence of failures of town planning.

The solution proposed by the Adam Smith Institute (1983) was the dismantling of the planning system, the retention of a certain amount of urban and rural conservation legislation, a return to the Victorian system of regulation through public health legislation and legal covenants, and the use of property law to resolve land-use conflict. A substantial degree of centralisation was also advocated, removing power from local government. This prescription was typical of those put forward by the right-wing analysts of town and country planning, though perhaps a little more extreme than most. Its central tenet was that partnership with the private sector might be a useful halfway house, but there was a clear case for root-and-branch reform of the system. We will examine first the evidence that the post-1979 Conservative governments pursued the more radical option.

*Radical change*

Thornley (1991) suggests that some of the town and country planning initiatives of the three Thatcher governments were designed, either implicitly or explicitly, to bypass or simplify the existing system. As such, we can classify these changes as major surgery. They aimed to circumvent completely the town and country planning machinery or replace existing legislation with new measures of a more streamlined nature designed to restructure the system in a way which would prioritise private-sector demands. For the most part, these radical changes were closely associated with certain of the urban initiatives that we discussed in Chapter 7. This integration of the urban planning system with broader urban initiatives provides an indication that the Conservatives wished to incorporate the planning system more fully into their approach to urban regeneration but, as we saw in Chapter 7, it does not necessarily mean that a coherent urban *policy* was emerging.

Urban Development Corporations provided the main means by which the Conservatives attempted to circumvent the town and country planning machinery (Thornley, 1991, ch. 8). We have discussed these creations in Chapter 7 and need not revisit our discussion here. We can, however, consider *Special Development Orders* (SDOs), a measure which the Conservatives made considerable use of both within and outside Urban Development Areas. SDOs were actually created by the Town and Country Planning Act, 1971, and gave the Secretary of State for the Environment the power to alter the General Development Order. Prior to 1979, SDOs had generally been used negatively – they had been used to restrict rather than extend the General Development Order. The Conservatives shifted the focus to positive planning and used SDOs to give blanket planning permission for a particular development or in a particular area; their potential in UDCs was particularly identified in Section 148 of the Local Government, Planning and Land Act, 1980 and they provided a key mechanism by which UDCs were enabled to bypass local planning restrictions.

SDOs constitute an excellent example of what Healey (1992) sees as the essential flexibility of the planning system. A pre-existing measure was turned to the political, market-orientated purposes of the government. For the Conservatives, SDOs could be represented as a method of positive intervention intended to stimulate economic development and debureaucratise the planning process; from a more critical perspective they stifled public participation and increased the power of the Secretary of State at the expense of local people. They were thus symptomatic of Thatcherite tendencies towards the centralisation of power, the emasculation of local government and the promotion of decision-making freedom for the developer.

Thornley (1991, ch. 9) represents Enterprise Zones (Chapter 7) as an attempt to simplify and streamline the planning process which stopped short of outright circumvention. He suggests that they rested on the (Hayekian) principle of replacing the bureaucratic discretion of planners with a general legal framework governing development activity. Despite the shortcomings of the practical application of this principle in Enterprise Zones, it also underpinned a later device: *Simplified Planning Zones* (SPZs). These entered the statute books in the Housing and Planning Act, 1986, although their form and nature had been under debate for several years before. They constituted, and indeed continue to constitute, an experiment in the partial deregulation of the planning process, giving 'advance planning permission' for specific uses or all uses within a zone designated by a local authority, a developer or the Secretary of State for the Environment. The zone and the nature of the simplification is subject to the final approval and close monitoring of the Secretary of State and has a ten year life; there are no inducements to developers or firms to locate in an SPZ other than the potential advantages of streamlined processes, but most SPZs are in areas which also attract some form of grant.

Both Lloyd (1987) and Stungo (1985) note that SPZs give flexibility in use change and leave detail to the developer. Thus they may assist in promoting economic regeneration. On the other hand, they retain the local authority link and, at least prior to the Planning and Compensation Act, 1991, required fairly extensive public participation exercises before they could be created. These exercises slowed the process and also raised expectations regarding consultation after the completion of the designation process – expectations which were, of course, contrary to the very principle of the SPZ. In contrast to SDOs, SPZs were therefore a more contradictory measure; their effectiveness in remoulding planning along pure Thatcherite lines is limited.

### Restyling planning

We will now turn our attention to the ways in which the post-1979 Conservative governments sought to modify rather than to overturn the town and country planning system. We will deal with these modifications in three stages, corresponding roughly to the periods of the three pre-1992 governments.

### Facilitating the private sector

As we have suggested above, New Right planning thought was particularly concerned with the perceived deficiencies of the structure planning system. Inevitably, one of the first actions of the new Conservative government in 1979 was to simplify that system. The process was streamlined and reorientated towards the needs of industry; plans were to anticipate and not to interfere with market trends; social engineering and redistributive questions were to be excluded and the central focus was to be on issues of land-use (Jowell, 1983). The move towards an integrative but prescriptive structure planning framework was thus abandoned in favour of a return to a more circumscribed role.

Development control also drew the attention of reformers. The system, which had remained substantially unchanged since 1947, was held to be insufficiently flexible for the needs of the construction industry of the 1980s. In particular it was too slow and offered too much scope for discretion on the part of the planning bureaucracy. An early initiative was the introduction of performance indicators; delay could be measured and league tables published of authorities which were taking too long to process applications. Circular 22/80 from the Department of the Environment (DoE, 1980) addressed the question of discretion through an emphasis on a general liberalisation of control. A pre-existing presumption of permission was reiterated and design controls were relaxed; the needs of small businesses (the imagined saviours of urban economies) were to be given favourable attention, and attitudes to non-conforming uses were to be liberalised. At the same time the GDO was extended. The sum effect of these modifications was to make it easier to obtain a relatively swift planning permission free from onerous conditions. This, at a time of deep recession, made it easier for industrial development to begin in places where it might earlier have been refused. However, it did little to enhance the built form of cities, removed important aesthetic controls and was of limited real importance in ensuring the economic regeneration of inner cities (Robson, 1988, pp. 92–3).

The landmark legislative instrument of the first Thatcher government was the Local Government, Planning and Land Act, 1980. This Act provided both a consolidation of early Thatcherite initiatives in its subject areas and also a position statement on the expected directions for policy development. Three themes in particular can be noted regarding town and country planning. First, the attack on structure planning was to be pursued. Reserve county-level powers of development control regarding conformity to structure plan proposals were to be reduced and districts were to be allowed to draw up local plans in advance of structure plans, thus constraining their content. Second, the scope for participation and consultation was to be reduced. This measure was designed to speed the planning process. Third, the role of local authorities in redevelopment was to be limited. Land registers of public land holdings were to be set up, surplus public land was to be sold to the private sector, and, as we noted above, the Community Land Act was repealed.

*Consolidation*

The second phase in the Conservative restyling of the town and country planning system saw the consolidation of the earlier modifications and further incorporation of private sector needs within planning legislation. DoE Circular 1/85 (DoE, 1985b) placed additional limits on the use of conditions when granting planning permission and sought to circumscribe the growing practice, known as *planning gain* or a *section 52 agreement*, of granting planning permission in return for an agreement on the part of the applicant to undertake in addition a development specified by the local authority (Alterman, 1990). This measure gave extreme freedom to developers at the expense of the public sector, a process which was extended in 1987 with the institution of a new Use Classes Order which amalgamated offices and light industry into a single class and allowed the subdivision of non-dwelling premises. Flexibility was the declared goal and small businesses the targeted beneficiary.

The Local Government Act, 1985, precipitated major modification of the structure planning system. The abolition of the metropolitan counties and the Greater London Council (see Chapter 9) created unitary local government; the separation of structure plans from local plans and development control was no longer possible. Instead, each of the new unitary authorities was to produce a *Unitary Development Plan* (UDP). The strategic framework for the UDPs was to be provided by central government through the medium of a guidance note. As Bristow (1985a, 1985b) argues, UDPs, while welcome as a long-overdue integration of land-use planning instruments, were to prove problematic in practice in that they have downgraded the strategic element and decontextualised development plans.

A particularly clear example of the reorientation of town and country planning towards the overt facilitation of private-sector needs was evident in the proposals of the 1985 White Paper *Lifting the Burden* (DoE, 1985c). The aims of this document were to lift the burden which was inhibiting the growth of private-sector business and slowing the recovery of the economy; the 'burden', it was suggested, was in part a consequence of the planning system. A more appropriate planning machine should balance the needs of development and developers with the interests of conservation. The guidance of the structure and local plan should be only one of the themes to be taken into account when deciding whether or not to approve a development. Equally, if not more, important would be a knowledge of market trends, and market needs would constitute a strong ground for appeal against refused permission. A subsequent Circular summarised the situation succinctly: 'Planning control is not intended to enable local planning authorities to intervene in the normal operation of market forces' (DoE, 1986, para. 11).

A policy of liberalisation had been clearly established and consolidated through the standard Thatcherite tactics of popularism (regulation as burden), removal of discretion, and centralisation. The cost was essentially the loss of opportunities for grass-roots participation and the ability to control the excesses of developers.

### Maturity

By 1987 the Conservatives had achieved many of their targets regarding the modification of the town and country planning system. Some areas continued to receive attention but contradictions to standard notions of New Right perspectives on town and country planning also began to emerge.

Opposition to the structure planning process continued unabated and there were rumours of the impending abandonment of structure plans in late 1987. These were borne out by the recommendations of the White Paper, *The Future of Development Plans* (DoE, 1989), in which it was proposed to extend the UDP system to the entire country, with local plans providing the basic land-use planning framework within loose constraints set by central and county-level strategic guidance. However, notwithstanding this ideologically motivated pressure for liberalisation and debureaucratisation, it became evident that those interests which the Conservatives were endeavouring to help – the property developers – actually valued a clear planning framework within which to conduct their activities. By 1991 the shift had occured and the land-use planning framework was actually extended by the requirements of the *Planning and Compensation Act*, 1991. This retained structure plans and additionally compelled local authority districts to prepare local development plans (Jones, 1991).

In the area of development control, modifications to the Use Classes Order in 1987 benefited office developers (Oatley, 1991) while a new GDO in 1988 continued the process of relaxing controls for industry. At the same time, however, the new GDO strengthened control in that most conservative of areas: conservation. The *Town and Country Planning Act*, 1990 consolidated this legislation and emphasised a strong concern that there should be an effective planning system for dealing with both urban and rural conservation issues. The *Planning and Compensation Act*, 1991 continued this theme of contradiction by enacting further changes to the GDO to give greater freedom with regard to demolitions but, in line with the Citizen's Charter, imposing greater requirements concerning publicity.

The linkage of traditional Conservative conservationism with the ecological concern of the late 1980s and 1990s (Elkins and Mclaren, 1991) represented another clear political drift to which the planning system and its Conservative interpreters had to respond. Again, action was mixed. On the one hand, as we shall see below, there was significant strengthening of conservation and landscape protection measures through the provisions of European legislation and the Environmental Protection Act, 1990. On the other, much of the ecological pressure resulted from urgings external to the British political scene and from such influences as the impact of economic recession. Furthermore, Government commitment was unsteady; compulsory registration of contaminated land, introduced in the Environmental Protection Act, was abolished in 1993 when it was discovered to be blighting urban land. Presumably the blight consequent upon ecological awareness was less acceptable than the blight flowing from the loss of potential development revenues in the private sector.

We would suggest, overall, that the characteristic of the third stage in Conservative town and country planning was the paradox of a return to planning. Healey (1992, p. 412) substantiates this argument in her contention that 'By 1990, the case for the adaptive flexibility of the system seemed to be proved right, as the emphasis once again shifted back to balancing market considerations with a concern for environmental quality and community development'. The planning machinery which the Conservatives used to achieve their political agenda during the 1980s is essentially the same as that which they are now using to address the agendas of the 1990s.

Furthermore, the basic elements of the planning system remain much as they were in 1947; there is still development control legislation and there are still land-use plans – although their nature is much changed.

From a Conservative point of view, much was achieved in the 1980s in terms of reorientating the planning system to market needs. This was most clearly evident in the death of strategic planning (Breheny and Hart, 1989) and the deregulation of development control in order to enhance the significance of private-sector interests. The costs of these changes was equally clear: greater centralisation, decreased participation, the removal of the social from the planning agenda, and (Ambrose, 1986) overt favouritism to the needs of capital. The 1990s appear to be characterised by something of a reaction to this reorientation; the process of remoulding town and country planning to Conservative ideals continues, but those ideals now include at least a rhetoric of ecological awareness and participatory planning.

**Planning in action**

We now turn our attention to two case studies of the impact of post-1979 Conservative planning. We will examine the extent to which the changes identified in the previous pages have contributed to the success or failure of attempts to, first, regenerate inner urban areas, and, second, manage urban growth.

*Planning for urban regeneration*

We will focus on one particular problem in regenerating inner urban areas, a problem which stems from the process of industrial change. Around the central historic, office or shopping districts of many cities lie derelict sites formerly occupied by warehouses, industrial buildings or, less frequently, industrially-related office buildings. These earlier businesses have tended to decentralise to suburban or rural locations, have gone bankrupt, or have simply become redundant. British examples would include Victoria Station, Manchester (Healey *et al.*, 1988, p. 68), Salford Quays (Law, 1988), Spitalfields, Bishopsgate Goods Yard and Paddington Canal Basin in London (Frost and Spence, 1991a, 1991b; Vlessing, 1991),

Liverpool North Docklands (MacDonald, 1989), the oft-cited planning case-study of Coin Street, London (Brindley *et al.*, 1989, ch. 5) and a host of other areas.

These vacant sites constitute a considerable target for regeneration activity. As Robson (1988, p. 148) noted, there were 4035 hectares of derelict land in Manchester in 1982. Vacant sites also constitute an attractive target; vacant land near a city centre, often in public ownership and usually within a deprived community, would appear to be an ideal location for development aimed at revitalising the urban economy. Where the vacant land takes the form of a single large site or a few large sites the goal of regeneration can appear deceptively simple. The reality is somewhat different. Vacant land usually comprises numerous relatively small and scattered parcels requiring consolidation, clearance and decontamination (Champion and Townsend, 1990, p. 177).

The post-1979 Conservative governments addressed this challenge primarily through what Brindley *et al.* (1989) have termed *leverage planning*. This involved the use of public investment in derelict areas to stimulate the private sector property and land market. Our discussion over the past few pages should show clearly that much of the reorientation of town and country planning towards private-sector needs was specifically designed to ensure leverage. Although the major elements of the leverage strategy were the urban initiatives which we reviewed in Chapters 5 and 7, their effective operation was closely intertwined with the liberalisation of town and country planning legislation. The key characteristic of the leverage approach to town and country planning was that it offered little scope for formal participation. Brindley *et al.* (1989) suggest that its antithesis was *popular planning*. This approach emphasised the conflict during the Thatcher years between the jointly-held goals of developers and governments committed to free market principles, and the more interventionist and redistributive aspirations of local communities. The key difference was that popular plans sought to reclaim the social dimension of planning and escape the straitjacket of confinement to land-use questions. They thus attempted to turn the clock back to an earlier, pre-Conservative, or even idealist, form of planning.

Popular planning exhibited the hallmarks of the politics of resistance to the new orthodoxy in planning. Perhaps as a structural concession to participation, it was occasionally successful, although such an outcome could usually be traced to a sympathetic local authority, professional support, tactical concessions to economic themes and macroeconomic circumstances which disabled the private sector. Numerous examples can be cited: see Ehyatt (1987) for a general review, Brindley *et al.* (1989, ch. 5) on the Coin Street development, Alty and Darke (1987) on Sheffield and Brownill (1990b) for a critical assessment. The relevant issues are clearly evident in the case of fiftyfour hectares of mainly derelict land owned predominantly by British Rail at King's Cross Station, London (Kynoch, 1989: Springay, 1989; Parkes and Mouawad, 1991; Catterall, 1992). A scheme by the London Regeneration Consortium (LRG) for an office city was opposed by the King's Cross Railwaylands Group, a popular planning umbrella for 400 local groups. The popular planning group had the support of the local authority and conducted a highly professional alternative 'planning for real' exercise incorporating detailed cost benefit analyses of their own and competing schemes. They argued for a socially responsible regeneration of their community and obtained concessions from the LRG. However, the basic principle of the LRG scheme remained unaltered and the property slump of the early 1990s ensured that, in any case, no development took place.

We would contend overall that the emphasis on urban initiatives during the 1980s was such that town and country planning was forced into a back seat as a tool for the promotion of urban regeneration. It did, however, retain a background importance. First, planning legislation such as SPZs and SDOs, while not entailing direct subsidisation of the private sector, provided a means of speeding up the planning process in areas of derelict land. Second, as we noted earlier, the repeal of the Community Land Act, 1975 effectively terminated the potential for the public sector to lead regeneration by virtue of owning land. The introduction of public-land registers and the enforced sale of public-land assets provided the basis for the private sector to enter the land market for what had, as again we indicated earlier, largely been public-sector land holdings. Third, popular planning, by exploiting the remaining bases for public participation and consultation within town and country planning legislation, highlighted the need for more flexible frameworks for assessing the ecological and social benefits that would not usually be incorporated into the narrowly economistic cost–benefit framework of leverage planning.

By the start of the 1990s this more conciliatory approach was gaining some ground as Conservative planning adjusted to recession and, in its mature phase, rediscovered community and social needs, integrated ecological awareness, and gave the concept of partnership a new priority. As we saw in the previous section, the new ecological awareness was not without contradictions, nor were people and social factors firmly back on the agenda. However, there was an acknowedgement that town and country planning mechanisms had a part to play in regenerating urban derelict land. Nowhere was this clearer than in the plans, announced in March 1993, for the regeneration of the East Thames Corridor. Plans to develop thirty miles of Thames-side land to the east of London, providing up to 128 000 new homes and 182 000 new jobs will entail land decontamination costs of £200–385 million. A Task Force (see Chapter 6) will co-ordinate this process and the town and country planning mechanism will provide the day-to-day structure for the developments; it all shows undoubted ecological awareness and is a mostly appropriate use for a blighted area. However, apart from infrastructural transport costs, funding is expected to come from the private sector. That, in a recession, seems problematic.

## Managing urban growth

The containment of urban growth has been a traditional theme of town and country planning legislation. We will examine containment under the post-1979 Conservative governments by means of a discussion of the fortunes of the green belt (Elson, 1986). Green belts (Chapter 2) were intended to contain the outward growth of metropolitan areas. Such a notion was problematic for the post-1979 Conservatives. It constituted regulation and interfered with the presumption that obstacles to economic growth should be removed. Ideological imperative was matched, however, by the political importance of the Conservative shire vote with its advocacy of rural conservation and opposition to significant encroachment on open country. There was thus a conflict between what Brindley *et al.* (1989) have called '*trend planning*' – the enablement of private sector development in areas of growth, and their concept of '*regulative planning*' – the use of the full powers of planning to conserve the environment in similar areas.

The situation was complicated by three further factors. First, the operation of the green belt policy had not been problem-free. Development had tended to 'leapfrog' the green belt and take place in more distant small towns and rural areas (Cherrett, 1982). Conflicts had become frequent between districts enforcing green belt designations through the use of development control powers and other bodies seeking development opportunities (Cherry, 1989). Second, green belts were not necessarily wholly composed of land fully deserving protection. Third, by the 1980s, the office, retail and high-technology industry sectors were all increasingly looking for green-field sites, and the demand for housing sites was also escalating, especially in South-East England.

Diverse commentaries on green-belt policy during the 1980s suggested the need for reform. The Adam Smith Institute (1983) recommended general relaxation and liberalisation in tandem with a greater role for central government. This prescription can be interpreted as an attack both on local government and on regulation. More interestingly, the Regional Studies Association, a body representing *inter alia* professional and academic planners, argued that green belts had failed to meet economic and social needs and required revision (Herrington, 1990; see Haslam, 1990, for criticisms of this position). They recommended the replacement of green belts with 'green areas' in which legislation would seek both to protect and to enhance high quality landscapes. At the same time, they suggested a less rigid attitude to development within the current green belt.

Although commentaries therefore appeared to favour liberalisation, the governmental response was less clear. Significant differences appeared between the protectionist and the market lobbies. Thornley (1991, pp. 213–14) and Elson (1986) provide particularly clear expositions of this conflict, while Ambrose (1986, ch. 7) outlines Patrick Jenkin's 1983/4 attempt to liberalise green belt policy in response to Consortium Developments' proposals for a ring of fifteen new 'country towns' around London and the argument that environmental interests were checking the progress of market deregulation. The late 1980s saw the protectionist lobby in the ascendant as the government began to address 'green issues' (Cabinet Office, 1990) and European Community legislation concerning environmental impact assessment came into effect.

By the 1990s this shift was increasingly evident in local authority plans: cycleways, sustainable transport strategies, wildlife habitat preservation and many other 'green' approaches were proposed and officially sanctioned. This apparent reverse to the general market-isation of planning can be linked to the contradictions of the 'mature' phase of Conservative planning which we identified earlier. In part it undoubtedly also had a vote-buying element, both with regard to traditional Conservatives and the new ecological vote – although the fact that the Department of Transport was prepared to drive a road through an Area of Outstanding Natural Beauty and Special Scientific Interest in a relatively safe Conservative constituency (Winchester) indicated limits to the new awareness.

Whatever the political debates, there was major growth on the outer flanks of green belts during the 1980s. Healey *et al.* (1988) record major case studies in South Manchester and the West Midlands. Between 1981 and 1987 350 000 new houses were built in outer South-East England (SERPLAN, 1989). The spirit of the green belt was eroded by the purchase of isolated mansions for corporate headquarters and agricultural land for tax farming (Munton, 1983). 'Nodal developments' on motorway junctions were extensive: science parks (Herrington, 1984, p. 38; Massey and Wield, 1992; Henneberry, 1992), out of town retail parks (Herrington, 1984, p. 40), amusement parks; and, of course, housing (Cheshire and Sheppard, 1989) all contributed extensively to the urbanisation of land on the fringes of the green belt.

The town and country planning system could do little to counter this process. Indeed, the modifications which we outlined earlier in this chapter meant that the process was actually made easier. Private-sector land needs were to be accommodated rather than delayed by the planning system. Thus, the downgrading of structure plans meant that the opposition of Wiltshire County Council to the growth of Swindon could be overturned on grounds of market need (Bassett and Harloe, 1990). Some counties continued to try to limit development to local needs but, notwithstanding the protectionist lobby in the government, the pressure from development interests and their advocates was persistent. Only in the late 1980s, with the onset of recession and the slump in the housing and office markets, did it slacken.

The enduring contradictions between the market and the protectionist position are amply illustrated by Michael Heseltine's

1991 London Lecture. Referring to his vision of a South Thames Corridor New Town, he said:

> Here's a challenge for the next decade. From Greenwich Peninsula perhaps to the Medway Towns a new London will be born . . . This will all require radical new approaches to development – using initiatives we have been developing elsewhere we must enhance the green areas to the east of London; and be imaginative in making new ones. We will protect the Green Belt. (Heseltine, 1991b)

This vision later developed into the proposals for an East Thames Corridor development which we have already mentioned. By proposing development east of London, it was intended to lessen pressure to the west where it is most intense; the East Thames development was announced at the same time as a proposal to build a 13 000-population private country town at Micheldever in Hampshire was vetoed. The East Thames development was also proposed on largely derelict land; except for the areas around Rainham and Dartford it will not offend existing conservation areas. However, bodies such as the Town and Country Planning Association, Friends of the Earth, and the Council for the Protection of Rural England were all less than confident that, without extensive state intervention, the proposal would succeed.

### Assessment

We have already, at several points in this chapter, made reference to the theoretical debates raised by the town and country planning system. We will now briefly offer an overview of the ways in which different theoretical traditions would view that system. We will also offer an assessment of the coherence of town and country planning as a policy area in the period since 1979.

Hayek (1960, ch. 22) offers the clearest exposition of neo-liberal views concerning the town and country planning system. The Adam Smith Institute (1983) provides a more focused view. The substance of both perspectives is that town and country planning is a manifestation of excess state intervention. It stifles market innovation and limits the scope for private-sector action; it is part of the problem of urban decline. Even prior to 1979, this view had affected the evolution of town and country planning. Many of the post-1979 developments can be seen as neo-liberal attempts to 'roll back the state' and enable the private sector. The retention of a town and country planning system and, some would argue, its mild renaissance in the 1990s was partially a reflection of the continuing impact of a neo-conservative conservation lobby. It also reflected the enduring pragmatism of those involved in the practical application of New Right dogma; the town and country planning system, whatever its shortcomings, offered a means by which voting individuals could both foresee and attempt to protect their own living conditions.

For Marxists, the planning system might be represented as a triumph of state intervention, protecting people from the excesses of a private sector determined to extract maximum use value from the land. Such a cosy conclusion would be at odds with the facts. More pertinent would be a Marxist interpretation which drew attention to the continuing and unequal conflict between capital and the state over the scope and direction of town and country planning. Furthermore, such an analysis might note the extent of the interest group which constitutes the development lobby and its congruence with the needs of industrial and development capital. In the period since 1979, the transformation of the system to a state of general accord with private-sector interests would accord with Marxist notions of a state apparatus attuned to the needs of capital; the renaissance of planning in the 1990s would be a concession designed to ensure the legitimacy of this restructured system.

Pluralist research has had much to say about town and country planning. Simmie (1974, 1981) has provided particularly sophisticated analyses drawing mainly on neo-pluralist perspectives. The notion that town and country planning is a simple matter of negotiating outcomes between equals is clearly untenable. Not only is the negotiation process managed within the town and country planning framework, it is also not a negotiation between equals. Early disquiet about the powers of the 'planocracy' (see page 180) can now be replaced by misgivings about a system in which, quite clearly, private-sector needs are now paramount and the scope for public participation is limited.

Table 8.1 attempts to apply our framework for policy analysis to the general assessment of urban planning under the post-1979 Conservative governments. The urban was defined primarily in physical terms as a built-up area with the functional attribute of being the centre of market activity and therefore, in Conservative terms, a target for activity. Such activity was guided largely by the tenets of neo-liberal theory. This theoretical approach was, however, tempered by a paradox: the state was required in order to ensure the application of neo-liberal theory in an environment where there was a strong history of state intervention. State direction was required to reduce state action.

This paradox came out most clearly in the analysis of the problem which the Conservatives perceived town and country planning should be addressing. This problem was not a substantive physical problem, and it was certainly not a social problem; rather it was a

**TABLE 8.1 Post-1979 urban planning: an assessment**

| | Urban Planning 1979–92 |
|---|---|
| Conception of 'urban' | An area of mixed land use; essentially physical definition; locus of market activity; little concern with the social |
| Theoretical approach | Mix of *laissez-faire* neo-liberalism and central direction |
| Nature of problem | Regulatory and statist nature of pre-existing planning system |
| Explanation | Rigidity of pre-existing state-centred system |
| Aim of policy | Contradictory: deregulate, introduce flexibility, centralise; conserve or develop |
| Mechanisms | Simplification, circumvention, facilitation and modification |
| Resourcing | Reducing |
| Management | Mainly local but increasingly centralised |
| Political support | Partisan |
| Legislation | Local Government, Planning and Land Act, 1980; successor legislation including consolidation through numerous Circulars |
| Monitoring | Relatively extensive but often *ad hoc* |

systemic problem – town and country planning itself. It was rigid and contradictory to the general goals of the Thatcher project. It needed to be simplified, reduced, avoided or abandoned. However, at the same time, it was essential to the preservation of the sort of (generally non-urban) vision of Britain which was espoused by the still-powerful traditional Conservatives who comprised much of the Conservative electorate. The solution was the preservation of a reduced and refocused system within a broad framework which was to a considerable extent unchanged. The planocracy was dismantled and local discretion was limited. Legislative change was extensive but, with the exception of the 1980 Act, largely achieved through consolidation and incremental marginal change. Monitoring was encouraged, but often limited to the imposition of performance indicators designed to speed decision-making.

**Conclusion**

We have covered a great deal of material in this chapter. Town and country planning has been revealed as a basic operational tool underlying and intimately associated with many of the grander urban initiatives. It has undergone many changes during the Thatcher years, changes which have radically altered the idealist vision of planning embodied, albeit imperfectly, in the 1947 and 1968/71 systems. In particular, we have argued that town and country planning since 1979 has been characterised by a growing accommodation with private sector and market needs, by a reaction to the perceived excesses of a local state bureaucracy, and by a degree of centralisation which has had the consequence of removing some pre-existing provisions for public participation and consultation. We have suggested that there may have been some weakening of this position in more recent years. While the Conservative transformation of planning was initially a fairly coherent project, its contradictions and apparently lessening radicalism in later years suggest that it would be unwise to identify a single coherent Conservative town and country planning policy. Its close integration with other urban initiatives is an interesting development but the verdict on these measures, which we set out in Chapter 7, means that planning does not contribute much to the overall case for an emerging urban policy.

# 9 Local Government and Urban Policy

Many, if not all, of the initiatives and policies we have reviewed in the preceding chapters have had an effect on local government. In some cases, local authorities have been intimately involved in the development and carrying-out of policy. In other cases, policies, or their consequences, have been imposed upon local authorities. In either case there have often been major consequences involving the reorientation of local authority activity. This was particularly the case during the Thatcher years (Rhodes, 1988; Moon and Parnell, 1989); there was a major restructuring of central–local relations, with the powers of the centre being generally, but often not without cost, enhanced at the expense of the local government.

Our major concern in this chapter is to outline the role of local government in 'urban policy'. Our focus will be particularly on the period after 1979. We shall:

- Consider the changing structure of local government with regard to urban areas.
- Analyse the impact of transformations in the nature of central-local relations.
- Assess the role of local government in national urban initiatives.
- Review attempts at local government-led economic development.
- Evaluate the effects of privatisation on local authorities.

In addressing these tasks we confront an enormous literature. While our analysis will, of necessity, involve reference to wider themes, we would urge the reader who requires a more general introduction to local government to consult a general text on the topic, for example Kingdom (1991), Stewart and Stoker (1989) or Stoker (1991).

## The structure of local government

The modern system of local government developed gradually during the nineteenth century, acquiring a degree of permanence via legislation enacted towards the end of the century and in the first decades of the twentieth century (Kingdom, 1991, ch. 2). In essence these reforms created a two-tier county/district system in rural areas and single multi-purpose county borough authorities in urban areas To all intents and purposes, except for the reform of London government in 1965, this system remained largely unchanged until the reforms initiated by the Local Government Acts of 1972 came into force in 1974.

The reforms of 1974 were the product of major debates during the 1960s over the future and role of local government (Dearlove, 1979). Redcliffe-Maud (1969) argued a corporatist position and recommended large, mainly single-tier, local government units in order to encourage the development of more efficient and effective management. This implied a greatly reduced number of local authority units based on city commuter areas (see Chapter 1) and would have challenged the Conservative political power-base in the shires; consequently it was rejected by the 1970 Conservative government. What emerged in 1972 was a compromise: a two-tier system (County/District in England and Wales; Region/District in Scotland) was retained, but responsibilities within the system were distributed differently in 'metropolitan' and 'shire' areas. This decision essentially replicated the one that had been made for London local government in 1965 when the Greater London Council (GLC) and London boroughs had been created.

The 1965 and 1974 reforms were extremely controversial. From the point of view of urban local government, three themes deserve particular mention. First, as was also the case with the contemporaneous reorganisation of the National Health Service, there were disputes over the ability and effectiveness of the tiers to handle the responsibilities which they were allocated; local responsiveness was stacked against strategic oversight. Second, the reorganisation was resented by many medium-sized urban areas. Previously these areas had had sole responsibility for their own local government as county boroughs; after 1974 they became subordinate to counties with little experience of the needs of urban areas. Third, the boundaries of some new authorities were opposed. Some were challenged as they removed historic separations: the absorbtion of parts of Cheshire into Greater Manchester, and Sutton Coldfield into Birmingham. Others were not only ahistorical, they were also culturally challenging: the artificial creations of Cleveland, Humberside and Avon.

From the beginning, the 1965/1974 system lacked a degree of legitimacy in the eyes of some politicians and many residents. However, it remained largely untouched until 1986. In that year urban government in the GLC and the metropolitan counties was reformed and responsibilities devolved to multi-purpose district-level authorities. The statutory role of the GLC and the metropolitan counties was abolished (Pickvance, 1991). However, the aspirations of the larger provincial cities, former county boroughs such as Nottingham and Bristol, regarding self-government, remained unsatisfied.

By 1992 the future of the non-metropolitan local government was under consideration, with the most likely outcome being the creation of single tier (*unitary*) authorities. Initial views from the DoE seemed to favour the county tier being abolished in England (DoE, 1991e) and the regional tier in Scotland. In Wales a mixture of pre- and post-1974 structures totalling twentyone unitary authorities was announced in March 1993 to replace the existing system from April 1995 (*Guardian*, 2.3.93).

## Central–local government relations

### Financial conflict

In the years when the post-1945 consensus reigned supreme and the welfare state was being established and expanded, local government was also growing. When the consensus broke down in the mid-1970s (see Chapter 4) local government was inevitably affected by the associated public expenditure crisis. As early as 1974 there were requests from central government that local government should restrain its spending. Initially it was hoped that local government would voluntarily reduce its spending; however, the gravity of the situation meant that, by 1976, cash limits were being introduced to force reductions in expenditure on recalcitrant local authorities. These actions were, relatively speaking, quite successful. They led to a reduction in local government expenditure as both a percentage of GDP and of total public expenditure by 1979.

The incoming 1979 Conservative government viewed state intervention and public expenditure as an anathema, arguing that both should be significantly reduced if freedom, choice and the entrepreneurial spirit were to be enhanced. Moreover, local government was viewed as overly bureaucratic and unsympathetic to business (especially small businesses). The new Secretary of State at the DoE, Michael Heseltine, demanded immediate cuts in local government expenditure, even though the financial year was already underway, and future cuts and reductions in human resources. Local government largely failed to comply with these demands and the stage was set for one of the major confrontations of the 1980s: the 1980s crisis in central–local relations (Travers, 1986; McVicar and Atkinson, 1985; Butcher *et al.*, 1990, ch. 4; Stoker, 1991, ch. 8).

In essence the 1980s crisis centred on central government attempts to reform the system whereby local authorities were financed. This system involved three elements: grants from the centre; locally-raised income (originally the rates, later the community charge and more recently the council tax); and other locally-raised funds (user charges, council house rents, etc.). Government attempted to limit its grant to local authorities and to relate the grant to centrally-assessed, and published, spending limits for each local authority. If a local authority chose to spend more than its centrally assessed target it would lose grant and the cost would fall disproportionately on local ratepayers who would then, theoretically, vote out over-spending (usually Labour) councils.

This attempt to reduce local government expenditure did not work in the anticipated way because only about one-third of voters actually paid full rates and, thus, most voters could vote for high spenders without having to bear the financial consequences. The Labour Party not only held on to councils but also won control of new ones. A series of *ad hoc* responses to this problem created financial chaos as grant systems were modified, and in some cases discarded, after the financial year had begun, and local authorities developed methods of creative accounting to circumvent new controls on their spending. The *Rates Act*, 1984, was an interim and arguably desperate attempt by government to reassert control (McVicar and Atkinson, 1985). The community charge and its replacement the council tax were further steps along the road to greater central control over local expenditure (Butcher *et al.*, 1990; Stoker, 1991). It would appear that these reforms worsened the position of low-resource urban authorities and, within them, made the position of the poor even worse (Ridge and Smith, 1990; Hills and Sutherland, 1991).

By 1988, the cumulative pressures from the centre had led to some significant reductions in local government spending. This had been accomplished at the considerable cost of a deterioration in central–local relations, most notably with a group of left-wing Labour councils but also with more moderate Labour councils and some Conservative-controlled ones. It was the first group which assumed most significance. During the first two post-1979 Conservative governments there was a rise in the number of urban authorities on the 'new urban left' practising what has been termed *municipal socialism* or *local socialism* (Boddy and Fudge, 1984; Gyford, 1985; Lansley *et al.*, 1989). This rather disparate group had its bases in urban local authorities such as the GLC, inner London boroughs, Sheffield and, in a rather different way, Liverpool. Its intention was to develop alternative strategies from those of the Conservative government and demonstrate that a socialist alternative existed and could be implemented at local level. Defeats over rate capping, abolition of their power bases in the GLC and the metropolitan counties and a third, overwhelming, Conservative electoral victory in 1987 limited their effectiveness and impact and led to a less confrontational approach.

By the early 1990s relations with the centre had improved considerably compared with the mid-1980s. However, this did not simply represent a change on the part of the localities. To an extent, even before Margaret Thatcher's resignation as Prime Minister, there was evidence of a softening on the centre's part. In 1991/2 local authorities in England planned to spend £0.9 billion more than the centre believed necessary (CM 1908, 1992, p. 113) and the debacle of the community charge led the centre to provide just over £4 billion in additional finance (CM 1908, 1992, p. 113) to moderate the political fallout. Although the current recession and demands for expenditure restraint may lead to new conflicts, it would appear that the worst of the financial crisis of central–local relations is now over. Local government has adjusted to a period of austerity, and central government has become more accommodating to local needs. However, as part of its determination to contain and reduce public expenditure, it would appear that the limits which the centre has imposed on the spending of many local authorities for 1993/4 will cause considerable hardship. While it is unlikely that a return to the sort of confrontations which characterised the mid-1980s will be seen, the emergence of renewed antagonisms between centre and locality cannot be ruled out.

*Political conflict*

It would be wrong to see finance as the sole issue causing central–local conflict. The new urban Left saw itself as the only real opposition to Thatcherism between 1983 and 1987. Margaret Thatcher saw this as a challenge to the authority of government, parliament and, perhaps most importantly, herself. This she was clearly not prepared to tolerate and her initial scepticism towards local authorities soon turned into outright hostility. Thus, despite all the DoE's attempts to justify abolition of the GLC and metropolitan counties (DoE, 1984), the underlying motive for changing the structure of urban local government was political.

While London and the Metropolitan areas did not subsequently descend into the chaos some predicted, there is no evidence that the reforms achieved appreciable expenditure reductions, that service provision moved closer to people, or that the system became any less complex and easier to understand as a multiplicity of statutory and *ad hoc* coordinating bodies emerged to provide services (James, 1990; Travers, 1990; Leach and Game, 1991).

We can see this destruction of local government as part of a wider attempt to restructure the welfare state during the 1980s. As Hambleton (1990, p. 98) has argued: '[the] government's key concern has been to undermine the role of local government in providing redistributive services'. This fits quite comfortably with New Right notions of 'rolling back the frontiers of the state' and unleashing entrepreneurial activity by removing the dead hand of state regulation. As far as Margaret Thatcher was concerned, local government exhibited some of the worst examples of these market-restraining tendencies.

Again, however, the situation became less confrontational by the late 1980s. Ridley, 1988 (see also Brooke, 1989) foresaw the emergence of the *enabling authority*. This refers to a situation in which local government does not actually provide services, but, instead, co-ordinates their delivery, whether by purchase from the private sector, the financing of voluntary groups to provide services, or through collaborative ventures with the private sector; in other words, it takes a strategic overview. As an enabling body local government becomes the provider of last resort. Accompanying the move to enabling has been a stress on the need to reform the internal management structures of local government to make them more cost effective, flexible and responsive to consumer demand (see Brooke, 1989; DoE, 1991f). This last issue – the consumer – emerged, along with the notions of empowerment and decentralisation, with considerable force in the early 1990s with Prime Minister John Major's stress on Citizen's Charters.

Bulpitt (1986) provides a useful summary of the processes driving the restructuring of central–local relation, drawing on the experiences of the first years of post-1979 Conservative government. He suggests that the *dual polity*, whereby the centre focused on 'high politics' (e.g. foreign affairs) while leaving low politics (e.g. local government) to occur within an automatically regulated and insulated domestic sphere, broke down in the late 1970s, and much of what occurred in the 1980s was part of an attempt to create a new polity. Thus the reforms to both local government structure and finance were part of an attempt to create a local government functioning 'automatically', in line with centrally-defined New Right criteria, and thereby leave the centre free to concentrate on high politics. In the long run, these attempts failed. First, they were, and continue to be, extremely time-consuming for the centre as well as politically damaging. Second, local government still overspends and local authorities are still able to resist and make life difficult for the centre.

## Local government and urban initiatives

Until the late 1960s (see Chapter 2) local authorities played a major role in attempts to deal with urban problems. In effect they were the lead agencies. Central government, in consultation with local government, supplied the statutory powers and the majority of the resources. Local authorities were mainly left to decide upon the timing and the extent of action. Legislation was largely 'permissive' (Griffith, 1966).

When specific urban initiatives began to emerge (see Chapters 3 and 4) local authorities had important roles. Arguably the greatest dominance of local government in urban regeneration schemes occurred in the Partnerships established in the later 1970s. In these, the centre entered into an explicit partnership with selected local authorities while giving a range of other local authorities access to additional Urban Programme funds. There was clearly an intention to involve local authorities in the regeneration of urban areas in partnership with the centre by providing them with additional powers and offering extra (albeit inadequate) resources. Although the Partnerships also offered the centre a means of exercising considerable influence over policy development at local level, what is important is that central government believed it was legitimate that local authorities be involved in attempts to regenerate their areas.

During the 1980s, for reasons outlined in the previous section, central government began to question the legitimacy and efficacy of local government *vis-à-vis* urban regeneration, preferring to rely upon the private sector. For much of the period the centre attempted to import private-sector methods, with limited success, into both central and local government. Local authorities were seen as overly bureaucratic and as stifling enterprise via planning and rates policies. Consequently, many of the urban initiatives which emerged during the 1980s specifically aimed to bypass local authorities, reduce their powers, and allow the centre to intervene more directly in the management and co-ordination of local government urban regeneration activity. Even initiatives which set out specifically to involve local authorities (e.g. Estates Action, City Challenge) sought to establish criteria which local government had to accept in order to participate and receive the benefit of additional resources. These criteria gave the centre greater control over the detail of schemes and required private sector participation.

Despite this progressive exclusion of local government from urban regeneration initiatives during the 1980s, the Audit Commission (1989) made it clear to the government that there remained a role for local authorities in urban regeneration and economic development. Local government participation was to take place within a framework which accepted the primacy of private sector-led growth as the main long-term answer to urban decline (Audit Commission, 1989, p. 1). Central government in the 1990s appears to accept this argument. In urban initiatives, such as City Challenge, where local government was closely involved, it was on the understanding that there should also be a significant level of private-sector involvement. Overall it is thus fair to say that, for much of the 1980s, local government was marginalised with regard to centrally-developed urban initiatives and that its involvement in the 1990s is on terms which favour private-sector development over social needs.

## Local economic development policies

While it is true to say that for most of the 1980s central government urban initiatives deliberately set out to marginalise local authorities, this does not mean that local government passively accepted this marginalisation. Increasingly during the 1980s local authorities attempted to devise local economic development policies to help revive their areas. Much attention has been focused on the actions of left-wing labour authorities in this regard but, as research by Mills and Young (1986) and Sellgren (1990) has shown, a wide range of authorities, urban and rural, Conservative as well as Labour controlled, became involved in local economic development during the 1980s.

Although a tradition of municipal involvement in industrial policy can be traced back to Fabian arguments, the activities of Victorian municipal leaders, and the development of council 'trading estates' (see Boddy and Fudge, 1984), it is doubtful if these writings and experiences exerted much influence on the initiatives that emerged during the 1980s. These initiatives had much more to do with the new urban Left (see above) and resistance to the free-market, anti-statist direction of central government policy (Parkinson, 1989). They provided local support for local people and were therefore popular – at least with those who benefited if not with those who footed the larger shares of the local rate bill. They also arguably represented a realisation by local authorities that the needs of industry should be acknowledged as being central to economic rejuvenation. For the Conservatives, such activity was problematic; it regulated and artificially manipulated the operation of the free market, sustained local governments in power which were opposed to central government, and entailed considerable public expenditure. Boddy (1984) has pointed to a division between what he terms mainstream and radical initiatives for local government-led economic development. We will use this distinction to analyse what has taken place.

*Moderate strategies*

Moderate local government strategies for economic development focused on simple publicity designed to attract investment to the local area. This would usually be coupled with aid regarding start-up or transfer costs and assistance with finding premises. Some of the funding for this activity came from the monies raised from the *Section 137* levy, a discretionary sum which local authorities were able to raise specifically for economic development purposes through the provisions of the Local Government Act, 1972, which allowed the product of a 2p rate to be used to benefit the local area. Where possible, local authorities would also assist enterprises in tapping available central government initiatives (see Chapter 6), and accessing European funds such as the EC Regional Development Fund and the EC Social Fund (see Chapter 11).

Short (1984, pp. 162–5) suggests that the moderate approach was often essentially a promotion, through the pages of the quality, trade and financial press, of the economic advantages (location, available workforce, local skills, aid incentives, etc.) of an area. Sometimes it involved consortia of local authorities, but more generally it was undertaken singly. Small firms were the prime target, though the hope was to attract larger employers. Unfortunately, evidence suggests that firms which responded to moderate strategies often stayed only as long as the subsidy lasted. The assumption that longer-term economic benefit resulted can be challenged (Robson, 1988, p. 137).

Boddy (1984) argues that the moderate strategy firmly positioned local authorities in a role underpinning the private sector. Private industry rather than public investment was perceived as the route to economic regeneration, and the local government task was to enable the private sector by socialising the costs of production thus freeing private industry from obstacles to profit in return for jobs. Moderate strategies for economic development do not therefore challenge the centrality of the free market although they do constitute intervention in a relatively limited sense.

Mills and Young (1986) charted the shift of moderate approaches from a reliance on premises-based aid to a more people-centred approach in the early 1980s. This shift initiated an emphasis which has continued into the 1990s. The accent moved to such issues as training and the provision of advice to both industrialists and potential employees. Local authorities themselves often undertook internal reorganisations to set-up and equip 'industrial development offices'. Though these bodies retained a concern with land acquisition on behalf of the private sector the emphasis was increasingly on a public–private partnership to ensure the availability of an appropriately skilled workforce for the needs of the local economy.

## Radical approaches

More radical and interventionist initiatives for local-government-led economic development began to emerge from the new urban Left in the early 1980s (Mawson and Miller, 1986). These initiatives had some similarity with mainstream approaches in their concern to exploit available central and European funding, but they differed from mainstream approaches over the way in which the role of the private sector was conceptualised; they challenged the primacy of the private sector and the market.

In the radical approach the local state would intervene in and against the market in order to restructure the local economy in the interests of labour rather than capital (Duncan and Goodwin, 1985, 1986). The approach closely integrated social factors into strategies of regeneration, giving them equal, if not greater, weight than economic factors. Radical approaches also saw the public sector, through its employment and purchasing power, as a stimulus for economic change in its own right. Local authorities were to re-examine their operations and reorientate their activities to take into account and benefit the local economy.

Direct intervention in the labour market through provision of training, subsidies and planning agreements was the route taken by most local authorities pursuing radical strategies (Short, 1984, p. 125). The key factor differentiating these authorities from those pursuing moderate strategies, apart from their leftwards political inclination, was the fact that the intervention was direct and active, rather than passive. The lack of social responsibility consequent upon unfettered operation of the free market was seen as a cause of economic decline. Regulation and, above all, intervention, was perceived to be necessary. Responsible employment practices and popular involvement in industrial management were sought and proposals for the development of indigenous industries and skills were set out.

The development of radical approaches reached its height in the metropolitan counties and the GLC. Following initial work by local employment and economic development offices, five large *enterprise boards*, modelled to an extent on the Scottish and Welsh Development Agencies, were created by the local authorities with a specific brief to use all available public-sector leverage to facilitate both public and private investment to develop their respective local economies. The Greater London Enterprise Board (GLEB), the West Midlands Enterprise Board (WMEB), West Yorkshire Enterprise Board, Lancashire Enterprises Limited, and the Merseyside Enterprise Board were able to command considerable financial power through the use of pension funds and Section 137. This, they believed, would give them sufficient financial muscle to intervene in the market place via planning agreements with firms, and even attract finance from the major investment institutions and banks. The strategy was, however, flawed. The sums which the enterprise boards were able to raise were crucially dependent on the size of the local rate base. Sums concordant with often utopian aspirations and over-large bureaucracies were to be borne by local people; people who, in view of the deprived nature of the metropolitan areas, were often relatively unable to shoulder the financial burden of funding.

After the abolition of the GLC and metropolitan counties the local enterprise boards (LEBs) survived but in a restructured and less generously financed form. Cochrane and Clarke (1990) note that, by the late 1980s, LEBs had moved much closer to the private sector and were increasingly accepting market criteria as their operating principles. Lawless and Ramsden (1990) provide a case study of Sheffield which illustrates how the authority moved, in the centre's eyes, from being a radical pariah in the early 1980s to becoming a model authority in the late 1980s. This shift in the ethos of the LEBs was part of a much wider move towards public–private partnership (see Chapters 5, 6 and 7). Effectively, the public sector returned, in a more sophisticated manner, to underwriting the costs of private development (Boyle, 1989; Moore, 1990). LEBs were, however, hamstrung by Part V of the *Local Government and Housing Act*, 1989, which seriously reduced the scope and range of local government's economic interventions and led, in some cases, to the abolition of LEBs (Bradshaw, 1990; Hayton, 1991). Despite the apparent late-1980s *rapprochement* between central and local government, the centre remained unwilling to allow local government a full role in local economic (and urban) regeneration unless it participated on the centres' terms.

*Case study: the Greater London Enterprise Board*

While other enterprise boards pursued rather different strategies (see Mawson and Miller, 1986; Cochrane, 1986; Cochrane and Clarke, 1990; and Coulson, 1990 for accounts), the GLEB represented the most advanced attempt at developing a local economic strategy. Its successes and failure represented the highpoint of the movement.

The GLC put together the most comprehensive and wide-ranging strategy of local economic intervention (GLC, 1985, 1986a, 1986b). Yet, despite its apparent sophistication and elaborately-worked-out system of intervention, its effects were questionable. It is debatable whether the GLEB really understood how the market operated or how to intervene in it to affect market behaviour. Perhaps inevitably, given the complexity of the markets affecting London, the GLEB responded to change and opportunity in a reactive, defensive, manner. It allowed the market to dictate the context in which its actions took place.

Despite great hopes of economic and social restructuring, GLEB was always bedevilled by a tension between economic and social intervention. The former increasingly won out. Many of the larger firms which the GLEB initially helped were on the verge of bankruptcy and required significant refinancing and internal restructuring. This not only raised allegations of utopianism, but also carried social costs in that it was likely to involve significant job loses. Similarly, attempts to pursue policies of greater worker involvement and equal opportunities quickly came into conflict with wider economic imperatives as well as encountering worker and trade union resistance (Cochrane, 1987). Attempts to foster the development of indigenous small businesses could not hope to replace the losses caused by the closure of large firms and conflicted with the wider aims of GLC social policy as the small businesses frequently did not have a good record on employment and equal opportunity policies. Ultimately, as Cochrane (1983) and Boddy (1984) among others have noted, the GLEB's activities were almost wholly defensive in nature; the structural forces they were attempting to deal with were far beyond their capacities to counter.

*An alternative? The Glasgow Eastern Area Renewal Project*

The Glasgow Eastern Area Renewal Project (GEAR) is included here as it provides a useful example of an approach to urban renewal in which local government was an official partner with the central state. GEAR was established in 1976 in Glasgow's run down east end, an area which had experienced high levels of population loss, unemployment and levels of multiple deprivation. In its original conception, it was very much a product of the conditions which led to the 1977 White Paper and the setting up of the Partnerships in England (see Chapter 4). It relied heavily upon the focused and co-ordinated actions of several central and local government bodies, but was primarily a joint city council and Scottish Development Agency (SDA) operation.

Despite its potential for developing an effective means to implement a coherent approach to urban problems in Glasgow, GEAR did not get off to a good start. It lacked an overall framework and a clearly structured plan, the management structures of the project were slow to evolve and it was mainly funded by top-slicing other programmes (Wannop and Leclerc, 1987a, 1987b; Wannop, 1990). McArthur (1987) has also argued that it failed to appreciate that unemployed people were some of the most vulnerable on Clydeside given their lack of qualifications and the types of skill they possessed. This meant that whatever employment was created was likely to go to people from outside the area. It also meant that GEAR needed a clear training and employment strategy – which it did not have.

The election (largely by the English) of a Conservative government in 1979 inevitably meant that the social and employment targeting aims of GEAR would be challenged. As the 1980s progressed, as in England, greater stress was placed upon small-business development and the creation of an environment conducive to the entrepreneur. Unfortunately this seems to have been of little benefit to the people (particularly those without jobs) living in the GEAR area (McArthur, 1987). As one local wryly commented, what appears to have been achieved is 'prettier street corners for the unemployed to stand on' (quoted in Brindley *et al.*, 1988, p. 138).

Paralleling these changes was an attempt to increase owner-occupation via sales of council housing, refurbishment and new building. Sales of council housing proved even less successful in the GEAR area than in Scotland as a whole and, while new building for owner-occupation and refurbishment by housing associations achieved some success, the overall tenure structure of the GEAR area had not changed significantly when the project formally came to an end in 1987 (Clapham and Kintrea, 1987; Maclennan, 1987).

Booth *et al.*, (1982) claim that GEAR added little to public investment that would not have occurred without its declaration. Moreover, as the 1980s progressed, attention began to switch away from Glasgow and its inner areas towards other cities and peripheral housing estates (Pacione, 1990). In Glasgow new forms of urban initiative considered more congruent with government aims were developed. These included the environmental projects associated with the tenure of the city as European City of Culture, and Glasgow Action, a city-centre-focused, property-led form of public–private partnership in which the needs of the private sector were given unquestioned priority (Boyle, 1989).

While GEAR is often referred to as a potential alternative model of urban regeneration, it seems to us that there is, in the end, little to be gained from trying to imitate it. The lack of central–local conflict so characteristic of England during the 1980s is heartening, but in the end does not seem to have had any particular benefits for Scottish urban areas nor to have led to more significant levels of public participation as claimed by the former Secretary of State for Scotland, Malcolm Rifkind (Scottish Office, 1988, 1990). Furthermore, Brindley *et al.* (1989, ch. 7) argue that the effective lead authority in GEAR was the SDA, and not Glasgow Corporation. The SDA usurped the local government role although an appearance of partnership was maintained. Far from exemplifying an alternative, incorporated role for local government in urban economic regeneration, 'GEAR was no less an intrusion into traditional local government in Glasgow than were the UDCs in England' (Robson, 1988, p. 198).

*Appraisal*

In the final analysis most local authority economic development strategies have had serious flaws. All have tended to be over-optimistic, have failed either to understand or realistically assess the forces they were attempting to counter, and have lacked adequate definitions of the social and economic criteria on which intervention was to be based. As Hambleton (1990, p. 81) has noted, 'The evidence suggests that a general rise in local economic activity does not necessarily result in a "trickle down" of employment benefits to disadvantaged groups. A weak links exists between local employment growth and the level of unemployment.'

Strategies have generally lacked a comprehensive local labour market design which has analysed the local labour market and developed policies congruent with that analysis (Campbell, 1990). Such a strategy would allow developments that could build on and develop the skills available in the area, develop jobs appropriate to the skills present in the area and direct jobs towards local people. Without such a policy, local economic development runs the risk of merely subsidising the private sector, allowing it to dictate the type and pace of development, focus on flagship schemes that attract the wrong types of job for the area, and widening already-existing social divisions (Massey, 1990).

So does this mean that local-government-led economic development has been a waste of time? It is difficult to make an objective assessment and drew unambiguous conclusions. Both Coulson (1990) and Foley (1992) have highlighted the methodological problems involved in measuring economic development and jobs created purely as a result of local actions, and the difficulty of comparing different local strategies. Given the nature of the national and international forces which local strategies are forced to confront, it would be surprising if they had more than, at best, a marginal effect on instigating local economic growth and job creation. However, it may be that local authorities can create conditions which will retain or attract investment of some sort. Locally orientated purchasing policies could be of assistance, particularly to small firms in a local economy, as might pro-active education, training and employment policies designed to give people a real chance of getting whatever jobs are created.

One route by which the local authority role may develop in future years is the *growth coalition* (Logan and Molotch, 1987). Developed in the USA, this concept sees land as the key commodity in the generation of growth in a local area. Harding (1991) reviews the applicability of the work to the UK. The mobilisation of the local state over land assembly and usage forms the basis for a coalition. Each locality attempts to enhance land values to encourage locally-based growth and to attract inward investment. In the UK, the public sector, through its land ownership and planning powers, can act as the pivot around which growth coalitions may form. Recent reforms to the powers of local government and planning legislation, the creation of organisations such as UDCs, and the growth of public–private partnerships may create conditions for UK growth coalitions to emerge (Harding, 1991; see also Hambleton, 1990, ch. 13; and the essays in Judd and Parkinson, 1990).

**Privatisation**

Privatisation, in the context of this chapter, refers essentially to an increasing private-sector involvement in the financing, provision, delivery, management and regulation of erstwhile public services. For the post-1979 Conservatives, it represented a counter to perceived excesses of public expenditure and a tool by which the political effectiveness of opponents in local government could be blunted. It was a relatively minor plank of the 1979 government's programme but a central element of the work of two subsequent governments; legislative impacts during the mid- and late 1980s effectively recast public–private roles in local government.

As we have seen earlier in this chapter, the early years of the Thatcher governments had seen much rhetoric about reducing public expenditure but little actual success. In particular, central government departments had been unable or unwilling to cut their expenditure and anticipated reductions had not been forthcoming. To demonstrate continued commitment to reducing public expenditure, new approaches were required; if central departments could not co-operate, then local government would have to shoulder the burden. The material covered in this section can be interpreted in this light: outright abolition and massive cuts were politically unacceptable; change was to be presented in the form of a reorientation towards efficiency. The position was that local government as it was then constituted was inherently inefficient in terms of its financing, structure and service delivery.

We have already considered the issues of finance and structure. It was issues of service delivery that were to be most affected by privatisation. Local government service delivery, it was claimed, lacked innovation and was rendered inefficient by 'restrictive' trade union practices running counter to perceived needs for flexible workforces (Walker and Moor, 1983). The notion that local governments were accountable to their electorate for ensuring efficient service delivery was also held to be inadequate. As we saw in earlier sections, the 'service-dependent poor', who made most use of services, paid least as a consequence of tax and rate rebates, and benefit systems. Yet, through superior numbers, they were able to sustain in power local governments committed to high expenditure on services. This situation offended New Right thinking on three counts. First, fiscal accountability was peripheral. Second, it encouraged the 'nanny state'. Third, it interfered with the operation of the free market; some local governments increasingly sought to use public expenditure to create 'jobs and services' which the populist New Right thought non-essential (Forsyth, 1980, 1983). The antidote was the nebulous concept of 'value for money' whereby all expenditure would require justification, generally with due regard to New Right ideology, and where the private would usually be preferred to the public as an agent for service provision, if not finance.

A wide range of approaches to privatisation can be identified. Heald and Steel (1982) limit themselves to two key types: *liberalisation* and *denationalisation*. The former refers to situations where rules and regulations are reduced, recast or abolished with the aim of facilitating private-sector growth and entryism to markets previously dominated by the public sector. Examples would include the deregulation of national and local bus services in the early 1980s (Davis, 1984) and, more recently, the proposed deregulation of British Rail. The latter relates to the outright sale of local or, more generally, national governmental assets. Example would include the 'sale' of British Telecom and, on a local scale, the sale of local authority houses. Barnekov *et al.* (1989, p. 160) favour a four fold categorisation: selling-off public assets; liberalisation; charging; and contracting-out. The first two are essentially the same as Heald and Steel's key types. *Charging* has a straightforward definition: services should cover their costs through use charges. *Contracting-out* is more complex. It refers to a situation where local government lets a contract for service provision on the basis of a competitive tender but (usually) retains some regulatory role. Pirie (1985) and Kolderie

(1986) suggest yet more detailed categorisations. Readers seeking detail on the sale of council houses or the emasculation of local government in UDCs or HATs should consult Chapters 5 and 7; these forms of privatisation will not be revisited here.

We will, however, consider contracting-out. The Conservatives of the mid-1980s attached major importance to this strategy. Local authorities were encouraged to relinquish the provider role in a number of key service areas in favour of a new role as contract manager and regulator, overseeing private-sector providers. This transformation was neither self-generated nor wholesale. As the Treasury Economic Report for 1982 stated:

> The decision to contract-out the provision of local services is the responsibility of the local authority, however they are being encouraged to do so as a means of reducing the costs to their ratepayers while meeting standards. (Treasury, 1982)

This 'encouragement' had its origins in the 1979 Conservative election manifesto, but the key legislative instrument was the Local Government, Planning and Land Act, 1980. Part 3 of that Act established the principle of *competitive tendering*: local authorities were to seek tenders from the open market for contracts to deliver highway maintenance, sewage, housing construction, and housing maintenance services. Their *direct labour organisations* (DLOs), meant that local government manual workers who had previously undertaken these tasks on an 'in-house' basis, were made to compete for their jobs. The Secretary of State for the Environment was awarded powers to ensure fair competition and quash anti-competitive practices.

During the first post-1979 government, the Conservatives essentially limited their action to identifying cases of local government waste and stressing the savings which could be made through contracting-out. The actual take-up of contracting-out remained low during the second Thatcher government. Labour authorities maintained ideological opposition with 'hard Left' councils such as Liverpool articulating trenchant 'jobs and services' perspectives linking their roles as public-sector employers with their aims and responsibilities regarding economic regeneration. Labour-controlled local authority organisations – such as the Association of Metropolitan Authorities – and the trade unions funded campaigns against contracting-out, drawing attention to contractors' failures (TUC, 1984, 1986) while other studies castigated the employment practices of contractors (Hastings and Levie, 1983), 'regulated competition' (Hartley and Huby, 1985) and failures to take account of the true costs of contracts (Parker, 1990). Many DLOs also won competitive tenders, thus keeping service provision in-house.

By 1985 surveys in the *Local Government Chronicle* were able to indicate that, at most, some 10 per cent of councils had actually contracted out a service. While Conservatives could argue that this limited impact concealed the reality of a situation in which market discipline had been successfully imposed upon local authorities, resulting in a new-found efficiency, Labour were able to see it as an indication that DLOs were more in tune with the reality of public-sector needs. In geographical terms, the take-up was also patchy. Urban areas tended to be more attractive to contractors as a result of their more developed service needs and existing infrastructures. Moon and Parnell (1986) record greatest take-up in southern England in resort and suburban areas, and councils with clear Thatcherite orientations. In an overall sense, it would appear that, notwithstanding some loss-leader tenders designed to open-up markets, private-sector concerns only won contracts when they had the ideological support of the local council and the local DLO was either not interested or, in a few cases, truly inefficient.

The provisions of the 1980 Act were subsequently extended to refuse collection, vehicle and grounds maintenance, and to the catering and cleaning DLOs. A Green Paper (DoE, 1985d) set out the initial proposals, estimated the value of the services concerned at £2.5 billion, and promised future extensions to include profession-ally-led services such as architecture, legal services and computing. Parker (1990) sees the 1985 Green Paper as an indication of governmental exasperation at the low take-up of contracting-out. It met with considerable resistance from local authorities of all political persuasions, not surprisingly perhaps, as it was introduced at a time when, because of the abolition of the metropolitan county councils and the GLC, central–local relations were at a low ebb. The attempt to force the hand of local government was delayed until after the 1987 general election and passed into legislation in the *Local Government Act*, 1988. This act was subsequently extended to include sports and leisure facility management and included a clause giving the Secretary of State for the Environment the power to add additional services subject to Parliamentary approval.

It would be incorrect of us to dismiss contracting-out as a phenomenon of little impact. It was important on two counts. First, it undoubtedly acted as a catalyst to greater efficiency. The tendering process and the explicit threat of privatisation forced local government to examine the cost-effectiveness of their DLOs (Audit Commission, 1989). Second, and as a consequence of the first point, the contracting-out legislation led local government to consider seriously alternative approaches to service provision and to review its role as prime provider. By the early 1990s, the boundaries between the public and the private sectors were far more blurred than the initial impact of contracting-out would have suggested.

In urban areas contracting-out had a considerable impact on the formerly large DLOs. The price for efficiency and cost-effectiveness was job loss, poorer pay and bonus structures and less satisfactory working conditions (Ascher, 1987, pp. 105–10). Of course, some benefited from the introduction of private-sector working methods, but these people tended to be those in elite managerial positions (Dunleavy, 1986). Contracting-out initially divided blue- and white-collar town hall workers and hit hardest at the low-level routine aspects of service delivery rather than the high-level management functions. For those working-class cities and communities which were dependent on public-sector employment and those local authorities seeking to reduce the severest effects of recession on its population by maintaining a large DLO, the consequences were therefore profoundly negative. In later years, as the contracting culture became more pervasive, this impact spread to white-collar workers – unfortunately at the same time as recession hit the same employment sector.

Post-1979 Conservative policies of privatisation saw the abandonment of old notions of the role of local government. The idea of local government as a major direct employer was abandoned. Most importantly, the changes were characterised by the gradual but forced removal from local government of its provider role. This was replaced by a new approach in which a leaner local government managed private-sector providers using value-for-money concepts and acted as a guarantor of standards and a last-resort safety net. For urban areas the consequences were to limit the extent to which local government could, through its employment activities and its service provision, hinder the negative impacts of central government policies and the untrammelled operation of the free market.

**Assessment**

*Theoretical perspectives*

Pluralism is the unstated theoretical perspective which underlies the role of local government in Britain. However, only occasionally has it been explicitly used to analyse local government. The results (e.g. Newton, 1976) have tended to suggest that participation in local government has been fairly restricted and largely reflective of the needs of local élites. Pahl (1970) considered one élite: 'local gatekeepers'. He focused on the values, ideologies and actions of a relatively small group of public-sector managers and examined how their decisions reinforced, reproduced or counteracted inequalities caused by unequal incomes. The advantage of this approach was an explicit focus on key individuals within the local government system. Its disadvantage, as Pahl (1975, 1977) acknowledged, was a neglect of the wider structural context in which decisions were taken.

The work of Rhodes (1988, 1990) addressed elements of this deficiency by drawing on the literature on inter-governmental relations and policy networks (see Chapter 7). Out of this work emerged a more complex analysis of local government and its relations with other organisations. Both participation in and the activities of local government are by no means as unconstrained as traditional pluralist theory assumed.

Rarely have British analysts of local government felt the need to justify local government's existence in pluralist terms. When they have, their analyses have tended to focus on what *should be* rather than what *is* (Goldsmith, 1992). The arrival of the Thatcher government in 1979 and its apparent determination to clip the wings of local government forced an explicit defence of local government from a pluralist position. The most eloquent statement of this defence may be found in the work of Jones and Stewart (1985) in which they argue 'the case for local government'. In essence, their position is that local government is the only elected political authority apart from Parliament. Thus it plays a key role in the distribution of power and the prevention of unhealthy concentrations of power. Moreover, it responds to local needs, and plays a key role in allowing people to participate in the democratic processes.

From such a position, local government's participation in urban regeneration is absolutely crucial as it provides a means for local people to influence the development of projects and a method, albeit limited, of holding such developments to account. In a more general sense, local government can be seen as just one of a number of competing public, private and voluntary bodies/organisations participating in regeneration projects to influence the outcome.

During the 1980s New Right attitudes to local government were to see it as part of the problem – as bureaucratic, unresponsive, inefficient, obstructing the market, favouring special interests and therefore must be curbed. This approach was strongly influenced by the work of writers such as Hayek and the Public Choice School (see Chapter 1). All forms of state provision were seen as being inefficient, and local politicians and bureaucrats were thought to be simply out to serve their own interests via a process of empire-building.

New Right theorists were not, however, unremittingly hostile to local government. So long as it conformed to the basic principles of the limited/minimal state they were quite happy to support it. For instance, Hayek (1982: vol. 3, p. 146) argued:

> If all administration were under a uniform law it could not alter, and which nobody could change to make it serve specific administrative purposes, the abuse of legislation in the service of special interests would cease. Most services now rendered by central government could be devolved to regional or local authorities which would possess the power to raise taxes at a rate they could determine but which they could levy or apportion only according to general rules laid down by a central legislature . . . I believe the result would be the transformation of local and even regional governments into quasi-commercial corporations competing for citizens. They would have to offer a combination of advantages and costs which made life in their territory at least as attractive as elsewhere within the reach of its potential citizens.

In the UK, developments did not proceed as far as Hayek envisaged, and the dominant role for local government became that of 'enabling' (Ridley, 1988; Brooke, 1989; see above). More specifically with regard to urban regeneration, the notion of partnership with the private sector also assumed prominence.

Marxist theory has tended to view local government from a 'global' position. Until the mid-1970s it largely ignored local government, seeing it as the 'creature of the centre'. Cynthia Cockburn's study of local government was one of the first which drew explicitly upon Marxist theory. Her analysis of Lambeth saw local government (or the local state) as largely the 'national state writ small' (Cockburn, 1977, p. 47). In such an analysis the local state, like the national state, simply serves the interests of capital. Duncan and Goodwin (1988), whilst largely following Cockburn's analysis, developed one notion in her work: local government *may* provide an avenue for class struggle against the state. The strategies developed by the 'new urban Left' during the 1980s would appear to be examples. However, the demise of this 'movement' suggests that the space for struggle was more confined than they suggested.

Marxist articulations of the relation between local government and urban regeneration often simply see local authorities which co-operate with the private sector as underwriters of capital's profitability. Harvey (1989b, p. 8) has castigated such 'entrepreneurialism'. He argues:

The new entrepreneurialism typically rests . . . on a public–private partnership focusing on investment and economic development with the speculative construction of place rather than amelioration of conditions within a particular territory as its immediate (though by no means exclusive) political and economic goal.

Recent neo-Marxist analyses have focused on wider social and economic changes. Analyses of 'post-Fordism' and the post-Fordist state have been extrapolated to include local government (Stoker, 1990). This work argues that local government is becoming more flexible both organisationally and in terms of service provision. Interestingly, this has certainly parallels the 'enabling authority' argument referred to above; however, writers such as Cochrane (1991 and 1992) have suggested that recent developments in local government are more appropriately seen in the context of New Right attempts to restructure the welfare state to emphasise private-sector provision and the role of the 'responsible individual'.

*Policy coherence*

As can be seen from Table 9.1, what constitutes urban local government is rather vague. Empiricism and pragmatism have dominated. This is clearly illustrated in numerous governmental reports. For instance, the Redcliffe–Maud Report (1969) studiously avoided any definition of 'urban' and 'rural' and decided instead to use population figures to determine the type of authority appropriate to an area.

For much of the post-1945 era, the theoretical position of local government was seen as that of an essential element in a liberal pluralist democracy. It constituted an essential element in the dispersal of power and a way of responding to local needs and delivering services efficiently. Later, given the New Right's hostility to the state and local authorities' frequent opposition to the centre it became seen as part of the problem. Increasingly, it was argued that local government was an obstacle to the free market and that high local taxes and local bureaucracy had forced firms either to close and/or to relocate elsewhere. In short, local government became a problem.

Increasingly the basis of this problem was public expenditure. By the late 1970s many (usually Labour controlled) local authorities were being defined as 'overspenders'. The 1980s saw increased pressure for expenditure reductions at all levels of government but particularly at local level. Local authorities frequently did their best to thwart expenditure reductions and some even attempted to *increase* expenditure as part of a direct challenge to the authority of the Thatcher governments. As a result, the aim of policy towards (urban) local authorities during the 1980s was to marginalise them and give them as small a role as possible in urban regeneration. By the late 1980s the notion of an 'enabling authority' was becoming increasingly popular. However, such bodies were expected to be supportive of the private sector.

'Privatisation' was seen as one of the key mechanisms for reducing the scope of both the state in general and in local authority activities in particular. It aimed to create the basis for a thriving enterprise culture and help rejuvenate run-down local economies. For much of the 1980s it appeared that the only acceptable form of local government was the type which privatised/contracted out all its services, met once a year to assign contracts for service provision to

**TABLE 9.1   Local government and urban policy: assessment**

|  | Local Government and Urban Policy |
| --- | --- |
| Conception of 'urban' | Vague, although has some legal basis in Acts, e.g. Local Government Act, 1972; however, largely associated with 'built-up areas' |
| Theoretical approach | Initially a general belief in decentralisation – element of pluralist democracy and local service delivery; latterly seen as obstacle to enterprise society/culture and thus to urban regeneration. Since late 1980s recognition that local government has a (supporting) role to play |
| Nature of problem | Until mid-1970s not a problem – key part of welfare state and redistribution of 'wealth'; by mid-1970s part of public expenditure problem; since 1979 obstacle to free market and accused of forcing firms out of cities |
| Explanation | In post-1979 era seen as over-bureaucratic, unresponsive, unaccountable and often 'extreme', i.e. opposed Conservative governments' |
| Aim of policy | Post-1979 to greatly reduce actions and expenditure, thereby creating an 'enabling' form which will help attract firms back to cities |
| Mechanisms | Major programme of centralisation and contracting out. Encourage local authorities to form partnerships with private sector |
| Resourcing | Poor, often dependent upon section 137 levies or winning central funding on basis of private-sector inputs |
| Management | Subject to increasing value-for-money audits and other post-1979 management reforms |
| Political support | After considerable central–local hostility for most of 1980s a 'truce' declared, but along with urban 'policy' more generally still largely 'peripheralised' |
| Legislation | Considerable – but largely restrictive rather than supportive |
| Monitoring | Considerable – but frequently takes the form of strict central oversight or pressure to adopt cost-reducing measures |

private firms, and removed the obstructive local bureaucracy. By the late 1980s the notion of public–private partnership was more popular and, with the onset of a recession and the subsequent reductions in the opportunities for profitable private-sector developments, local authority participation become an essential element in rejuvenation schemes.

In most authorities resourcing was poor. Local economic policies, for example, were largely dependent upon Section 137 levies. Only in the larger metropolitan authorities could this raise significant funds. Throughout the 1980s pressure to reduce expenditure was intense as the centre believed that virtually all local authorities were profligate. There was intense pressure for local authorities to adopt private-sector management methods and give greater value for money. These principles were particularly applied to local economic policy; partnership with the private sector was part of the attempt to change local government's working culture, to make it more innovative and responsive.

The political environment in general and legislative measures in particular can best be described as hostile. Bodies such as UDCs were established in part to bypass and marginalise (Labour) local authorities, but also to demonstrate the inherent superiority of the private sector when it came to regeneration. By the late 1980s something of a truce had been declared although it would be difficult to say that the centre was actively supporting local economic regeneration policies other than in a tepid manner; the continuing prohibition on local labour clauses and the use of purchasing policies to favour local firms has meant that local authorities remain unable to ensure that local people benefit from regeneration.

Monitoring has most frequently taken the form of central pressure on expenditure, usually by reductions in central grants, but also by limits on the spending of individual authorities. Individual projects have often been subject to strict, and frequently arbitrarily imposed, spending limits. Within this context financial monitoring has increased considerably. However, there does not appear to have been a great deal of emphasis on the quality of outputs. In urban regeneration projects the stress has largely been on gearing ratios rather than jobs for local people.

**Conclusion**

Local government has undergone a process of restructuring during the 1980s. This restructuring was not only in terms of its involvement in urban initiatives but also in a much wider sense. The form that the restructuring took was specifically influenced by a New Right ideology that legitimated attacks upon the state, public expenditure and bureaucracy, and saw local government as the prime exhibitor of these 'problems'.

The fact that local government resisted and the centre made a series of blunders meant that we witnessed a long-drawn-out conflict which neither side could be said to have decisively won or lost. Compromises were made by both sides. As a by-product of these conflicts, local government was to a large extent excluded from new urban initiatives and its role in existing ones significantly circumscribed. These tendencies reached their height in *Action for Cities* (HMSO, 1988) which barely mentioned the role of local government in urban regeneration. Its successor documents (*Progress on Cities* and *People in Cities*) gave local government a somewhat more prominent role and, by the late 1980s, relations were beginning to improve slightly, as the centre began to relax a little as public–private partnerships emerged at local level. In Scotland, local government retained a much more significant role

What began to emerge in the later 1980s and early 1990s was an apparently more coherent view of local government linked to notions of empowerment, decentralisation and consumer choice – the so-called enabling authority. Whether this was anything more than an *ex post* rationalisation of developments is questionable; what is also in question is the extent to which the enabling authority will be able to meet its promises. The length and depth of the 1990s recession may limit the extent to which the private sector is willing and able to be enabled. Then, assuming it can find the resources, the centre may give local government, as the only player in the game, a larger role and greater freedom to pursue local strategies.

# 10 Race, Urban Problems and Urban Initiatives

By the end of the 1980s it had been estimated that non-white people made up just under 5 per cent or 2.6 million, of the UK's total population (Jones, 1993, p. 12). Of these people, about 2.2 million may be described as black or Asian. At the regional level the black and Asian population is unevenly distributed throughout the UK, with the vast majority concentrated in the South-East (including Greater London), the North-West and parts of the Midlands and Yorkshire (Jones, 1993, p. 16). At the subregional level we find a similar unevenness, with most black and Asian people living in urban areas, particularly in the major conurbations of England. Even within urban areas there is a high level of unevenness, with the black and Asian populations being highly concentrated in a small number of inner city areas where they have, on the whole, remained settled since the early 1950s (Jones, 1979; Robinson, 1991). This polarised spatial distribution is by no means accidental and relates to the nature of the employment and housing markets in which black and Asian people found themselves in the post-Second World War period.

On numerous occasions in this book we have referred to the long-term role that race has played in shaping the conception and development of urban initiatives. We gave particular attention to the theme in Chapter 2 in our coverage of the urban policy in the 1950s and 1960s. In this present chapter we bring together material from later years. We argue that, while issues relating to race have often been central to the development of urban initiatives, government, at both central and local levels, has often attempted to disguise this fact. Race has been subsumed as a factor within wider area policies designed to help all disadvantaged groups, black and white alike, within the chosen areas. Such a strategy has enabled the government to distance itself from the charge of using positive discrimination to favour the black population over its white counterpart. This chapter comprises four sections:

- An analysis of the changing ways in which the presence of black and Asian people has been constructed as a 'problem' since 1968.
- An examination of the interrelationship of race and urban initiatives.
- A consideration of the role of race in structuring the activities of urban local government.
- An exploration of two issues particularly pertinent to the conditions under which black people live in the inner cities: employment and housing.

## The construction of the race problem

Skin colour, spatial concentration and the latent conflict potential within the labour and housing markets made the black and Asian population easy targets for a widespread racism which emerged most overtly during the 1970s. We can trace this racism to the legacy of Empire; the potent image of the European taking civilisation and democracy to the 'unenlightened' parts of the globe created a widespread belief in the superiority of white races and the inferiority of black and Asian people. When the first post-war black and Asian immigrants arrived in the UK they faced a situation of racial stereotyping which was widespread throughout all levels of British society. This popular imagery was, however, only one side of the story. The government was also heavily involved in the construction of race as an official 'problem' in Britain.

As we saw in Chapter 2, the 1950s and early 1960s saw a racialisation of British politics in which the construction of race as a problem progressively intensified (Miles, 1990; Solomos, 1989, ch. 3). This racialisation was temporally and spatially uneven (Lunn, 1989) but, by the time of the 'race riots' of Notting Hill and Nottingham in 1958, it had permeated government thinking to the extent that political comment on the riots saw them as almost a natural response on the part of white people to an alien threat. As Miles (1984, p. 255) has noted, 'the 1958 riots were politically defined as being a consequence of New Commonwealth migration, a conceptualisation that was mediated through the idea of "race"'.

The immediate effect of racialisation and the 1958 riots was to clear the way for the Conservative government, despite its commitment to the notion of a Commonwealth of black, Asian and white equals, to take action to limit and control immigration into the UK and tie it to the needs of the economy via the Commonwealth Immigration Act, 1962. This Act had an important catalytic effect on the racialisation of British politics. As Sivanandan (1976, p. 358) has noted, 'The basic intention of the government, one might say, was to anchor in legislation an institutionalised system of discrimination against foreign labour, but because that labour happened to be black, it ended up by institutionalising racism itself'.

When Labour came to power in 1964 it supplemented the immigration-orientated 1962 Act with the Race Relations Act, 1965, which it represented as an attack upon racial discrimination. The 1965 Act continued the racialisation process and was, at the same time, severely limited. It dealt only with direct forms of discrimination, lacked adequate means of enforcement and excluded housing and employment. It was also posited on the basis that there was indeed a *numbers problem*: a Labour MP, Roy Hattersley, argued in the Commons that 'Integration without control is impossible, but control without integration is indefensible' (quoted in Solomos, 1989, p. 73). Control of immigration and action to counter discriminatory practices were thus seen as two sides of the same coin. However, the leadership of both the Labour and the Conservative parties were well aware that control was the issue which was popular with sectors of the key white working-class electorate. While neither party in leadership was to openly exploit race (at least until Mrs Thatcher in 1978 – see Rich, 1986), they could not ignore its electoral implications.

Race surfaced once again as a major political issue in 1968 (see Chapter 3). An influx into the UK of East African Asians with British citizenship appeared imminent. Enoch Powell dramatised the situation as a threat, playing upon white fears of an influx of an 'alien cultural horde' which might subvert Britain's place in the world, culture, sense of national identity and cohesion. He suggested that, as a result, tensions would be created which would unleash 'foaming rivers of blood' within British society (see Rich, 1986). At the same time, as Smith (1993, pp. 133–4) has noted, Powell also linked spatial location with race; he argued that great swathes of Britain's cities were in danger of being transformed into 'alien territory'. This confirmed a link between race and the inner city and effectively legitimised the use of race as a tool for the mobilisation of the electorate in respectable British political discourse.

Anti-discrimination legislation in the late 1960s clearly exhibited the notion of race as a problem. Attempts to assist the assimilation of immigrants into the host population via mechanisms such as providing extra English teachers for the children of immigrants under Section 11 of the Local Government Act, 1966, reflected a view that black and Asian children constituted a problem, and a concern that the white population should not feel threatened. Civil servants, parents and some educationalists were worried that, once the number of immigrant children in a school went above a certain level, white children would suffer some unspecified disadvantage. A Department of Education and Science Circular (DES 7/65) argued that:

> It is inevitable that, as the proportion of immigrant children in a class or school increases, the problems will become more difficult to solve, and the chances of assimilation more remote . . . Experience suggests . . . that . . . up to one-fifth of immigrant children in any group fit in with reasonable ease, but that if the proportion goes over one-third . . . serious strains arise . . . It will be helpful if the parents of non-immigrant children can see that practical measures have been taken to deal with the problems in the school, and that the progress of their own children is not being restricted by the undue preoccupation of the teaching staff with the linguistic and other difficulties of immigrant children.

Attempts were made by Labour governments to widen anti-discrimination legislation through the provisions of the Race Relations Acts of 1968 and 1976 but the emphasis remained on the need to control ever more strictly black and Asian immigration. This led to the passing of the Immigration Act, 1971 and the Nationality Act, 1981. This emphasis should be seen in the context of the rise of the National Front (NF) and other extreme right wing political organisations during the 1970s. Certain sections of the Conservatives' electorate defected to these overtly racist organisations, and in the mid-1970s the NF achieved a degree of success in local elections. It appeared that their presence might affect the Conservative vote in a number of marginal parliamentary constituencies and, in response, Margaret Thatcher appealed directly to fears that an alien (black and Asian) culture was threatening to 'swamp' the traditions and rights of the indigenous white population. While not overtly supporting policies such as repatriation, she did little to counter such ideas. Her actions won back successfully part of the Conservative electorate and gave her the personal support of key sections of the Party's neo-conservative right wing.

It is questionable to what extent this neo-conservative rhetoric on race was actually translated into practice during the 1980s (for differing views see Gordon (1989) and Mitchell and Russell (1989)). While immigration controls were tightened during the 1980s it is arguable that the issue was to a certain extent depoliticised. Control became part of the conventional wisdom and thus became a largely administrative issue. As a political issue, race politics switched more to questions of urban unrest; the 'numbers problem' remained but was given a supplementary construction as a *law and order threat* with black and (to a far lesser extent) Asian people being seen as the enemy within. Race also became ensnared in Conservative opposition to local government and state intervention; the attempts of 'loony left' local authorities to 'force' anti-racist policies upon an innocent and unsuspecting white population attracted particular disapproval.

## Urban initiatives and race since 1968

We have already seen how a particular context was created which defined the black and Asian presence in Britain as problematic and how, on the one hand, government used this to justify tighter immigration controls while, on the other, they argued that such controls should be accompanied by efforts to improve the lot of existing black and Asian communities. These attempts were accompanied by an official concern that the white population should not feel that black and Asian people were getting special treatment. We shall now examine the extent to which these contradictory tendencies influenced attempts through urban initiatives to counter race-based disadvantage in inner cities.

### *The Urban Programme and the Community Development Project*

The Urban Programme and the Community Development Project were the first genuinely urban initiatives and emerged in the later

1960s partly as a response to Powell's speeches, but also because of a fear that the racially-linked violence which some US cities experienced at the time might be repeated in Britain. They were introduced in a climate of political consensus over the necessity for immigration control. In the Parliamentary debates over the Urban Programme both the then Home Secretary, James Callaghan, and his opposite number on the Conservative side, Quentin Hogg (later to become Lord Hailsham), were at pains to stress the need 'to control the inflow of immigrants' (Hansard, vol. 768, 22.7.68, col. 42). However, there was also a prior acknowledgement 'that all our citizens have an equal opportunity in life' (ibid., col. 41). This conflict was typical of subsequent urban initiatives and clearly indicates the subliminal presence of race as a factor in structuring the development of programmes.

Both government and Opposition were at pains to play down this role. They sought to develop general urban initiatives which would catch within their nets the disadvantaged black and Asian communities without appearing to specifically favour them over their white counterparts. As Young (1983, p. 289) has noted: 'the Urban Programme was born to ambiguity'. Area-based policies were the perfect solution to the race dilemma; the hope was that, if areas contained significant numbers of black and Asian people, then they too would benefit from any additional resources directed towards the area.

In practice, despite the high concentrations of black and Asian people in inner areas, many actually lived outside declared areas. Moreover, the presence of immigrants was only one of a number of factors determining an area's qualification for the allocation of additional resources. As a review of the traditional elements of the Urban Programme (see Chapter 6) noted:

> Assisting ethnic minorities has been an implicit objective of the Urban Programme since its inception. However, it is only since 1974 . . . that this aspect has been consistently and explicitly publicised. Two types of project may be said to be meeting this objective: schemes which are aimed directly at ethnic minorities and others which are directed at a wider group but have a high proportion of ethnic minorities among their clients. (Quoted in Stewart and Whitting, 1983, p. 14)

Although, as the 1965 and 1968 Race Relations Acts implicitly recognised, more positive action was justified in order to counter racial discrimination, no government spokesperson seems to have been willing to make such an argument. What therefore occurred as regards race was a form of benign neglect; the government hoped that black and Asian people would benefit from the allocation of additional resources, but were not prepared to take any action which would ensure that they received such benefits.

A more sinister view is advanced by Bridges (1975 and 1981/2). He argues that early (and subsequent) urban initiatives were characterised by two functions. First, their location in the Home Office, which he describes as the 'Ministry of Internal Security', signified that they were primarily part of a concern with the maintenance of law and order. Second, they represented a move from indirect forms of control to a more direct attempt at managing the black and Asian populations. While it would be unwise to accept these simplistic arguments at face value, particularly as it was the DoE which actually became the lead department, it is equally unwise to dismiss them out of hand. As we have already argued, one of the functions of inner-city policy is a form of area crisis management (Pickvance, 1990) and initiatives may function as a form of conflict displacement. Thus, in the context of race, Stewart and Whitting (1983, p. 18) have argued that:

> The major concerns felt by ethnic minorities are about racism, discrimination, and relations with the police. Thus for many groups the Urban Programme, if understood at all, is at best a source of funds for useful community based activity and at worst a diversionary smokescreen to divert attention from the absence of a serious commitment to a multi-racial society.

### The 1977 White Paper

Shankland *et al.* (1977, p. 70) quote an earlier letter from the then Secretary of State for the Environment, Peter Walker, arguing for the need to discover the extent of multiple deprivation suffered by Britain's black and Asian populations. This curiosity was one of the background factors that eventually produced the 1977 White Paper

(HMSO, 1977). Yet race had only a walk-on part in the White Paper. Having identified racial discrimination as a key component of the 'urban problem', the White Paper went on to state:

> However, the attack on the specific problem of racial discrimination and the resultant disadvantages must be primarily through the new anti-discrimination legislation and the work of the Commission for Racial Equality. (HMSO, 1977, p. 4)

In the space of a few lines the issue of racial discrimination was introduced and passed on. It may be, as we noted in Chapter 4, that, as one of the possible reasons for this urban initiative was to win back and consolidate Labour's inner city electorate, the government foresaw electoral problems if it were to be seen to be overtly favouring black and Asian people in the inner city.

The anti-discrimination legislation referred to in the White Paper was the Race Relations Act, 1976. Young and Connelly (1981) note that central government failed to offer a vigorous lead regarding the implementation of this Act and left a great deal of discretion to local authorities. The Commission for Racial Equality, for its part, lacked both the powers and the resources to pursue anti-discriminatory activities. It also lacked the power to ensure that urban initiatives fully took into account the needs of black and Asian communities, and it could not force such considerations on to programmes run by central departments and local authorities. Rex (1982) notes that the Commission's concerns as regards urban initiatives were simply to ensure that ethnic minorities got their share rather than that the overall goals of policy took into account the plight of such minorities.

Rex (1981 and 1982) has also argued that the White Paper was inherently racist in that it failed to consider the effects of its proposed solutions to the inner-city problem upon the black and Asian communities living there. As regards the issue of race, the 1977 White Paper, rather than constituting a watershed, may therefore best be described as more of the same. Indeed, in some ways it represented an even more thoroughgoing marginalisation of race. This was most clearly seen when the department most closely concerned with race issues, the Home Office, was not allocated a presence at local level on the Partnership Committees established in the wake of the Inner Urban Areas Act, 1978.

*Race and post-1979 urban initiatives*

As we have already documented, the 1979 Thatcher government was hostile to the kinds of intervention envisaged by the 1977 White Paper. Indeed, under the new Conservative administration, the very idea of the state intervening specifically to direct economic development to urban areas and discriminate positively to assist black and Asian communities was ruled out by a combination of neo-liberal theory (the supremacy of the market and the need to treat individuals identically), and the hostility of key sectors of the Conservative electorate to Britain's black and Asian population.

*The Urban Programme*
During the 1980s the role of the Urban Programme in its various forms was reviewed and the emphasis switched to economic and environmental capital projects. This had a particularly severe effect upon the voluntary sector ventures which constituted the majority of the projects benefiting black and Asian communities (Harrison, 1989). Had it not been for the urban unrest of 1980 and 1981 it is highly likely that the Programme would have experienced severe cuts and would also have been more rigorously restructured (Young, 1983, pp. 291–2). In the event, the urban unrest delayed the restructuring and, in the two financial years following the unrest, spending actually increased. The further restructuring eventually occurred in 1985 and was accompanied by a further marginalisation of projects benefiting the black and Asian communities. As Munt (1991, p. 190) has argued:

> Black projects appear to have been disproportionately affected, by both the preference for economic schemes and a marked reduction in available revenue and, unlike the non-statutory sector in total, have not retained the percentage of approved UP expenditure.

The setting up of the Scarman Inquiry after the 1981 unrest, and the fact that the Programme was not restructured and cutback until 1985 can be seen either as an attempt by the government to meet some of the needs of the black and Asian communities or as a deliberate ploy to buy time as the government prepared itself to deal more efficiently with outbreaks of urban unrest. Solomos (1988, p. 209) has argued strongly for the second position:

> The promise of reform has been used as a symbolic political gesture to indicate official concern for the problems of the poor, youth unemployment, the racially disadvantaged or those living in depressed inner city areas. At the same time the strengthening of the police, both in terms of resources and powers, has been pushed through apace on the premise that a strong stance on law and order will create conditions in which violent disturbances are less likely to occur.

Some support for this analysis can be drawn from a consideration of the impact of the second, 1985, round of urban unrest. In contrast to 1980/81, the second round of urban unrest did little to halt the restructuring of the Urban Programme. This difference reflects a changing definition of the problem black and Asian communities. Scarman (1981), while refusing to acknowledge the existence of institutional racism, argued that the 1981 unrest had its roots in sustained economic and social disadvantages suffered by the black and Asian communities and aggravated by hostile policing methods. The 1985 unrest, on the other hand, did not bring forth any similar type of enquiry and the government defined it in terms of the activities of 'criminal minorities'. Attempts were made to define the unrest as the result of (black) drug dealers maintaining 'no-go areas' in which they could pursue their trade without fear of police intervention. Sections of the black community were effectively criminalised. By doing this government was able to deflect attention away from the root causes of unrest (Benyon and Solomos, 1990). As Solomos (1988, p. 187) has argued, these arguments were useful for the government because:

> First, they helped to focus attention on the supposed character-istics of inner city areas and their residents without looking at the history of how such areas had developed and the role of political and economic forces in the creation of 'ghetto' areas. Second they helped to reassure society at large that violence was the product of aberrant conditions in the inner city areas with a particular type of inhabitant, in other words the riots were 'atypical departures from a political process that is peaceful and rational'.

Reviewing experience of the UP and its effects on ethnic minorities in the 1980s Harrison (1989, p. 61) concluded:

> The preoccupations of DoE monitoring reflect priorities in policy. The relative lack of development of realistic measures of benefits for ethnic minorities suggests that ministers are little concerned with this aspect of the Urban Programme. After all, ethnic minorities represent only one target of the Programme, and at present there may be little political support for emphasising them.

*Other initiatives*

If we look at the other major initiatives which characterised the 1980s, the downgrading and marginalisation of social issues pointed out in Chapters 5–7, had clear consequences for the race issue. If these developments are examined there is little evidence of even marginal concern with race. Urban Development Corporations, Enterprise Zones, the various inner-city grants and property-led regeneration in general paid little or no attention to race or any other social issue (Munt, 1991).

The situation in Liverpool provides ample illustration. The Gifford Inquiry (1989) pointed out that Liverpool 8 (Toxteth), with its largely black community and high rates of unemployment, had largely been ignored by the Merseyside Development Corporation. Similarly, when Michael Heseltine, the then Secretary of State at the DoE, set up the Merseyside Task Force in response to the 1981 unrest, the concerns and needs of the black community received little or no attention (Ben-Tovim, 1988). Gifford (1989, p. 51) argued that all the initiatives, and the organisations which administered them on Merseyside:

> failed to develop ... adequate targeting mechanisms which ensures that main programmes and resources are bent towards the Black population. By and large the Black community has been excluded from access to these bodies.

Where the 'flagship' style projects typical of property-led development did take place, it was argued that 'the showpieces of the post-1981 period, the Liverpool Garden Festival and the Albert Dock development, had been irrelevant to the Black community although happening on its door-step.

Thus the assumption that trickle-down was the best way to aid deprived urban communities proved misplaced for the black and Asian communities (see Munt, 1991). The refusal to direct development and the by-products of development (e.g. jobs and housing) affected them particularly badly, often intensifying existing forms of discrimination.

## Race and urban local government

In the area where local government and 'urban policy' meet, a great deal is left to the discretion of the local authority with regard to race matters. Thus very wide variations in practice and attitude are found. The main instrument for action has been Section 11 of the Local Government Act, 1966 (see above and Chapter 2). Evidence suggests that some local authorities have remained unaware of the existence of Section 11 funds, and others have failed to direct their Section 11 monies towards black and Asian groups, preferring instead to supplement their mainstream programmes (Ben-Tovim, 1986; Cross *et al.*, 1988). Authorities which did take up Section 11 funds and direct them at black and Asian populations often saw their actions as evidence of an adequate commitment to race issues and failed to take further supplementary action; mainstream programmes were left untouched to run as before.

Some local authorities did go further. The development of positive *equal opportunities policies* was pursued by several councils. These local authorities were frequently attacked by both central government and the press, arguing that the white population was suffering as a result of discriminatory policies. A number of *causes célèbres* occurred, of which perhaps the most famous was the Honeyford case regarding equality of opportunity in education in Bradford. As Cross *et al.* (1988) point out, such reassessments of mainstream programmes were rare because it was precisely such attempts that were likely to come under attack from national politicians and press. This specific hostility, and the wider hostile climate in which local government found itself in the 1980s, were potent obstacles to the development of thoroughgoing equal opportunities policies.

The catalyst for the development of equal opportunities policies was the Race Relations Act, 1976. This gave local government the responsibility for ensuring that it pursued employment practices which were non-discriminatory, and the general task of promoting 'harmonious race relations' (see Young and Connelly, 1981, pp. 46–7, for a summary of these responsibilities; for an overview see Solomos and Ball, 1990). More controversially, some authorities also developed *anti-racist policies*. It is difficult to distinguish clearly between the two types of policy but, broadly speaking, equal opportunities policy entailed ensuring that no unlawful discrimination occurred, while anti-racist policy entailed more positive action to assist ethnic minorities.

The local authorities which began to develop equal opportunities policies in the wake of the 1976 Act were given very little guidance and support from the Home Office. They had a great deal of discretion in their interpretation of the law and were left largely to their own devices (Young and Connelly, 1981). When the Conservatives came to power in 1979 the rhetoric which accompanied their election suggested that it was unlikely they would be sympathetic to such policies. Indeed, many feared that they would abolish the Commission for Racial Equality and significantly reduce what little resources were directed towards equal opportunities. In the event, outright abolition did not occur but, as Solomos (1991a) notes, negative Conservative attitudes towards public expenditure and local government structurally constrained the context in which equal opportunities policies were developed.

In the later 1970s, demands for equality of opportunity were increasingly articulated through the election of black and Asian councillors in urban local authorities. Black and Asian communities demanded access to decision-making processes. Anwar (1990) has suggested, that what was granted was largely tokenistic and political parties, including the Labour Party, for which most black and Asian people vote (Layton-Henry, 1990), were unwilling to apply equal opportunities policies to themselves and examine their own internal structures and practices. This led to the development of black and Asian sections in the Labour Party in an attempt to move the concerns of black and Asian people to the centre of the party's policy agenda. These largely failed; the Labour leadership saw such activities as being electorally counterproductive.

Electoral pragmatism was, in fact, perhaps the key factor determining the salience of equal opportunities on the race policy agenda of the mid-1980s. Mitchell and Russell (1989) suggest that, while the neo-conservative wing of the New Right did not force many of their views on to the policy agenda, they undoubtedly blocked the development of certain types of policy – including the more positive variety of equal opportunities policy, anti-racist policy. Such initiatives were subjected to the most virulent attacks in the national and local media: Lewis (1988) described anti-racism as a 'mania', treating it as if it were a virulent virus which threatened to infect British society. Gordon (1990) and Gilroy (1990) provide overviews of these attacks and their effects. As a result of this opposition a number of authorities backed away from anti-racist policy and even equal opportunities policy.

In a more direct sense the 1980s saw reductions in the scope for local authorities to act for equal opportunities for black and Asian people. The Local Government Act, 1988, made it very difficult for them to use their purchasing and contracting-roles to promote equal opportunities policies in the private sector (Ball and Solomos, 1990). In terms of internal employment policies Young and Connelly (1981) note that equal opportunities had an insignificant impact, being subordinated to the wider employment and organisational needs of the local authority and diluted through fear of alienating white workers and unsettling the working routines of the authority. Ouseley (1984, 1990) has argued forcefully that, in consequence of all these factors, equal opportunities policies remained marginal to the power structures and decision-making centres of local authorities. In some authorities individual officers with responsibility for race relations were appointed, but they all too often found themselves isolated, both physically and in terms of proximity to decision-making, from the rest of the authority. As a result, their energies were diverted into dealing with relatively minor issues rather than forcing the local authority to examine the extent to which discriminatory practices were institutionalised within its own organisational structures, culture and mode of operation.

What should be clear from this brief coverage is that equal opportunities policies had, in real terms, a diminishing impact during the 1980s. While this partly relates to the context in which local government has found itself operating, we should not ignore the internal resistance to equal opportunities; local authorities themselves proved resistant to change and central government gave little in the way of positive guidance. This contrasts sharply with other situations, such as council-house sales, where pressures were placed on local authorities to conform with legislation, and central government gave a firm lead. One of the central problems facing the development of equal opportunities policies for black and Asian inner city residents has therefore been a lack of political will on the part of central government, perhaps best illustrated by the centre's unwillingness to develop its own equal opportunities policy.

## Employment

In Chapter 6 we noted the employment problems facing inner-city workers in general. We saw that there were few employment initiatives aimed specifically at the inner-city unemployed. There have been none targeted specifically at the black and Asian unemployed. During the 1950s and 1960s discriminatory practices forced black and Asian workers into particular industries and occupations. These industries were generally in the manufacturing sector and located in the inner city. They were particularly hard-hit by recession because they were often both outdated and badly located; they were hit by the twin processes of deindustrialisation and the urban–rural shift (Newnham, 1986; Brown, 1992). As a result, throughout the 1980s, there were very high rates of black and Asian unemployment in the inner cities (Benyon, 1984; Newnham, 1986).

Newnham (1986) points out that, even taking location and industrial sector into account, black and Asian unemployment is much higher than would normally be expected. In economic downturns black and Asian workers' unemployment has increased more rapidly than their white counterparts, reflecting the existence of a highly segmented labour market in which black and Asian workers, apart from occupying low-paid and low-status jobs, are also concentrated in the peripheral sector where jobs are easily shed. As Brown (1992, p. 52) notes, there is 'a high degree of racial segregation in the labour market'. Taken together, these factors suggest that there is systematic employer-based racial discrimination in the British labour market.

Given the higher propensity of black and Asian workers than their white counterparts to join trade unions, it might have been expected that the trade unions would have offered some defence against discrimination. However, Phizacklea and Miles (1992) point to further racism within the trade unions. Trade unions have been slow to respond to the needs of black and Asian workers, and all too often, when they have taken on board anti-discrimination policies, they have done so in a rhetorical way rather than mounting real attempts to counter discrimination. It would seem that unions share with employers many of the preconceptions regarding black and Asian workers; they too fear the white backlash.

Whilst these points are extremely disturbing in themselves, what is perhaps even more disquieting is that racial discrimination in employment has been documented for some considerable time. In the 1960s Daniel (1968) made it quite clear that black and Asian people were subject to systematic discrimination. Yet, over twenty-five years later, and despite three race relations acts, little seems to have changed (Newnham, 1986; Ohri and Faruqui, 1988). In the later part of the 1970s, and particularly after the urban unrest of 1980/1, the threat to law, order and social stability posed by unemployed and increasingly marginalised 'black youth' found its way on to the policy and political agendas (Solomos, 1988). Something of a moral panic (Hall *et al.*, 1978) led employment and training agencies to turn their attention to black youth.

Studies of employment schemes have suggested that black and Asian people are grossly under-represented on the employer-led training schemes which are most likely to lead to jobs at the end of the training period, and are concentrated on state-led schemes (Solomos, 1986; Wrench, 1987). Solomos (1988) argues that the state-led programmes are more concerned with keeping black and Asian youth off the streets than solving the underlying causes of their unemployment. As we have seen with regard to local and central government, little political will has been invested in the pursuit of equal opportunity employment policies within state organisations, so it was always highly unlikely that the state would intervene to reform the wider labour market. Moreover, the neo-liberalism which dominated government thinking during the 1980s made the possibility of intervention in the inner city labour market, or the wider labour market, extremely unlikely. It would have represented an interference in the operation of the free market, involved deploying the coercive powers of the state, and entailed the unequal treatment of individuals (Mitchell and Russell, 1989, pp. 176–80).

## Housing

As with employment, the existence of widespread racial discrimination in the housing system has been noted for some time (Rex and Moore, 1969; Daniel, 1968). Discriminatory forms have varied according to the tenure concerned but all have had the effect of severely limiting black and Asian people's access to decent living accommodation. Mullins (1989) has suggested that they may be disproportionately represented among the homeless.

Since at least the mid-1960s, but especially since 1979, owner-occupation has been the preferred tenure of successive governments and has been favoured accordingly. Yet as we have already suggested (Chapter 6) it may not be best suited to the requirements and incomes of inner-city residents (Karn *et al.*, 1985). Black and Asian owner-occupiers, in part due to their lower incomes, are disproportionately concentrated in the inner cities and occupy the worst-quality properties. Given low incomes, such owners often have insufficient resources to spend on general upkeep, repairs and improvements. This produces a vicious spiral in which the properties deteriorate rapidly. Moreover, black and Asian communities fail to benefit from the available state resources to aid housing refurbishment, and government has notably failed to develop strategies to reverse this situation (Ratcliffe, 1992).

Such problems have frequently been compounded by further factors. First, black and Asian buyers have been excluded from more conventional forms of housing finance. As Karn *et al.* (1985) and Philips (1987a) have argued, banks and building societies have frequently considered prospective black and Asian purchasers as unsafe lending risks, forcing them to go to non-conventional sources of finance which have increased their overall housing costs. In some cases in the 1960s and 1970s building societies employed a policy of 'redlining', whereby they refused to lend for property purchase in certain inner-city areas; often such areas contained high proportions of black and Asian owners (Ginsburgh, 1992).

Second, Karn *et al.* (1985) have also suggested that inner-city owners in general have not benefited from house price inflation to the same extent as their suburban counterparts. It is likely that, within the inner city, black and Asian owners have benefited even less and have thereby been denied the access to the temporary benefits which accompanied the house price inflation of the late 1980s. Finally, it seems that key gatekeepers in the housing market, notably estate agents, have frequently taken it upon themselves to steer black and Asian purchasers away from white suburban locations and towards predominantly black and Asian inner-city locations. This has assisted in the creation of a segmented market place (Ginsburgh, 1992) and has interacted with other forces to create a high degree of spatial and social polarisation which embodies racial (as well as class) residential segregation.

With regard to access to council housing, the failure of local authorities to respond to the needs of black and Asian people and the existence of systematic discrimination, on both an institutional and an individual level, in the allocation process is well documented (Henderson and Karn, 1984; Jacobs, 1985; Philips, 1987a, 1987b, 1988; Solomos and Singh, 1990; Ginsburgh, 1992). Black and Asian people have found it more difficult to gain access to public housing. When they *have* gained access they have been allocated the worst properties: for example, older flats concentrated on particular run-down estates in inner areas. Discrimination operates at both an individual and an institutional level and, while the former can be countered via anti-discrimination training, the latter is much more difficult to eradicate because it is deeply rooted in organisational structures and cultures which are particularly difficult to change without considerable political will and widespread organisational restructuring (Ouseley, 1990). Even where ostensibly committed authorities have attempted to bring about changes, few have been willing to follow through the implications of race equality polices and counter the racist reactions of the neighbours of black and Asian local authority tenants.

Overall there has been little substantial improvement in the position of black and Asian people within the council housing sector. Nor has owner-occupation been opened up to black and Asian people. In the area of housing, black and Asian people suffer not only from being concentrated in the inner-city but also from systematic discrimination because of race.

**Assessment**

*Theoretical perspectives*

In terms of the major theoretical approaches we outlined in Chapter 1, race has attracted considerable interest and controversy. Pluralist analyses of urban policy freely acknowledge the influence of race but have been unwilling to accept the conspiratorial analyses of authors such as Bridges (1981/2) who see urban initiatives as attempts to control potentially rebellious black urban populations. For pluralists, the marginalisation of race in urban policy is perhaps best understood in terms of Bachrach and Baratz's (1970) analysis of non-decision-making and the mobilisation of bias. Their study examined how the black poor in Baltimore were excluded from the political process. Even when they gained access to the policy-making arena, change was slow and unlikely to produce fundamental transformations in living conditions and life-chances. These conclusions apply equally to the UK, where black access to local political and policy-making processes has been slow, as well as both spatially and organisationally isolated.

New Right analyses of race combine elements of both neo-liberalism and neo-conservatism (e.g. Mishan, 1988a, 1988b; Lewis, 1988). The neo-conservative element is unusually strong and can be strongly linked to the central figure of Enoch Powell, an erstwhile Conservative minister. As Rich (1986, p. 52) notes, Powell linked 'the race and immigration issue . . . to a wider theme of conscious national reassertion in an effort to proclaim control over a national destiny he realised was rapidly passing from the hands of the British political elite'. The supposed effects of an 'alien wedge' on Britain mean multi-culturalism is strongly opposed. Furthermore, race is seen as a law-and-order problem through the threat which black populations ostensibly pose to the indigenous white society. Attempts to counter discrimination are strongly opposed (Savery, 1985; Lewis, 1988) because they affect the freedom of the indigenous population. According to Mishan (1988a, p. 18) racial harmony depends 'upon the characteristics and behaviour of the racial minorities themselves'.

As regards race and urban initiatives, neo-conservatives are mainly concerned with maintaining order and authority. The police will be expected to enforce law and order in inner cities and prevent the growth of no-go areas. Grants to community centres or for environmental improvements will be admissible in this process of creating an acceptance of political authority among black groups. But there is less likely to be sympathy for projects which preserve black culture and language, as this will be seen as hindering assimilation into the host community.

Neo-liberals also oppose cultural projects and additionally oppose anti-discrimination activity. The latter treats similar individuals in an inequitable manner. The threat to liberty is compounded because it is the state which usually carries out and enforces such programmes. As Mishan (1988b, p. 6) points out with regard to anti-discrimination policies, 'their implementation entails coercion and, to that extent at least, may be said to violate the canons of traditional libertarian doctrine'. Neo-liberals prefer to allow the market to counteract discrimination based on race. If an employer chooses not to employ black people, he/she will have a reduced pool of labour from which to draw, labour costs will increase and profits fall; 'the great virtue of . . . [the free market] is that it is colour-blind' (Lewis, 1988, p. 14). From this perspective, policies which discriminate in favour of urban areas in general are illegitimate and anti-discrimination policies designed to assist racial minorities doubly so.

Marxist analyses are, as we have noted, primarily concerned with analysing the economic tendencies of development within capitalism and the concept of class. Race has tended to be a secondary factor, subsumed within the notion of the 'reserve army of labour'. A key aspect of this type of analysis has been the role of the state and trade unions in using race to create divisions within the working class, thereby producing a more complex segmentation within urban labour markets (Harvey, 1989a, ch. 5). As a consequence of this generalised and sparse analysis, Marxist analyses of urban policy in Britain have generally had very little to say specifically about the issue of race. Phizacklea and Miles (1980) note the economic causality of the inner-city problem and how race has become socially constructed as part of this problem and assisted in confining the problem to specific spatial locations.

*Policy coherence*

As can be seen from Table 10.1 there has been little coherence in the relationship of race to urban policy. In keeping with the generally

**TABLE 10.1   Race and urban policy: an assessment**

| | Race and Urban Policy |
|---|---|
| Conception of 'urban' | Vague; area of dereliction in inner city; locus of unrest and 'deviant groups'; a political/social issue |
| Theoretical approach | No explicit theoretical approach; racism justified by assumed unreconcilable cultural differences |
| Nature of problem | 'Numbers problem', threat to British culture, to 'white' jobs, houses and education – danger of 'swamping'; law and order problem; concentrated in inner-city locations |
| Explanation | Influx of 'alien wedge' undermining British (white) society, particularly in inner cities |
| Aim of policy | Primary stress on control of numbers and control of potential unrest; secondary stress on reducing racial discrimination, although a refusal to acknowledge institutionalised discrimination |
| Mechanisms | Control mainly exercised via immigration laws/police; anti-discrimination actions mainly via public sector, particularly local government and initiatives such as UP |
| Resourcing | For control elements reasonably well financed; for anti-discrimination poor and unplanned, subject to wider cuts in local government and UP |
| Management | Immigration control highly centralised, policing less so; anti-discrimination activities largely marginalised – little strategic management for these |
| Political support | For immigration control and policing strong; often used to mobilise political support. For anti-discrimination actions fleeting: for instance support increased after urban unrest of 1981/8; otherwise marginalised |
| Legislation | Several pieces, e.g. Commonwealth Immigrants Act, 1962; Race Relations Act, 1976, although rarely mentioned in urban legislation, e.g. Inner Urban Areas Act, 1978. |
| Monitoring | Subject to general monitoring of urban initiatives; however, no strategic overview of race and little consideration of impact of wider policies. |

vague conceptualisation of the 'urban' noted in previous chapters, there has been a focus on derelict inner-city locations; this has been conflated with concerns about urban unrest and deviant/inadequate groups. There has usually been a tacit assumption of basic and unreconcilable cultural differences which can only be bridged when the immigrant community accepts the customs and mores of the host community. As a result, theory, problem definition and explanation have all largely been defined in terms of numbers; areas of British cities are considered to be in 'danger' of being transformed into enclaves of the Indian sub-continent, Africa or the Caribbean. There has been an increasing tendency to link this problem construction to law-and-order issues (Solomos, 1988).

As regards policy aims, mechanisms of operation, resourcing and management, the primary concern has been control and policing. Poorly-funded urban initiatives have rarely explicitly addressed issues of race. As we saw with the UP (Chapter 3), politicians and civil servants were unwilling to acknowledge that issues of race were central to the programme when it was launched in 1968 and it was not publicly admitted until 1974 that race was one of the factors structuring resource allocation (Stewart and Whitting, 1983). The 1977 White paper, after acknowledging the centrality of racial discrimination to the inner-city problem, then marginalised it. In the 1980s urban initiatives have been even more unwilling to address such issues; only in the wake of urban unrest have policy-makers been prepared to address issues of race and then largely in terms of social control. Bulpitt (1986) argued, correctly, that race has largely been peripheralised to bodies which have neither the powers, the resources, the will or the desire to tackle the problems of racial disadvantage and discrimination. Race was therefore essentially a political tool rather than a central concern of urban policy; it occasioned separate control-orientated legislation rather than an integrated and well-monitored legislative response through urban policy.

## Conclusion

Black and Asian people are highly concentrated within particular regions and urban areas. The origins of this concentration can be traced largely to the housing and employment markets which they generally first entered during the immediate post-Second World War period. Most black and Asian people still live in these original areas of settlement. Unlike their white counterparts they have not usually participated in the drift to the suburbs or the process of counterurbanisation. This would seem to imply powerful and systematic forces operating to retain sociospatial concentration.

We have argued that systematic discrimination provides this force and to illustrate this we have looked briefly at housing and labour markets. More widely, we have pointed to the varying ways in which the presence of black and Asian people in the UK has been constituted as a threat, shattering national unity, denying white people access to resources, and threatening law, order and social stability. This threat has been used to justify immigration control and, at times, intensify and strengthen policing in inner-city areas.

Since the mid-1960s immigration control has been accompanied by proclamations by the government of its intent to do something to improve the plight of black and Asian citizens. These attempts have, at best, been marginal and largely confined to peripheral initiatives. As Ball (1988, p. 18) argued, 'black and Asian communities are being given some crumbs from the table which keeps them busy and quiet; but . . . within the present structure there is no real potential for fundamental change'. Governments have been unwilling to declare that these marginal programmes are specifically directed at black and Asian populations for fear of offending their white electorates. This has posed particular problems for the Labour party who require black, Asian and white votes to win certain inner-city seats. The Conservatives, on the other hand, have been less concerned with electoral niceties because, on the whole, to win seats they have not required black and Asian votes, and the majority of their voters would be opposed to such actions. Only in situations where they have felt the rule of law and order to be challenged, as in the case of the urban unrest of the 1980s, have they given specific notice to race issues.

In such a context it is clear that urban initiatives have been used to give the appearance of doing something, to offer rewards to those who conform, and also to open cracks within the black and Asian communities, thereby marginalising lawless elements and directing attention away from the wider, more deeply-rooted causes of urban unrest and poverty among the black and Asian communities. By portraying urban unrest as a predominantly black and Asian phenomenon, which it clearly was not (Benyon, 1985), they have been able, coincidentally, to reinforce the stereotyping of black and Asian people as an alien presence within the inner-city.

# 11 Conclusion

This book has been centrally concerned with British urban policy. In this concluding chapter our first task will be to provide a brief but necessary acknowledgement that urban policy in Britain is not solely of British origin. We shall review the European Community's role in assisting urban regeneration, a role which, depending on parliamentary decisions in Britain, may increase towards the year 2000. The subsequent sections of the chapter will look back over the material we have covered. We shall reflect upon the utility of pluralist, Marxist and New Right perspectives for understanding urban policy. Finally, using the general policy analysis framework outlined in Chapter 1, we will offer an overall assessment of urban policy in the post-1945 period.

## The European dimension to urban regeneration

From its inception, the European Community (EC) has been concerned with the creation of a free market within which member states can compete on an equal footing. One of the central elements in the creation of an EC-wide free market was the removal of national or local forms of 'protectionism' by which less-developed countries protected their markets or richer countries gave too much support to their weaker regions. However, the EC also recognised that inequalities both between and within member states were likely to be exacerbated by the operation of the freemarket. As a result, a form of regional policy emerged and a number of *Structural Funds* were created in order to counteract inequalities and aid affected areas (Harrop, 1992, ch. 6; Hall and van der Wee, 1992). Two structural funds are of particular relevance to urban policy: The European Regional Development Fund (ERDF) and The European Social Fund (ESF).

### The European Regional Development Fund

The ERDF was first established in 1975 and then considerably expanded in 1987, when its funds were increased in the wake of the

Single European Act, 1986. From 1987 to 1992 ERDF expenditure increased from 7 billion to 14 billion ECU (Harrop, 1992, p. 149). This increase reflected a recognition of the need to alleviate the impact of the Single European Market on weak regions, declining industries and their workers. As part of this increase, expenditure became more focused and planned.

The six principle targets of ERDF expenditure are: under-developed regions, regions in industrial decline, long-term unemployment, youth unemployment, the adaptation of agricultural structures, and the development of rural areas (*Journal of Regional Policy*, 1992, pp. 559–60). For urban policy, the primary concern is with regions in industrial decline. In recent years the UK has been one of the major beneficiaries of assistance under this heading (*Journal of Regional Policy*, 1992, p. 559, table A); in 1992/3 Britain's share of the ERDF was £958m (*Guardian*, 15.2.93).

ERDF industrial decline funding has recently been expanded to include adjacent areas such as: 'urban communities with an unemployment rate at least 50% above the Community average which have recorded a substantial fall in industrial employment' *Journal of Regional Policy*, 1992, p. 561). However, it is intended to complement national regional expenditures; it is meant to be in addition to, rather than a replacement for, national regional expenditure. This stance has been enforced rigorously' in recent years and there has been a move away from the funding of individual projects towards rolling multi-year programmes which are part of structural changes that will facilitate a region's participation in the free market. Furthermore, EC regional funds are small when compared to national regional expenditure. As Brunskill (1990, p. 23) has noted: EC funding can be expected to have no more than a marginal effect on Britain's economic problems, but it does however act as a catalyst to funding from other sources'.

*The European Social Fund*

The ESF is not concerned with social policy as traditionally understood in the UK; it does not directly tackle poverty and income redistribution. It focuses on labour market issues and, in particular, on increasing 'the occupational and geographical mobility of workers in the Community' (Molle, 1990, p. 434).

Once again, such expenditures are intended to make the free market operate more efficiently and effectively. As a side effect, they may ameliorate the consequences of industrial decline and unemployment but, like the ERDF, they are 'supply-side' measures which were not designed to compensate or protect regions and workers from the consequences of their uncompetitive industries and infrastructure. The aim is to help people adjust to new circumstances and to become genuinely competitive. Given this, it is almost inevitable, particularly since Greece and Portugal joined the EC, that the greater part of the ESF has been directed towards poorer, less-developed 'southern' countries.

*The UK*

As with so many other aspects of the EC, the ERDF and ESF have been viewed rather cautiously from within the UK. As a result, Britain has been somewhat slow to take advantage of the opportunities offered by the funds. Moreover, the 'supply-side' nature of the ERDF and ESF conflict with traditional views of social and regional policy in the UK which have traditionally been concerned to redress/ameliorate inequalities. This situation has been complicated by the fact that during the 1980s the Thatcher governments viewed regional policy *per se* as an interference with the market but, at the same time, saw EC structural funds as a way to replace UK funds. The latter tactic created considerable tension between Brussels and Whitehall.

In recent years the EC has attempted to counter its image as a highly centralised but intrusive body which interferes in the government of individual countries. As part of this strategy there has been an increasingly attempt to have 'maximum regard for local circumstances' (*Journal of Regional Policy*, 1992, p. 578). For regional policy this has meant a 'partnership' between Brussels and national, regional and local governments. However, in the UK:

> the involvement of the central government in taking the lead on drafting and editing plans and programmes was considerably greater than in other countries . . . England, in particular, is distinctive since there are no regional councils or other regional administrations responsible for the planning regions. There is also a lack of experience of Regional Economic Planning compared to

other EC countries. Consequently, the UK Local Authorities were much more junior partners in the planning process than elsewhere. (*Journal of Regional Policy*, 1992, p. 579).

This situation was exacerbated by the tensions which existed between central and local government for much of the 1980s (Chapter 8).

Some authorities, however, did recognise the advantages of going to Europe. Early in the 1980s Birmingham City Council lobbied hard to be declared an Assisted Area (to qualify for UK regional assistance). This was essential to qualify for the ERDF. When Assisted Area status was achieved in 1984 they immediately directed their attention to Brussels and have taken an increasingly pro-active stance ever since, going so far as to actually open an office in Brussels. As Martin and Pearce (1992, p. 500) have noted of Birmingham:

A key feature of . . . the approach was the way in which it [the council] began to look towards the EC Commission as a potential source of funding for economic regeneration leading to a shift from a predominantly national view to an increasingly international perspective on the city's economic problems and their solution.

By 1987 Birmingham had received £78 million from the ERDF and, in 1988, it received a package of £203 milion in aid extending to 1991 and consisting of £128 million from the ERDF, £31 million from the ESF and £44 million in loans (Martin and Pearce, 1992, p. 500).

Birmingham is an example of one of the more active local authorities in the UK as regards the EC. But it and many other authorities have been hampered by their late entry into the 'policy networks' which constitute the ERDF, ESF and associated funds. Many other local authorities have not even begun to tap into these resources and the national government has been rather slow to encourage them, being mainly content to portray Brussels as a 'bureaucratic nightmare' or 'gravy train'. Furthermore, not only has the UK's centralised administrative structure and the absence of a British tradition of regional planning inhibited the participation of subnational government in EC schemes, so too has the national government's attitude to EC funds. In February 1993 it was

reported that the EC commissioner with responsibility for the
~~was withholding~~ almost £1 billion in ERDF aid from Britain
~~till~~ the government demonstrated that EC funds were not being
used to replace domestic expenditures (*Guardian*, 15.2.93). Only
after prolonged negotiation was an agreement between reached
between Brussels and Whitehall.

Although EC funding is small in relative terms and is unlikely to
have a major impact on the scale of the UK's urban and regional
problems it can, therefore, have a significant impact on individual
localities and projects. Indeed, one of the recent features of EC aid
has been to encourage innovative and collaborative regeneration
projects between areas in member states. By the late 1980s central
government had also begun to recognise the benefits that could
accrue to particular areas if a more positive attitude was taken
towards ERDF and ESF funding. Overall, however, we should not
expect the EC to have a major impact on urban regeneration in the
UK: the funds are too small; Britain is relatively rich and thus can
only expect a small percentage share; the UK has been slow to
exploit what opportunities are available and has been late entering
the 'policy networks', British administrative structures and central–
local relations have been unhelpful; and, finally, the funds
themselves are not designed to support urban regeneration as such
– their major concern is with the facilitation of the free market and
the creation of a 'level playing field' within the Community on which
all members can compete as equals.

## Understanding urban policy

During the course of this book we have suggested theoretical
interpretations of the material in each chapter, drawing upon the
three approaches outlined in Chapter 1. In this section we shall offer
an overview of post-war developments from each of the
perspectives.

### Pluralist perspectives

Pluralist interpretations of urban change and policy during the
1950s and 1960s, while valuable, tended to focus purely on group

interaction. As a result, they neglected not only the institutional and organisational context but also the wider structural context within which group interactions occurred. British work in the 1970s bore out this deficiency (Simmie, 1974; Newton, 1976): certain groups were systematically excluded from the decision-making process and others given privileged access. Relevant theoretical constructs were non-decision making and bias mobilisation (Bachrach and Baratz, 1970) and symbolism (Edelman, 1977). These raised crucial issues concerning power, decision-making and the means utilised by key groups to marginalise certain issues and groups.

Such neglected issues were of particular importance during the 1950s and 1960s. New towns were being established and major urban redevelopment schemes were taking place but affected populations were rarely consulted or listened to. Whole communities were dispersed throughout cities or to estates beyond the green belt without considering the effects on family and kinship (Young and Wilmott, 1962). Developments seemed to owe more to the conceptions of councillors and professional groups (e.g. planners and architects). They effectively structured access to the decision-making process and thus outcomes (Dunleavy, 1981b; Atkinson, 1989). Citizen participation was only marginal. It was restricted to commenting on already made plans and offering suggestions for minor alterations. Agendas had been well and truly set; participation was a 'symbolic' act. It integrated the governed into the decision-making process, thereby gaining their consent, but was restricted to details of minor matters.

The abandonment of strategies of wholesale urban redevelopment was not primarily as a result of pressures from those affected. This indicates a practical limitation of pluralist theory. Instead, by the late 1960s, the enormous costs involved in redevelopment were becoming all too clear to the government; the policy shift was a consequence of financial necessity. It coincided with the 'discovery of the urban problem' and resulted in the emergence of area-based policies such as the UP, CDPs and Inner Area Studies. Pluralists were able to explain these sequences of events by taking a more critical focus on the decision-making process. Lindblom (1977) suggested that the state was not some neutral arbiter and that some groups (e.g. business) had privileged access to the decision-making process. This perspective, 'neo-pluralism', involved something of a *rapprochement* with forms of Marxism.

Simmie's (1981) study of Կ
control in Oxford provides us
*rapprochement*. While acknowleԁ
ments on class and class struggle,
compatible with pluralism. He argues
have privileged access to the state. This
allows him to conclude that:

> [His] analysis illustrates a primarily corporatist power structure ın
> the making of land-use planning decision. In those decisions
> concerned with land used for production purposes, the power
> structure was based on economic conditions of imperfect
> competition. In those decisions concerned primarily with the
> provision of goods and services, the power structure illustrated
> somewhat similar political conditions which were labelled
> imperfect pluralism. (Simmie, 1981, p. 306)

Extending this perspective to urban development more generally
would indicate that key economic groups (e.g. property developers,
building firms, investment institutions) play a central role in
structuring the (re)development process. Other groups (e.g. local
residents) contribute to 'imperfect pressure group politics', and on
occasion win out (e.g through 'popular planning', see Chapter 8),
but even during the 1970s their influence was marginal.

During the 1980s 'imperfect pluralism' appeared to become even
more imperfect. Successive Conservative administrations attempted
to exclude previously incorporated parts of the political process, in
particular local government. They gave priority to the interests of
developers and builders by creating organisations, such as UDCs,
which marginalised or bypassed those they wished to exclude.
Pluralist theory required further modification. Work on policy
networks (Rhodes, 1988) offered stimulating possibilities: inter-
governmental networks in some cases facilitated policy-making and
in others constrained it. Rhodes (1988) pointed out that urban
policy threatened too many already well-established policy networks
and, as a result, was never able to establish a policy network of its
own (this point is equally applicable to the 1977–9 Labour
government urban initiative).

From a current pluralist perspective the relative ineffectiveness of
urban policy may thus be seen in part as a result of the failure to

establish a policy network which could secure the financial and political commitment concomitant with the scale of the problem. At the same time, developments during the 1980s would also seem to support Lindblom's (1977, p. 172) argument that: 'in any private enterprise system, a large category of major decisions is turned over to businessmen . . . They are taken off the agenda of government'. Pluralism can therefore contribute usefully to the understanding of urban policy, particularly when it comes to understanding inter-group and inter-organisational relations. Where it is perhaps at its weakest is in understanding the structural origins of power and the limits that are placed upon inter-group and inter-organisational activity. These shortcomings are problematic given the global nature of the forces which have created urban decline and the context within which urban regeneration occurs.

*New Right perspectives*

New Right theory remained marginal to academic and political discourse for much of the post-1945 era. It was only after 1975 that it achieved a degree of prominence. This new prominence should not be attributed to the intrinsic explanatory power of New Right thought; it mainly reflected a sense of disenchantment and frustration with the social democratic consensus and, more importantly, the failure of that consensus to 'deliver the goods'. Thus the New Right 'phoenix' rose out of the ashes of social democracy. Its diagnosis of Britain's problems, urban problems included, can be traced back to restrictions on individual liberty, the rise of collectivism, and the displacement of the free market. The growth of the state is a fundamental aspect of the problem; the solution is to reduce the role of the state to a minimum, thereby enhancing individual liberty and the role of the market, and, at a stroke, resolving society's problems.

The neo-conservatism variant of New Right thought has had little to say about the exact form that regeneration of the inner city areas should take. Its principle concern with such areas has been in terms of the threat which they pose to social order and social and cultural cohesion (Chapter 10). Race has played a significant role in creating such threats. The concept of the 'underclass' has also (re)surfaced in a variety of neo-conservative discourses, stressing the threat which displaced and marginalised groups pose to bourgeois social institutions. Neo-conservatives have been concerned to contain such problems through a mixture of law and order and assimilation policies. In general there have been few specific policy suggestions other than to lament the decline of traditional working-class communities and families. The post-war redevelopment schemes are blamed for much of the destruction, but so too is the free market; there is an emphasis upon organic change and a distrust of an unrestricted free market with its unpredictable consequences.

Neo-liberals, on the other hand, have been more strident in their assertions that the answer to all problems is an unrestricted free market and a minimal state. Thus the crisis in Britain's inner urban areas derives from the undermining of market processes; Chisholm and Kivell (1987) see the key to urban regeneration as lying in the revival in a free market in land, removing planning controls and greatly reducing the role of local government. Government, both central and local, and the programmes it has initiated are seen as part of the problem. The redevelopment policies of the 1950s and 1960s, and post-war planning policies, were an unwarranted, and ultimately disastrous, interference in the operation of the market and a constraint on individual liberty. The outcomes were forms of redevelopment which no one wanted and the creation of an 'inner city wasteland'.

Many of the urban policies pursued by the Thatcher governments appeared to be attempts to put neo-liberalism into practice. However, as we, and some neo-liberal critics, have noted (Davies and Butler, 1986; Stoney, 1987), these initiatives were not so much the state withdrawing and allowing the free market to operate as the state's role being restructured and the operation of firms under-written by state funds. As Stoney (1987, p. 30) has noted:

> Left to itself, the marketplace has decided what activities are profitable and self-sustaining . . . One wonders how much a vote-catching syndrome has underpinned the EZ, FP and other programmes of development aid which have been tried since 1980. If such a motive has predominated, it has been demonstrably ineffective in many Northern areas, including Merseyside and the North-West.

A fundamentalist neo-liberal would argue that the market, left to its own devices, will produce the best results. Market failure largely derives from the interference, and distorting effects, of state intervention. The pragmatic nature of Thatcherism led it to retreat from fundamentalism in its application of neo-liberalism to urban problems. In consequence, the purity of the solution was affected and, not surprisingly, the urban policies were not the hoped-for complete success; they were insufficiently liberal. As we move through the 1990s John Major's governments seem to be continuing and even enhancing the strategy of pragmatism. The result is unlikely to be an effective urban policy. The long-term crisis of public expenditure which had clearly emerged by the beginning of 1993 and seems likely to set limits on almost everything the state does, means it is unlikely that Major will feel able to reduce state involvement to the extent that the neo-liberals would argue necessary.

*Marxist perspectives*

Marxists have tended to stress the structural causes of urban decline, arguing that uneven development is an inherent aspect of capitalism on a global, national, regional and even city level. Most Marxist analyses have increasingly stressed the global context (Thrift, 1987) and highlighted the difficulties faced by the government at both national and local levels in trying to counter these forces (Cochrane, 1983). So long as capitalism, and thus uneven development, continues, some nations, regions and cities will flourish while others will decline in a never-ending cycle. In this situation capital will seek to take advantage of variations in the costs of production between different spatial locations on a national and international scale (Massey, 1984). The role of the state is to underwrite capital's needs and where necessary to exercise its relative autonomy in order to assure the survival of capitalism. On occasion this may entail social control, or as Pickvance (1990) has termed it 'territorial crisis management'. On a more local scale, Harvey (1989b) has argued that the conditions ushered in by the economic crisis of the 1970s and the rise of neo-liberal regimes have forced cities to adopt a strategy which he terms 'urban entrepreneurialism' in which they compete to attract investment and jobs from globally mobile multinational capital.

The various urban initiatives were thus conceptualised in terms of their relevance for production, reproduction and class struggle. Small area initiatives such as CDPs were seen as an attempt at social control, whereby the behaviour of deviant individuals and communities was rendered compatible with the capitalist work ethic. Marxists dismissed these initiatives as irrelevant (Rees and Lambert, 1985) or as attempts to tinker with the 'problem' without actually acknowledging its true nature or committing commensurate resources. Even the 1977 Labour government's initiative, while recognised as a radical conceptual break with the past, was questioned on the grounds that: 'it should be apparent that we cannot legitimately separate out the fate of the cities from what was happening in the wider economy or from the state's responses to these wider changes' (Rees and Lambert, 1985, p. 142). The strategy followed by the post-1979 Conservative governments *vis-à-vis* cities was seen as being subordinate to a wider strategy aiming to regenerate Britain's national economy (Rees and Lambert, 1985, pp. 156–9). EZs, UDCs and FPs were seen as attempts to reduce government expenditure, as free market experiments and as traditional, albeit highly selective, forms of state intervention designed to underwrite capital accumulation (Shutt, 1984).

Whilst Marxism is particularly strong at analysing structural causes it is at its weakest when applied to processes of decision-making. There is an inevitable tendency to see everything in terms of capital accumulation and the class struggle and reduce local developments to mere reflections of more abstract forces (e.g. Cockburn, 1977). The work of authors such as Simmie (1981) and Rhodes (1988) provide valuable examples of the type of analysis which Marxists have rarely been able to produce.

In overall terms, an assessment of the utility of the different theoretical approaches to the understanding of urban policy would have to acknowledge that each has its merits and demerits. None, on its own, has proved adequately coherent as an explanatory framework. Each has required modification as events have unrolled. We would reject the idea that we can pick and mix the different theories to provide a hybrid wonder theory. Rather, we would contend that there is no single correct theoretical approach from which to begin: each has its strengths and weaknesses and can learn from dialogues with the others.

**Assessing urban policy**

*Conceptualising urban*

No post-1945 government had an adequate conceptualisation of the urban. While recognising the inherent difficulties in defining the urban, it is notable that recent governments have even failed to make significant use of the increasingly sophisticated work on Local Labour Market Areas developed by bodies such as CURDS (see Chapter 1). This work might at least have allowed the government, however imperfectly, to begin to conceptualise the nature of local decline and how it intertwined with and was determined by regional, national and international factors.

In fairness, we should note that our own usage of terms has lacked the consistency we recommend. At various times in this book we have referred to 'urban' at other times 'inner city' problems. This is a reflection of a deep-rooted uncertainty regarding the definition of urban and the spatial location of 'urban problems'. By even talking of 'urban problems' there is a danger of conveying the impression that such 'problems' are found only in urban areas and that their causes are contained within these areas. Such an analysis runs the risk of detaching urban areas and their problems from the society in which they exist and from the wider structural causal mechanisms which have generated these urban problems. There is no easy solution to these issues. Even when adopting the local labour market as the basic unit of conceptualisation we remain aware that this must:

> be seen as historically and geographically contingent . . . [and] in the end contingent upon processes of capital accumulation and the circulation of associated revenues in space and time. (Harvey, 1989a, p. 159).

*Theory*

The development of a coherent theoretical approach to urban problems could conceivably allow a more integrated strategic approach to urban decline. This would undermined the reliance on the area approach so characteristic of many urban initiatives, expose the fact that problems cannot be limited to discrete locations, and require a much greater commitment of resources and political will. For governments, the untheorised, uncoordinated area approach has the advantage of keeping urban problems down to manageable proportions which require only limited amounts of resources, avoid any difficult questions and do not raise the issue of structural reforms to deal with urban problems.

Following Massey (1984) and Harvey (1982, chs 12, 13) we would argue that urban growth and decline are two sides of the same coin, intimately and irrevocably interrelated and underpinned by national and international factors. Consequently the urban policy of a nation state cannot be developed in ignorance of wider structural factors. Furthermore, a national commitment to a particular theoretical orientation cannot be successful when significant subnational forces are opposed or, more importantly, when a governmental fails to commit itself wholeheartedly to the particular approach and its consequences. Thus, while the post-1979 New Right analysis of urban problems had a certain theoretical coherence, notwithstanding its curious amalgam of neo-liberalism and neo-conservatism, it was doomed to failure because the Conservatives were unable to operationalise their strategy without the significant contradiction of state intervention to both 'kick-start' initiatives and ameliorate their effects.

For these reasons we see urban initiatives as symbolic; set up to mitigate the worst excesses of urban decline and demonstrate governmental concern without raising fundamental questions or grasping the nettle of consequences. The economic costs of intervention and the social costs of non-intervention were more than governments were prepared to risk.

*The nature of the problem*

The years since 1945 have seen considerable changes in the manner in which urban problems have been conceptualised. For much of the period from 1945 to the mid-1960s the emphasis was on decentralisation of population and industry, and the redevelopment of the cities at lower densities; the problem was largely conceptualised in physical terms. This conceptualisation existed within the social democratic consensus which assumed that poverty had been eradicated by full employment and the welfare state, and that the costs of decentralisation and redevelopment could be borne by an expanding economy. Strictly speaking there was not an urban problem as such; merely a maldistribution of population and industry and a physical problem of obsolescent and decaying housing.

In the mid-1960s a concern began to emerge that there was still an element of residual urban poverty. However, this did not involve a challenge to the prevailing conceptualisations as any remaining poverty was blamed on the (deviant) behaviour of individuals and communities. These individual and social pathologies were thought to be confined to discrete and limited urban areas. Towards the end of the 1960s this conceptualisation of the problem began to be questioned, most notably by the Community Development Projects and the Inner Area Studies. The results of their research undermined the pathological explanations and questioned the widely-held views concerning (physical) decentralisation and redevelopment. As a result, these policies were downgraded and the focus switched to a 'structural approach'. The 1977 White Paper stressed the role of economic and environmental decline, the social problems this caused, and the need to reverse such processes and ameliorate the resulting social problems. Despite this recognition of the wider structural causes of urban problems, an area focus to urban initiatives still retained a central role. Post-1979 Conservative governments have, in part, maintained this structural conceptualisation while placing greater emphasis on the need for economic and physical rejuvenation; downgrading the social element while surreptitiously reintroducing the pathological conceptualisation.

Thus the understanding of the urban problem has changed over the post-war period. Throughout the period, however, the problem has always been seen as spatially discrete. In the late 1960s the discussion was of 'pockets of poverty'. By the late 1980s the problem was limited to areas which had been bypassed by the 1980s' 'economic miracle'. In conceptual terms there has therefore been a longstanding marginalisation and residualisation of the problem; it has been represented as being *small*, perhaps for fear of the fact that any genuine recognition of the scale of the problem would involve the commitment of enormous resources to counter it.

*Explanation*

For the period up to the mid-1970s the predominant explanation of urban problems cited a maldistribution of population and industry and sought a more spatially even distribution. This was, for a brief period, accompanied by an explanation that effectively blamed the problems of inner cities on the pathological behaviour of their residents. By the mid-1970s the recognition of the wider structural nature of the problem shifted the key role in explanation to processes such as deindustrialisation and the urban–rural shift. The flight from the inner city of capital, the middle classes and the more affluent working classes was acknowledged as a key element in the causation of economic, environmental and social decline. Thus, in terms of explanation, there had been, by the late 1970s, a switch from discrete urban explanations to a recognition of a wider structural explanation which was affecting all areas of urban life.

After 1979 there was a continued recognition of the wider issues. Indeed, for much of the 1980s the importance of specifically urban decline was played down as part of the wider problem of national economic decline. The solution to the latter, allowing the market to reassert itself, would inevitably bring about the solution to the former. The causes of national decline were thus the causes of urban decline. Explanations stressed the negative impact of state intervention, in particular the planning and regional policies of previous governments, in forcing the withdrawal of capital from the cities. There was, however, also a return to 'blaming the victims' for their plight, particularly black communities, but also a disparate range of other groups such as the 'underclass' and single-parent mothers. Post-1979 Conservative explanations for urban decline were therefore characterised by internal inconsistency; a structural analysis was retained but social pathology reasserted itself to facilitate the stigmatisation of certain cities and particular groups and locations within cities.

*Aims and mechanisms*

In the period up to the mid-1970s the central aim of urban policy was to redistribute industry and population more evenly. The primary mechanisms for the attainment of this aim were state subsidies and restrictions; the use of planning, regional and new town policies. This involved the use of 'carrot and stick' techniques on the part of the state. When the Community Development Projects and the Urban Programme were set up an additional aim was introduced: to help 'problem' individuals and communities to help themselves by the government injecting small amounts of additional resources. The discrediting of this approach and the adoption of a structural diagnosis shifted the aim to one which argued that industry and population had to be attracted back to cities. This stance has been dominant since 1977, although since 1979 there has been a much greater stress on the role of the private sector as the key mechanism for achieving change, and on the need for individuals and communities to take responsibility for their situation.

In practice, restructured forms of state intervention continued to have an importance after 1979. These, however, were largely focused on enabling development at certain key sites (e.g. the Docklands) which were deemed particularly attractive to the private sector; property-led development is the general term we have used to describe this form of development. The mechanism whereby the urban poor would benefit from these developments was generally known as 'trickle-down'. Although difficult, if not impossible, to substantiate, it may also be that some smaller state resource inputs were used in a symbolic sense to defuse the 'urban crisis'. Running through both approaches was a strong role for central government; local government was increasingly marginalised as regards urban initiatives during the 1980s. By the early 1990s, the onset of the longest and deepest recession in post-1945 British history forced the government to acknowledge that the private sector and the associated trickle-down mechanism could not be relied upon to rejuvenate urban areas and solve urban problems. This led to a new emphasis on public–private partnerships, in which a more compliant local government was to be allowed to participate so long as it made the correct noises regarding the role of the private sector.

*Resourcing*

As soon as the myth of permanent economic growth was exploded and the level of public expenditure became seen as a problem in the mid-1970s, it was inevitable that great pressure would be placed on resources for any state-generated policy. The exploding of this myth coincided with the early urban initiatives (the Community Development Projects, the Urban Programme) which were consequently poorly funded. By the time of the post-1977 Labour initiatives, direct funding was grossly inadequate when compared to the scale of the problem. However, it was argued that more resources could come from 'bending' the Rate Support Grant and the general budgets of central government departments to benefit the inner cities. This attempt at alternative financing did not work, nor was it ever likely to work.

Since 1979, funding has, on the whole, continued to be inadequate. Individual projects such as the Docklands have been given favourable treatment and certain programmes have been protected in response to pressure – for example, the Urban Programme in the immediate aftermath of the 1981 urban unrest. On the whole, however, the emphasis has been on using public funds to lever private investment. This approach to resourcing had some success, most notably in areas located in booming regions of the national economy which were attractive to the private sector and therefore arguably did not need public funds. As soon as the economic down-turn arrived, this flow of private investment abruptly froze and began to withdraw. Overall, in the 1980s, whatever planning there was as regards resources relied very heavily upon attracting the private sector. This allowed capital to determine the location, timing and amount of urban regeneration.

*Management, politics and legislation*

Up to the end of the 1960s the management of urban problems was left largely in the hands of bodies such as local authorities, New Town Corporations and the Department of Industry in its various incarnations. There was little in the way of overall strategic management. By the early 1970s the enthusiasm for corporate management was beginning to have an effect and, during the Heath government, experimental urban initiatives using this form of management were set up – the Comprehensive Community Programmes. By persuading local authorities to identify problems, prioritise them and then (re)focus their resources on these problems, it was hoped that the problems could be solved with only minimal additional resources. In essence, this approach also informed the post-1977 Labour government strategy, particularly the formation of the Partnerships.

After 1979, management was strongly emphasised. Public-sector management methods were seen as being inherently inefficient and private-sector methods as inherently superior. At all levels of government considerable emphasis was placed upon financial management and the devolving of responsibility to the lowest practicable level where aims and targets could be identified. Wherever possible, responsibility was to be handed over to the private sector which would, it was held, inevitably manage and utilise resources more efficiently, effectively and economically, thereby giving greater value for money. Where the state sector was still to play a role it either imported private-sector individuals to run programmes or had to adopt the 'right' managerial structures to guarantee that limited resources would achieve more. Thus the Urban Programme was subject to regular management reviews and, at local level, City Action Teams and Task Forces were given a key role in co-ordinating local regeneration activities.

At no time during the post-1945 era has there been serious cross-party and cross-departmental commitment to addressing urban problems. Inter-party differences over the mechanisms to combat the problems have counteracted a joint recognition of the structural nature of the problems. Attempts to ensure that all governmental organisations assessed their policies and programmes *vis-à-vis* their effects on urban problems have also failed; they have been unwilling to adapt organisational structures, working procedures and resources to benefit urban areas and, as such, have acted as a major constraint on the development of a strategic and co-ordinated approach to the problems.

Notwithstanding the hopes raised by *Action for Cities* (HMSO, 1988b) these deficiencies have been growing during the post-1979 period. They are most clearly evident when we examine the legislative base of the various urban initiatives that we have discussed. The decentralisation and redevelopment policies of the 1940–60 period had a fairly sound legislative base. Initiatives such as the Urban Programme and the Partnerships were also anchored in specific pieces of legislation which granted regeneration organisations new powers. Since 1979 most legislative developments have been tacked on to other pieces of legislation or introduced through the use of circulars. Despite the proclaimed need to 'do something about those inner cities', the Conservatives have still to enact a comprehensive and visible statement of their intentions regarding urban problems.

*Monitoring*

Until the election of the first Thatcher government in 1979 the official monitoring of urban initiatives seems to have been poor, although substantial academic work exists. Since 1979, more resources have been put into monitoring and evaluation exercises and their sophistication has increased considerably. The exercises which have been funded have, however, been intellectually limited. They have focused almost exclusively on individual programmes or initiatives, and mainly on quantitative outcomes. As a result there has been a general failure to address overarching issues of urban decline, and attention has been deflected away from wider, bigger and politically unacceptable issues which might begin to address the root causes of the urban problem. Furthermore, the post-1979 monitoring and evaluation has been essentially a record of achievement; it has been largely uncritical and has given little attention to the distributional effects of policies: that is, to the question of who has benefited. Given the neo-conservative tendencies in the post-1979 governments, this is not surprising. For a government-funded study to criticise the government has become extremely unusual.

## Conclusion

We are left with the impression that, at no time in the post-1945 era, can one realistically talk of a coherent urban policy. Initiatives which have sought to benefit urban areas have seldom been purely urban. Nor have they exhibited the clarity and coherence of purpose which should be expected of a policy.

In every period we have covered in this book there has been a failure to conceptualise the nature of the problem, political support has been half-hearted, organisational structures and interests have obstructed the development of coherent policy, and resource availability has been minimal. Government-led strategies have failed as have the so-called private-led strategies of the 1980s.

While in some ways this is to be expected, we have argued that attempts have also been made to downgrade and marginalise the importance of urban problems, to define them in ways which limited the problems to manageable proportions and served a symbolic purpose. At various times there have also been a number of urban initiatives running simultaneously, sometimes in parallel, sometimes intersecting, but usually uncoordinated. Furthermore, the continued focus on discrete areas has meant that there has never been any likelihood of a concerted attack upon the causes of urban decline. Urban initiatives have therefore had a variety of simultaneous and often conflicting functions. They have reflected the needs of the government of the day and have deflected attention away from the root causes of urban problems.

At the time of writing it is just over twenty-five years since the first urban initiative was launched and a genuine *urban policy* still eludes us. As Spencer (1987, p. 9) has noted: 'There is . . . no national urban policy in any meaningful sense – there are individual programmes, but no overarching policy framework'. Nor have urban problems decreased over those twenty-five years. Certain areas of British cities have improved – London Docklands is a stunning example of how a run-down area can be physically and socially transformed within the space of decade – but the types of development that we have witnessed have, at best, merely displaced problems, if not actually exacerbated them, and created new ones.

# Guide to Further Reading

Each chapter of this book has been written in such a way as to provide a comprehensive review of the theoretical and empirical literature on urban policy in Britain. This guide seeks to provide a set of key readings for students seeking a 'next step' in their exploration of particular subjects or themes.

### Chapter 1   Analysing Urban Policy

Newby's chapter in Worsley's *The New Introducing Sociology* (Newby, 1987) provides an accessible introduction to material on the nature of the urban. A more detailed discussion is in Saunders (1979, part 1; 1981). The latter also rehearses the relevant theoretical perspectives, although a clearer introduction can be found in Dunleavy and O'Leary (1987). Edelman (1977) provides an elderly but adequate assessment of the policy process.

### Chapter 2   Post-War Urban Problems and the Rediscovery of Urban Poverty

An excellent flavour of the optimism and aspirations of the period covered in this chapter is provided by Crosland (1964). Abel-Smith and Townsend (1965) chart the darker side of the dream: the rediscovery of poverty. A useful outline of the contemporary urban problem and state responses to it is set out in the earlier chapters of McKay and Cox (1979), while Higgins (1978) offers a useful analysis of the initiatives in the USA.

### Chapter 3   First Steps: Urban Initiatives and Urban Problems in Early 1970s Britain

The material covered in this chapter is the subject of a considerable literature. The reader interested in comparing accounts should consult Lawless (1979, 1986) or Higgins *et al.* (1983). Middlemas (1991) provides a comprehensive political history of the economic crisis of the mid-1970s.

### Chapter 4   The Watershead? Urban Policy 1977–79

Readers wanting a full understanding of the material covered in this chapter should go to the source: HMSO (1977). Useful commentaries are provided by Nabarro (1980), Higgins *et al.* (1983), and Parkinson and Wilks (1983,

1986). An interesting part case study, part commentary is Sills *et al.* (1988). Gamble (1988, ch. 3) describes the rise and fall of the social democratic consensus.

## Chapter 5  Urban Problems since 1979: The Conservative Approach

Ranelagh (1991) and Gamble (1988) provide good overviews and assessments of Thatcherism. Perhaps the best general coverage of the urban problems covered in this chapter is offered by Champion and Townsend (1990). The general Conservative approaches to these problems are covered by Barnekov *et al.* (1989); Storey and Johnson (1989) examine the role of small businesses in an accessible fashion.

## Chapter 6  Reshaping the Urban Policy Inheritance

Regional policy is reviewed by Smith (1989) and Prestwich and Taylor (1990). Sills *et al.* (1988) provide useful coverage of the urban programme, although developments in the latter part of the 1980s and in the 1990s are best studied from the primary sources. Primary sources also provide the best material on City Challenge and the City Grant, although De Groot (1992) is worth consulting on the latter. An overview of housing policy is provided by Atkinson and Durden (1990), while Atkinson and Lupton (1990) is a summary of employment-related initiatives.

## Chapter 7  Urban Initiatives since 1979: Innovation, Consolidation and Assessment

We have provided copious references to this chapter; the interested reader should follow these up to get an in-depth understanding of the material which we have covered. Particularly useful studies are PA Cambridge (1987) and Talbot (1988) on EZs; Stoker (1989) on UDCs; and Davies and Butler (1986) on FPs; Barnekov *et al.* (1989) provide an excellent overview. *Action for Cities* or *New Life for Urban Scotland* are essential reading for their upbeat presentations of government action on urban areas.

## Chapter 8  Urban Planning under Conservatism

We have signposted appropriate further reading extensively in this chapter. For readers seeking a comprehensive understanding of the town and country planning system we recommend Rydin (1993). Thornley (1991) is the outstanding account of the Thatcher years; Healey (1992) provides a recent update and Brindley *et al.* (1989) can also be recommended. Elkin and McClaren (1991) is a good overview of the emerging ecological urban politics of the 1990s.

**Chapter 9  Local Government and Urban Policy**

Stoker (1991) and Wilson *et al.* (1994) provide useful analytical overview of local government. Lansley *et al.* cover municipal socialism while Ridley (1988) explores the countervailing concept of the enabling authority. Cochrane and Clarke (1990) review LEBs, while privatisation is well covered by Ascher (1987) and adequately updated by Parker (1990).

**Chapter 10  Race, Urban Problems and Urban Initiatives**

The work of Solomos affords comprehensive coverage of the issues discussed in this chapter; Benyon and Solomos (1987) provide a useful collection of essays on the urban riots of the 1980s, while Solomos on his own offers effective studies of employment (1986) and housing (1991b). Sivanandan (1976) and Lewis (1988) provide an interesting contrast of theoretical perspectives, while urban policy is covered by Stewart and Whitting (1983) and Munt (1991).

# Bibliography

Abel-Smith, B. and Townsend, P. (1965) *The Poor and the Poorest*, Occasional Papers on Social Administration (Bell, London).

Adam Smith Institute (1983) *Omega Report: Local Government Policy* (ASI, London).

Adcock, B. (1984) 'Regenerating Merseyside Docklands', *Town Planning Review*, vol. 55 (pp. 265–89).

Altermann, R. (1990) 'Developer Obligations for Public Services in the USA: Some Policy Implications for British Planners', in Healey, P. and Nabarro, R. (eds), *Land and Property Development in a Changing Context* (Gower, Aldershot).

Altvater, E. (1973) 'Notes on Some Problems of State Intervention II', *Kapitalistate*, no. 2 (pp. 76–83).

Alty, R. and Darke, R. (1987) A City Centre for People: Involving the Community in Planning for Sheffield's Central Area, *Planning Practice and Research*, vol. 3 (pp. 7–12).

Ambrose, P. (1976) 'British Land-use Planning: A Radical Critique', *Antipode*, vol. 8 (pp. 2–14).

Ambrose, P. (1986) *Whatever Happened to Planning?* (Methuen, London).

Anwar, M. (1990) 'Ethnic Minorities and the Electoral Process', in Goulbourne, H. (ed.), *Black Politics in Britain* (Avebury, Aldershot).

Ascher, K. (1987) *The Politics of Privatisation* (Macmillan, London).

Ashcroft B. and Taylor, J. (1979) 'The Effects of Regional Policy on the Movement of Industry in Great Britain, in Mclennan, D. and Parr, J. (eds), *Regional Policy* (Martin Robertson, Oxford).

Atkinson, R. (1989) 'Housing Policy, Owner Occupation and Central-Local Relations: A Case Study of Slum Clearance and House Improvement in Portsmouth, 1945–1978' (unpublished PhD thesis, University of Kent).

Atkinson, R. and Durden, P. (1990) 'Housing Policy during the Thatcher Years', in Savage, S. and Robbins, L. (eds), *Public Policy under Thatcher* (Macmillan, London).

Atkinson, R. and Lupton, C. (1990) 'Towards an Enterprise Culture? Industrial and Training Policy', in Savage, S. and Robbins, L. (eds), *Public Policy under Thatcher* (Macmillan, London).

Audit Commission (1989) *Urban Regneration and Economic Development: The Local Government Dimension* (HMSO, London).

Audit Commission (1991) *The Urban Regeneration Experience – observations from local value for money audits* (HMSO, London).

Association of London Authorities and Docklands Consultative Committee, (1991) *10 Years of Docklands: How the Cake Was Cut* (ALA/DCC, London).

Bachrach, P. and Baratz, M. (1963) 'Decisions and Nondecisions: an analytical framework', *American Political Science Review*, vol. 57 (pp. 641–51).

Bachrach, P. and Baratz, M. (1970) *Power and Poverty* (Oxford University Press).

Bacon, R. and Eltis, W. (1976) *Britain's Economic Problems: Too Few Producers* (Macmillan, London).

Bains (1972) *The New Local Authorities: Management and Structure* (The Bains Report) (HMSO, London).

Baker, K. (1990) *The Responsible Individual* (Conservative Political Centre, London).

Balasurbramanyam, V. and Rothschild, R. (1985) 'Free Port Zones and the United Kingdom', *Lloyds Bank Review*, no. 158 (pp. 20–31).

Ball, H. (1988) 'The limits of influence: Ethnic Minorities and the Partnership Programme', *New Community*, vol. 15 (pp. 7–22).

Ball, W. and Solomos, J. (eds) (1990) *Race and Local Politics* (Macmillan, London).

Banfield, E. (1974) *Unheavenly City Revisited* (Little, Brown, Boston, Mass.).

Banham, R. *et al.* (1989) 'Non-plan: an experiment in freedom', *New Society*, March, 435–42).

Barnekov, T. *et al.* (1969) *Privatism and Urban Policy in Britain and the US* (Oxford University Press).

Barrett, S. and Fudge, C. (eds) (1981) *Policy and Action* (Methuen, London).

Bassett, K. and Harloe, M. (1990) 'Swindon: The Rise and Decline of a Growth Coalition', in Harloe, M. *et al.* (eds), *Place, Policy and Politics* (Unwin Hyman, London).

Batley, R. (1989) 'London Docklands: An Analysis of Power Relations between UDCs and Local Government', *Public Administration*, vol. 67 (pp. 167–87).

Begg, I. *et al.* (1986) 'Economic and Social Change in Urban Britain and the Inner Cities', in Hausner, V. (ed.), *Critical Issues in Urban Economic Development*, vol. 1 (Clarendon, Oxford).

Ben-Tovim, G. *et al.* (1986) *The Local Politics of Race* (Macmillan, London).

Ben-Tovim, G. (1988) 'Race, Politics and Urban Regeneration: Lessons from Liverpool', in Judd, D. and Parkinson, M. (eds) *Leadership and Urban Rgeneration* (Sage, London).

Bentley, G. (1992) 'The Real City Challenge', *Local Work*, no. 34 (pp. 1–5, 7).

Benyon, J. (1984) 'Unemployment, Racial Disadvantage and the Cities', in Benyon, J. (ed.), *Scarman and After* (Pergamon, Oxford).

Benyon, J. (1985) 'Going Through the Motions: The Political Agenda, the 1981 Riots and the Scarman Inquiry', *Parliamentary Affairs*, vol. 38 (pp. 409–22).

Benyon, J. and Solomos, J. (eds) (1987) *The Roots of Urban Unrest* (Pergamon, Oxford).

Benyon, J. and Solomos, J. (1988) 'The Simmering Cities', *Parliamentary Affairs*, vol. 41 (pp. 402–22).

Benyon, J. and Solomos, J. (1990) 'Race, Injustice and Disorder', in MacGregor, S. and Pimlott, B. (eds), *Tackling the Cities* (Clarendon, Oxford).

Berry, F. (1974) *Housing: The Great British Failure* (Charles Knight, London).

Birch, D. (1979) *The Job Generation Process* (MIT Program on Neighborhood and Regional Change, Cambridge, Mass.).

Blackaby, F. (ed.), (1979) *Deindustrialisation* (Heinemann, London).

Blake, P. (1977) 'Britain's New Towns: Facts and Figures', *Town and Country Planning*, February (p. 94).

Boddy, M. (1984) 'Local Economic and Employment Strategies', in Boddy, M. and Fudge, C. (eds), *Local Socialism* (Macmillan, London).

Boddy, M. and Fudge, C. (eds) (1984) *Local Socialism* (Macmillan, London).

Bogdanor, V. (1983) 'The meaning of Mrs Thatcher's Victory', *Encounter*, vol. 60/61 (pp. 14–19).

Bond, P. (1991) 'Alternative Policies in the Inner City', in Keith, M. and Rogers, A. (eds), *Hollow Promises* (Mansell, London).

Booth, S. *et al.* (1982) 'Organisational Redundancy: A Critical Appraisal of the GEAR Project', *Public Administration*, vol. 60 (pp. 56–72).

Boyle, R. (1989) 'Partnership in Practice', *Local Government Studies*, vol. 15 (pp. 17–28).

Boyle, R. and Rich, D. (1984) 'Urban Policy and the New Privatism in the United States and Britain', *Public Administration Bulletin*, no. 45 (pp. 22–36).

Bradshaw, P. (1990) 'Urban Development Corporations and Enterprise Boards Revisited', *Local Economy*, vol. 5 (pp. 214–24).

Breheny, M. and Hart, D. (1989) 'The Death of Strategic Planning', in Breheny, M. and Congdon, P. (eds), *Growth and Change in a Core Region* (Pion, London).

Bridges, L. (1975) 'The Ministry of Internal Security: British Urban Social Policy 1968–74', *Race and Class*, vol. XVI (pp. 375–86).

Bridges, L. (1981/2) 'Keeping the Lid On: British Urban Social Policy 1975–81', *Race and Class*, vol. XXIII (pp. 171–85).

Bright, G. *et al.* (1988) *Small Businesses and the Rebirth of Enterprise in Britain* (Conservative Political Centre, London).

Brindley, T. *et al.* (1989) *Remaking Planning* (Unwin Hyman, London).

Brinks, J. and Coyne, J. (1983) 'The Birth of Enterprise', *Hobart Paper* No. 98 (IEA, London).

Bristow, M. (1985a) 'How Unitary is Unitary? Some Comments on the New British Unitary Plan System', *Built Environment*, vol. 11 (pp. 30–4).

Bristow, M. (1985b) 'Some Questions on Unitary Development Plans', *Regional Studies*, vol. 19 (pp. 59–61).

Brittan, S. (1975) 'The Economic Contradictions of Democracy', *British Journal of Political Science*, vol. 5 (pp. 129–59).

Brittan, S. (1980) 'Hayek, the New Right and the Crisis of Social Democracy', *Encounter*, vol. 54 (pp. 31–46).

Brooke, R. (1989) *Managing the Enabling Authority* (Longman, London).

Brookes, J. (1989) 'Cardiff Bay Renewal Strategy – Another Hole in the Democratic System', *The Planner*, January (pp. 38–40).

Brown, C. (1992) 'Same Difference: The Persistance of Racial Disadvantage in the British Employment Market', in Braham, P. *et al.* (eds), *Racism and Antiracism* (Sage, London).

Brownill, S. (1990a) *Developing London's Docklands: Another Great Planning Disaster* (Paul Chapman, Liverpool).

Brownill, S. (1990b) 'The People's Plan for the Royal Docks: Some Contradictions in Popular Planning', in Thornley, A. (ed.), *Radical Planning Initiatives* (Gower, Aldershot).

Brunskill, I. (1990) *The Regeneration Game*, Industrial Policy Paper 1 (Institute of Public Policy Research, London).

Buchanan, J. and Tullock, G. (1965) *The Calculus of Consent* (University of Michigan Press, Ann Arbor, Mich).

Buck, N. and Gordon, I. (1987) 'The Beneficiaries of Employment Growth: An Analysis of the Experience of Disadvantaged Groups in Expanding Labour Markets', in Hausner, V. (ed.), *Critical Issues in Urban Economic Development*, vol. II (Clarendon, Oxford).

Bulpitt, J. (1986) 'The Discipline of the New Democracy', *Political Studies*, vol. XXXIV (pp. 19–39).

Butcher, H. *et al.* (1990) *Local Government and Thatcherism* (Routledge, London).

Butler, E. *et al.* (1985) *The Omega File* (ASI, London).

Butler, E. and Pirie, M. (1983) *Freeports* (ASI, London).

Cabinet Office (1990) *This Common Inheritance*, CM 1200 (HMSO, London).

Cadman, D. (1982) 'Urban Change, Enterprise Zones and the Role of Investors', *Built Environment*, no. 7 (pp. 13–19).

Cambridge Economic Policy Review (1982) 'Employment Problems in the Cities and Regions of the UK', *Cambridge Economic Policy Review*, vol. 8, no. 2.

Campbell, M. (1990) 'Towards a Local Labour Market Strategy', *Local Economy*, vol. 5 (pp. 4–14).

Carley, M. (1991) 'Business in Urban Regeneration Partnerships: A Case Study in Birmingham', *Local Economy*, no. 6 (pp. 100–15).

Carr-Hill, R. and Chandra-Boreham, H. (1988) 'Education', in Bhat, A. *et al.* (eds), *Britain's Black Population*, 2nd edition (Gower, Aldershot).

Carter, B. *et al.* (1987) 'The 1951–55 Conservative Government and the Racialisation of Black Immigration', *Immigrants and Minorities*, vol. 6 (pp. 335–47).

Castells, M. (1977) *The Urban Question* (Arnold, London).

Castells, M. and Henderson, J. (1987) 'Techno-economic Restructuring, Socio-political Processes and Spatial Transformation: A Global Perspective', in Henderson, J. and Castells, M. (eds), *Global Restructuring and Territorial Development* (Sage, London).

Catterall, B. (1992) 'All Aboard for Another Docklands?', *New Statesman & Society*, January 10 (pp. 16–17).

Champion, A. and Green, A. (1987) 'The Booming Towns of Britain: The Geography of Economic Performance in the 1980s', *Geography* (pp. 97–108).

Champion, A. and Green, A. (1992) 'Local Economic Performance in Britain during the late 1980s: The Results of the Third Booming Towns Study', *Environment and Planning A*, vol. 24 (pp. 243–72).

Champion, A. and Townsend, A. (1990) *Contemporary Britain* (Arnold, London).

Champion, A. *et al.* (1987) *Changing Places* (Arnold, London).

Cherrett, T. (1982) 'The Implementation of Green Belt Policy', *Gloucestershire Papers in Rural and Local Planning* (GCAT, Gloucester).

Cherry, G. (1974) *The Evolution of British Town Planning* (Hill, Leighton Buzzard).

Cherry, G. (1989) 'The Green Belt: Strategy for the Urban Fringe in British Planning', *Geographica Polonica*, vol. 56 (pp. 75–80).

Cheshire, P. and Shephard, S. (1989) 'British Planning Policy and Access to Housing', *Urban Studies*, vol. 26 (pp. 469–85).

Chisholm, M. and Kivell, P. (1987) *Inner City Waste Land*, Hobart Papers 108, (IEA, London).

Christie, I. and Rolfe, H. (1992) 'The TECS and Inner City Regeneration', *Policy Studies*, vol. 13 (pp. 54–63).

Church, A. (1990) 'Transport and Urban Regeneration in London Docklands', *Cities*, vol. 7 (pp. 289–303).

Clapham, D. (1985) 'Management of the Local State: The Example of Corporate Management', *Critical Social Policy*, vol. 14 (pp. 27–47).

Clapham, D. and Kintrea, K. (1987) 'Public Housing', in Donnison, D. and Middleton, A. (eds), *Regenerating the Inner City* (RKP, London).

Clegg, S. (1989) *Frameworks of Power* (Sage, London).

Cloke, P. (1977) 'An Index of Rurality for England and Wales', *Regional Studies*, vol. 11 (pp. 31–46).

Cochrane, A. (1983) 'Local Economic Policies: Trying to Drain an Ocean with a Teaspoon', in Anderson, J. *et al.* (eds), *Redundant Spaces in Cities and Regions* (Academic Press, London).

Cochrane, A. (1986) 'Local Employment Initiatives, in Lawless', P. and Raban, C. (eds), *The Contemporary British City* (Harper and Row, London).

Cochrane, A. (ed.), (1987) *Developing Local Economic Strategies* (Open University Press, Milton Keynes).

Cochrane, A. (1991) 'The Changing State of Local Government', *Public Administration*, vol. 69 (pp. 281–302).

Cochrane, A. (1992) 'Restructuring the Local Welfare State', paper presented to a conference 'Towards a Post-Fordist Welfare State?', Teeside University.

Cochrane, A. and Clarke, A. (1990) 'Local Enterprise Boards: The Short History of a Radical Initiative', *Public Administration*, vol. 68 (pp. 315–336).

Cockburn, C. (1977) *The Local State* (Pluto, London).

Colenutt, B. (1992) *Social Regeneration* (Centre for Local Economic Strategies, Manchester).

Colenutt, B. and Tansley, S. (1990) *Inner City Regeneration* (Centre for Local Economic Strategies, Manchester).

Community Development Project (CDP) (1977a) *Gilding the Ghetto* (CDP Inter-Project Team, London).

Community Development Project (CDP) (1977b) *The Costs of Industrial Change* (CDP Inter-Project Team, London).

Community Development Project (CDP) (1974) *Inter-Project Report* (Information and Intelligence Unit, London).

Confederation of British Industry (CBI) (1988) *Initiatives Beyond Charity: the report of the CBI Task Force on Business and Urban Regeneration* (CBI, London).

Cooke, P. (ed.) (1989) *Localities* (Unwin Hyman, London).

Cordon, C. (1977) *Planned Cities* (Sage, London).

Coulson, A. (1990) 'Evaluating Local Economic Policy', in Campbell, M. (ed.), *Local Economic Policy* (Cassell, London).

Cowling, M. (1990) 'The Sources of the New Right', *Encounter*, vol. LXXXV (pp. 3–13).

Cox, A. (1979) 'Administrative Inertia and Inner City Policy', *Public Administration Bulletin*, no. 29 (pp. 2–17).

Cox, A. (1984) *Adversary Politics and Land* (Cambridge University Press).

Crosland, A. (1964) *The Future of Socialism* (Jonathan Cape, London).

Cross, D. (1990) *Counter-Urbanisation in England and Wales* (Gower, Aldershot).

Cross, M. *et al.* (1988) *Black Welfare and Local Government: Section 11 and the Social services* (Centre for Research in Ethnic Relations, University of Warwick).

Cullingworth, J. (1975) *Environmental Planning*, vol. 1 (HMSO, London).

Cullingworth, J. (1980) *Environmental Planning*, vol. 4 (HMSO, London).

Cullingworth, J. (1985) *Town and Country Planning* (George Allen & Unwin, London).

Dahl, R. (1961) *Who Governs? Democracy and Power in an American City* (Yale University Press, New Haven, Conn.).

Dahl, R. (1982) *Dilemmas of Pluralist Democracy* (Yale University Press, New Haven, Conn.).

Dale, R. (1989) 'The Thatcherite Project in Education: The Case of the City Technology Colleges', *Critical Social Policy*, vol. 9 (pp. 4–19).

Daniel, W. (1968) *Racial Discrimination in England* (Penguin, Harmondsworth).

Daniels, P. (1987) 'The Geography of Services', *Progress in Human Geography*, vol. 11 (pp. 433–47).

Daniels, P. and Bobe, M. (1992) 'Office Building in the City of London: A Decade of Change', *Area*, no. 24 (pp. 253–8).

Darwin, J. (1990) *The Enterprise Society: Regional Policy and National Strategy* (Centre for Local Economic Strategies, Manchester).

Davies, T. and Mason, C. (1986) 'Shutting Out the Inner City Worker, *SAUS Occasional Paper*, 23 (SAUS, Bristol).

Davies, W. and Butler, E. (1986) *The Freeport Experiment* (ASI, London).

Davis, E. (1984) 'Express Coaching since 1980: Liberalisation in Practice', *Fiscal Studies*, vol. 5 (pp. 47–60).

Dawson, J. and Parkinson, M. (1991) 'Merseyside Development Corporation 1981–1989', in Keith, M. and Rogers, A. (eds), *Hollow Promises* (Mansell, London).

Dean, H. and Taylor-Gooby, P. (1992) *Dependency Culture* (Harvester Wheatsheaf, Hemel Hempstead).

Dearlove, J. (1979) *The Reorganisation of British Local Government* (Cambridge University Press).

Debenham, Tewson and Chinnock (1991) *Money Into Property* (Debenham, Tewson and Chinnock, London).

De Groot, L. (1992) 'City Challenge: Competing in the Urban Regeneration Game', *Local Economy*, vol. 7 (pp. 196–209).

Denman, D. (1980) *Land in a Free Society* (Centre for Policy Studies, London).

Dennis, N. (1972) *Public Participation and Planners' Blight* (Faber, London).

Dennis R. (1978) 'The Decline of Manufacturing Employment', *Urban Studies*, vol. 15 (pp. 63–75).

Department of Education and Science (DES) (1965) 'Circular 7/65 (HMSO, London).

Department of the Environment (DoE) (1980) *Development Control Policy and Practice*, Circular 22/80 (HMSO, London).

Department of the Environment (DoE) (1984) *The Abolition of the Greater London Council and the Metropolitan County Councils* (HMSO, London).

Department of the Environment (DoE) (1985a) *Urban Programme: Ministerial Guidelines* (HMSO, London).

Department of the Environment (DoE) (1985b) *The Use of Conditions in Planning Permissions*, Circular 1/85 (HMSO, London).

Department of the Environment (DoE) (1985c) *Lifting the Burden* (HMSO, London).

Department of the Environment (DoE) (1985d) *Competition in the Provision of Local Authority Services* (HMSO, London).

Department of the Environment (DoE) (1986) *Development by Small Business*, Circular 2/86 (HMSO, London).

Department of the Environment (DoE) (1988a) *Urban Policy and DoE Programmes* (HMSO, London).

Department of the Environment (DoE) (1988b) *City Grant Guidance Notes* (HMSO, London).

Department of the Environment (DoE) (1989) *The Future of Development Plans* (HMSO, London).

Department of the Environment (DoE) (1990) *The Urban Programme Management Initiative: A Consultation Paper on Proposed Changes* (HMSO, London).

Department of the Environment (DoE) (1991a) *Urban Programme. Annual Guidance 1992/93* (HMSO, London).

Department of the Environment (DoE) (1991b) *City Challenge* (HMSO, London).

Department of the Environment (DoE) (1991c) *General Note: Derelict Land Grants* (HMSO, London).

Department of the Environment (DoE) (1991d) *Derelict Land Reclamation Grant: Applicants Other than Local Authorities* (HMSO, London).

Department of the Environment (DoE) (1991e) *The Structure of Local Government in England: A Consultation Paper* (HMSO, London).

Department of the Environment (DoE) (1991f) *The Internal Management of Local Authorities in England* (HMSO, London).

Department of the Environment (DoE) (1992a) *Urban Programme Annual Guidance 1993/94* (HMSO, London).

Department of the Environment (DoE) (1992b) *City Challenge Bidding Guidance 1993–94* (HMSO, London).

Department of the Environment (DoE) (1992c) *The Urban Regeneration Agency* (HMSO, London).

Department of the Environment (DoE) (1992d) *City Grant Guidance Note* (HMSO, London).

Docklands Joint Committee (DJC) (1980) *London Docklands – Past, Present and Future* (DJC, London).

Docklands Consultative Committee (DCC) (1990) *The Docklands Experiment: A critical review of eight years of the London Docklands Development Corporation* (DCC, London).

Docklands Consultative Committee (DCC) (1992) *All That Glitters is not Gold: a critical analysis of Canary Wharf* (DCC, London).

Donnison, D. (1967) *The Government of Housing* (Penguin, Harmondsworth).

Donnison, D. and de Soto, P. (1980) *The Good City* (Heinemann, London).

Drewett, R. *et al.* (1976) 'British Cities, Urban Population and Employment Trends 1951–71, *DoE Research Report*, no. 10 (HMSO, London).

Duncan, S. and Goodwin, M. (1985) 'The Local State and Local Economic Policy', *Policy & Politics*, vol. 13 (pp. 227–53).

Duncan, S. and Goodwin, M. (1986) 'The Local State and Local Economic Policy: Political Mobilisation or Economic Regeneration', *Capital and Class*, vol. 27 (pp. 14–36).

Duncan, S. and Goodwin, M. (1988) *The Local State and Uneven Development* (Polity, Cambridge).

Dunleavy, P. (1977) 'Protest and Quiescence in Urban Politics', *International Journal of Urban and Regional Research*, vol. 1 (pp. 193–218).

Dunleavy, P. (1980) *Urban Political Analysis* (Macmillan, London).

Dunleavy, P. (1981a) 'Alternative Theories of Liberal Democratic Politics', in Potter, D. *et al.* (eds), *Society and the Social Sciences* (RKP, London).

Dunleavy, P. (1981b) *The Politics of Mass Housing* (Clarendon, Oxford).

Dunleavy, P. (1986) 'Explaining the Privatisation Boom: Public Choice Versus Radical Approaches', *Public Administration*, vol. 64 (pp. 13–34).

Dunleavy, P. and O'Leary, B. (1987) *Theories of the State* (Macmillan, London).

Dunn, R. *et al.* (1987) 'The Geography of Council House Sales in England 1979–1985', *Urban Studies*, vol. 24 (pp. 47–59).

Edelman, M. (1977) *Political Language* (Academic Press, New York).

Edwards, J. (1989) 'From Whitehall Strategy to Local Impact', in Aldridge, B. and Edwards, J. *Living with Inner City Policies* (Royal Holloway and Bedford New College, London).

Edwards, J. and Batley, R. (1978) *The Politics of Positive Discrimination* (Tavistock, London).

Ehyatt, A. (1987) 'Regenerating from the Local Level', *Town and Country Planning*, vol. 56 (pp. 232–4).

Elias, P. and Keogh, G. (1982) 'Industrial Decline and Unemployment in the Inner City Areas of Great Britain: A Review of the Evidence', *Urban Studies*, vol. 19 (pp. 1–15).

Elkin, T. and McLaren, D. (1991) *Reviving the City* (Friends of the Earth, London).

Elson, M. (1986) *Green Belts: Conflict and Mediation in the Urban Fringe* (Heinemann, London).

Erickson, R. and Syms, P. (1986) 'The Effects of Enterprise Zones on Local Property Markets', *Regional Studies*, vol. 20 (pp. 1–14).

Eyles, J. (1979) 'Area Based Policies for the Inner City', in Herbert, D. and Smith, D. (eds), *Social Problems and the City* (Oxford University Press).

Fagence, M. (1977) *Citizen Participation in Planning* (Pergamon, Oxford).

Fainstein, S. (1990) 'The Changing World Economy and Urban Restructuring', in Judd, D. and Parkinson, M. (eds), *Leadership and Urban Regeneration* (Sage, London).

Feagin, J. (1988) *Free Enterprise City* (Rutgers University Press, New Brunswick, NJ).

Fine, B. and Harris, L. (1979) *Rereading 'Capital'* (Macmillan, London).

Flynn, N. and Taylor, A. (1986a) 'Inside the Rust Belt: An Analysis of the Decline of the West Midlands Economy 1: International and National Economic Conditions', *Environment and Planning A*, vol. 18 (pp. 865–900).

Flynn, N. and Taylor, A. (1986b) 'Inside the Rust Belt: An Analysis of the Decline of the West Midlands Economy 2: Corporate Strategies and Economic Change', *Environment and Planning A*, vol. 18 (pp. 999–1028).

Foley, P. (1992) 'Local Economic Policy and Job Creation: A Review of Evaluation Studies', *Urban Studies*, vol. 29 (pp. 587–98).

Ford, J. (1992) 'The Damocles Sword', *Roof*, July/August (pp. 16–17).

Forrest, R. *et al.* (1979) 'The Inner City: In Search of the Problem', *Geoforum*, vol. 10 (pp. 109–116).

Forrest, R. and Murie, A. (1983) 'Residualisation and Council Housing', *Journal of Social Policy*, vol. 12 (pp. 453–68).

Forrest, R. and Murie, A. (1986) 'Marginalisation and Subsidised Individualism', *International Journal of Urban and Regional Research*, vol. 10 (pp. 46–65).

Forsyth, M. (1980) *Reservicing Britain* (ASI, London).

Forsyth, M. (1983) *The Myths of Privatisation* (ASI, London).

Fothergill, S. and Gudgin, G. (1982) *Unequal Growth: Urban and Regional Employment Change in the UK* (Heinemann, London).

Friedman, M. (1962) *Capitalism and Freedom* (University of Chicago Press, Chicago).

Frost, M. and Spence, A. (1991a) 'Employment Changes in Central London in the 1980s I: The Record of the 1980s', *Geographical Journal*, vol. 157 (pp. 1–12).

Frost, M. and Spence, A. (1991b) 'Employment Changes in Central London in the 1980s II: Understanding Recent Forces for Change and Future Development Cònstraints', *Geographical Journal*, vol. 157 (pp. 125–35).

Froud, M. (1985) 'New and small firms in the UK: An Analysis of the Policy Process', *Geoforum*, vol. 16 (pp. 369–86).

Fuller, R. and Stevenson, O. (1983) *Policies, Programmes and Disadvantage* (Heinemann, London).

Gamble, A. (1974) *The Conservative Nation* (RKP, London).

Gamble, A. (1988) *The Free Economy and the Strong State* (Macmillan, London).

Gibson, M. and Langstaff, M. (1982) *An Introduction to Urban Renewal* (Hutchinson, London).

Giddens, A. (1984) *The Constitution of Modern Society* (Polity, London).

Gifford (1989) *Loosen The Shackles*, The Gifford Inquiry (Karia Press, Liverpool).

Gilroy, P. (1990) 'The End of Anti-racism', in Ball, W. and Solomos, J. (eds), *Race and Local Politics* (Macmillan, London).

Ginsburg, N. (1992) 'Racism and Housing: Concepts and Reality', in Braham, P. *et al.* (eds), *Racism and Antiracism* (Sage, London).

Goddard, J. and Champion, A. (eds) (1983) *The Urban and Regional Transformation of Britain* (Methuen, London).

Goldsmith, M. (1992) 'Local Government', *Urban Studies*, vol. 29 (pp. 393–410).

Goldthorpe, J. *et al.* (1969) *The Affluent Worker in the Class Structure* (Cambridge University Press).

Goodwin, M. (1986) 'Locality and the Local State: Economic Policy for London's Docklands', *Urban and Regional Studies Working Paper* no. 53 (University of Sussex, Brighton).

Gordon, P. (1989) 'Citizenship for Some?', *Runnymeade Commentary* 2 (Runnymeade Trust, London).

Gordon, P. (1990) 'A Dirty War', in Ball, W. and Solomos, J. (eds), *Race and Local Politics* (Macmillan, London).

Gosling, P. (1992) 'Cities Braced for New Challenge', *Independent on Sunday*, 19 July (p. 31).

Grant, J. (1977) *The Politics of Urban Transport Planning* (Earth Resources Research, London).

Greater London Council (GLC) (1985) *The London Industrial Strategy* (GLC, London).

Greater London Council (GLC) (1986a) *The London Labour Plan* (GLC, London).

Greater London Council (GLC) (1986b) *The London Financial Strategy* (GLC, London).

Green, A. (1986) 'The Likelihood of Becoming and Remaining Unemployed in Great Britain, 1984', *Transactions Institute of British Geographers*, vol. 11 (pp. 37–56).

Green, D. (1982) *The Welfare State: for Rich or for Poor* (IEA, London).

Green, D. (1987) *The New Right* (Wheatsheaf, Brighton).

Greenwood, R. and Stewart, J. (1974) *Corporate Planning in Local Government* (Charles Knight, London).

Griffith, J. (1966) *Central Departments and Local Authorities* (George Allen & Unwin, London).

Guttmann, R. (1976) 'State Intervention and the Economic Crisis: The Labour Government's Economic Policy 1974–5', *Kapitalistate*, no. 4/5 (pp. 225–70).

Gyford, J. (1985) *The Politics of Local Socialism* (George Allen & Unwin, London).

Hall, P. *et al.* (1973) *The Containment of Urban England* (George Allen & Unwin, London).

Hall, P. (1977) 'Green Fields and Grey Areas', *Proceedings of Royal Town Planning Institute Annual Conference* (Royal Town Planning Institute, London).

Hall, R. and van der Wee, D. (1992) 'Community Regional Policies for the 1990s', *Regional Studies*, vol. 26 (pp. 499–509).

Hall, S. *et al.* (1978) *Policing the Crisis* (Macmillan, London).

Hall, S. (1983) 'The Great Moving Right Show', in Hall, S. and Jacques, M. (eds), *The Politics of Thatcherism* (Lawrence and Wishart, London).

Hall, S. and Jacques, M. (eds) (1983) *The Politics of Thatcherism* (Lawrence and Wishart, London).

Hallsworth, A. and Bobe, M. (1993) 'How the Interest Rate Cut Ate the Docklands Canary', *Area*, vol. 25 (pp. 64–9).

Ham, C. (1992) *Health Policy in Britain* (Macmillan, London).

Ham, C. and Hill, M. (1984) *The Policy Process in the Modern Capitalist State* (Wheatsheaf, Brighton).

Hambleton, R. (1977) 'Urban Policy', *The Planner*, no. 63 (pp. 163–5).

Hambleton, R. (1981) 'Implementing Inner City Policy: Reflections from Experience', *Policy and Politics*, vol. 9 (pp. 51–71).

Hambleton, R. (1990) *Urban Government in the 1990s: Lessons from the USA* (SAUS, Bristol).

Hambleton, R. (1991a) 'The Regeneration of US and British Cities', *Local Government Studies*, no. 17 (pp. 53–69).

Hambleton, R. (1991b) *Another Chance for Cities*, Papers in Planning Research, no. 126 (Department of City and Regional Planning, University of Wales, Cardiff).

Hamnett, C. (1979) 'Area Based Explanations', in Herbert, D. and Smith, D. (eds), *Social Problems and the City* (Oxford University Press).

Harding, A. (1991) 'The Rise of Urban Growth Coalitions UK-Style', *Environment and Planning C: Government and Policy*, vol. 9 (pp. 295–317).

Harloe, M. *et al.* (eds) (1990) *Place, Policy and Politics* (Unwin Hyman, London).

Harrington, M. (1962) *The Other America* (Macmillan, London).

Harris, R. (1988) *Beyond the Welfare State* (IEA, London).

Harrison, M. (1989) 'The Urban Programme, Monitoring and Ethnic Minorities', *Local Government Studies*, vol. 15 (pp. 49–64).

Harrop, J. (1992) *The Political Economy of Integration in the European Community*, 2nd edition (Edward Elgar, Aldershot).

Hartley, K. and Huby, M. (1985) 'Contracting-out in Health and Local Authorities', *Public Money*, vol. 5 (pp. 23–6).

Harvey, D. (1978) The Urban Process under Capitalism', *International Journal of Urban and Regional Research*, vol. 2 (pp. 101–31).

Harvey, D. (1982) *The Limits to Capital* (Blackwell, Oxford).

Harvey, D. (1989a) *The Urban Experience* (Blackwell, Oxford).

Harvey, D. (1989b) From Managerialism to Entrepreneurialism', *Geografiska Annaler*, vol. 71B (pp. 3–17).

Haslam, M. (1990) 'Green Belts and the Future', *The Planner*, vol. 76 (pp. 14–16).

Hastings, S. and Levie, H. (1983) *Privatisation* (Spokesman, London).

Haughton, G. (1990) 'Targeting Jobs to Local People: The British Urban Policy Experience', *Urban Studies*, vol. 27 (pp. 185–98).

Hayek, F. (1944) *The Road to Serfdom* (RKP, London).

Hayek, F. (1960) *The Constitution of Liberty* (RKP, London).

Hayek, F. (1982) *Law, Legislation and Liberty* (RKP, London).

Hayton, K. (1991) 'The Future for Local Authority Economic Development companies', *Local Government Studies*, vol. 17 (pp. 53–67).

Heald, D. (1983) *Public Expenditure* (Martin Robertson, Oxford).

Heald, D. and Steel, D. (1982) 'Privatising Public Enterprise: An Analysis of the Government Case', *Political Quarterly*, no. 53, 333–49).

Healey, M. and Clark, D. (1984) 'Industrial Decline and Government Response in the West Midlands: The Case of Coventry', *Regional Studies*, no. 18 (pp. 303–18).

Healey, M. and Clark, D. (1985a) 'Industrial Decline in a Local Economy: The Case of Coventry, 1974–1982', *Environment and Planning A*, vol. 17 (pp. 1351–67).

Healey, M. and Clark, D. (1985b) 'Industrial Decline, Industrial Structure and Large Companies: The Case of Coventry, 1974–1982', *Geography*, vol. 70 (pp. 328–38).

Healey, P. (1992) 'The Reorganisation of State and Market in Planning', *Urban Studies*, vol. 29 (pp. 411–34).

Healey, P. *et al.* (1988) *Land Use Planning and the Mediation of Urban Change* (Cambridge University Press, London).

Heclo, H. (1972) 'Review Article: Policy Analysis', *British Journal of Political Science*, vol. 2 (pp. 83–106).

Hegarty, S. (1988) 'Inner City Aid: The Figures behind the Hype', *Public Finance and Accountancy*, 9 January (pp. 7–10).

Henderson, J. and Karn, V. (1984) 'Race, Class and the Allocation of Public Housing in Britain', *Urban Studies*, vol. 21 (pp. 115–28).

Henneberry, J. (1992) 'Science Parks: A Property-based Initiative for Urban Regeneration', *Local Economy*, vol. 6 (pp. 326–35).

Hennessy, P. (1989) *Whitehall* (Secker & Warburg, London).

Her Majesty's Stationery Office (HMSO) (1940) *The Distribution of the Industrial Population* The Barlow Report (HMSO, London.

Her Majesty's Stationery Office (HMSO) (1967) *Children and their Primary Schools* The Plowden Report (HMSO, London).

Her Majesty's Customs and Excise (HMCE) (1984) *Free Zones: Guidance Notes for Users* (HMSO, London

Her Majesty's Stationery Office (HMSO) (1988) *Action for Cities* (HMSO, London).

Her Majesty's Stationery Office (HMSO) (1989) *Progress on Cities* (HMSO, London).

Her Majesty's Stationery Office (HMSO) (1990) *People in Cities* (HMSO, London).

Her Majesty's Stationery Office (HMSO) (1965) *The Housing Programme 1965–1970*, Cmnd 2838 HMSO, London).

Her Majesty's Stationery Office (HMSO) (1977) *Policy for the Inner Cities*, Cmnd 6845 (HMSO, London).

Her Majesty's Stationery Office (HMSO) (1983) *Regional Industrial Development*, Cmnd 9111 HMSO, London).

Her Majesty's Stationery Office (HMSO) (1988a) *DTI – The Department for Enterprise*, CM 278 (HMSO, London

Her Majesty's Stationery Office (HMSO) (1992) *DoE Expenditure Plans 1992–93 to 1994–95*, CM 1908 (HMSO, London).

Herrington, J. (1984) *The Outer City* (Harper and Row, London).

Herrington, J. (1990) *Beyond Green Belts* (Jessica Kingsley, London).

Heseltine, M. (1979) Secretary of State's Address, *Proceedings, RTPI Summer School* (RTPI, London).

Heseltine, M. (1983) *Reviving the Inner Cities* (Conservative Political Centre, London).

Heseltine, M. (1986) *Where There's a Will* (Hutchinson, London).

Heseltine, M. (1991a) Speech to Manchester Chamber of Commerce and Industry, 11 March.

Heseltine, M. (1991b) *The Future of London: The 1991 LWT London Lecture* (London Weekend Television, London).

Higgins, J. (1978) *The Poverty Business* (Blackwell, Oxford).

Higgins, J. *et al.* (1983) *Government and Urban Poverty* (Blackwell, Oxford).

Hills, J. and Sutherland, H. (1991) 'The Proposed Council Tax', *Fiscal Studies*, vol. 12 (pp. 1–21).

Holtermann, S. (1975) 'Areas of Urban Deprivation in Great Britain', *Social Trends*, no. 6 (pp. 33–47).

Hornsby, T. (1982) 'Urban Renewal: The Financial Institutions and Whitehall', *Management in Government*, vol. 4 (pp. 206–18).

House of Commons Employment Committee (HCEC) (1988) *The Employment Effects of Urban Development Corporations*, Third Report Session 1978–88, HCP327–1 (HMSO, London).

House of Commons Public Accounts Committee (HCPAC) (1989) *Urban Development Corporations*, Twentieth Report Session 1988–89, HCP385 (HMSO, London).

House of Commons Public Accounts Committee (HCPAC) (1990) *Regenerating the Inner Cities*, Thirty-third Report Session 1989–90, HCP215 (HMSO, London).

Howard, E. (1946) *Garden Cities of Tomorrow* (Faber, London).

Howe, G. (1979) 'Throw the Inner Cities Wide Open to Initiative', *Estates Times*, 14 September (pp. 10–11).

Hula, R. (1990) 'The Two Baltimores', in Judd, D. and Parkinson, M. (eds), *Leadership and Urban Regeneration* (Sage, London).

Hunt, D. (1990) Speech Given at British Urban Regeneration Association Conference, 13 February.

Hurd, D. (1988) 'Citizenship in the Tory Democracy', *New Statesman*, 29 September (p. 14).

*Inquiry into British Housing* (1991) (Joseph Rowntree Foundation, York).

Issac, J. (1990) 'The New Right and the Moral Society', *Parliamentary Affairs*, vol. 43 (pp. 209–26).

Jacobs, J. (1965) *The Death and Life of Great American Cities* (Penguin, Harmondsworth).

Jacobs, S. (1985) 'Race, Empire and the Welfare State: Council Housing and Racism', *Critical Social Policy*, vol. 13 (pp. 6–28).

James, S. (1990) 'A Streamlined City: The Broken Pattern of London Government', *Public Administration*, vol. 68 (pp. 493–504).

Jessop, B. (1980) 'The Transformation of the State in Post-war Britain', in Scase, R. (ed.), *The State in Western Europe* (Croom Helm, London).

Johnson, D. (1988) 'An Evaluation of the Urban Development Grant Programme', *Local Economy*, vol. 2 (pp. 251–70).

Johnson, N. (1990) *Reconstructing the Welfare State* (Harvester Wheatsheaf, Hemel Hempstead).

Jones, A. (1991) 'A New Importance for Development Plans', *Planning*, no. 932 (pp. 16–17).

Jones, G. and Stewart, J. (1985) *The Case for Local Government* (George Allen & Unwin, London).

Jones, P. (1979) 'Ethnic Areas in British Cities', in Herbert, D. and Smith, D. (eds), *Social Problems and the City* (Oxford University Press).

Jones, P. and Wild, T. (1991) 'Industrial Restructuring and Spatial Change in Britain and West Germany', in Wild, T. and Jones, P. (eds), *De-Industrialisation in Britain and Germany* (Anglo-German Foundation, London).

Jones, R. (1982) *Town and Country Chaos* (ASI, London).

Jones, T. (1993) *Britain's Ethnic Minorities* (PSI, London).

Joseph, K. and Sumption, J. (1979) *Equality* (John Murray, London).

Journal of Regional Policy (1992) 'Regional Policy and the European Community', *Journal of Regional Policy*, vol. 12 (pp. 557–83).

Jowell, J. (1983) 'Structure Plans and Social Engineering', in *Structure Plans and Local Plans: Planning in Crisis*, Occasional Papers in Planning and Environmental Law (Sweet & Maxwell, London).

Judd, D. and Parkinson, M. (eds) (1990) *Leadership and Urban Regeneration* (Sage, London).

Kamis, C. (1992) 'Wolverhampton', *Local Work*, no. 34 (pp. 6–7).

Karn, V. (1979) 'Low Income Owner Occupation in the Inner City', in Jones, C. (ed.), *Urban Deprivation and the Inner City* (Croom Helm, London).

Karn, V. *et al.* (1985) *Home-Ownership in the Inner City* (Aldershot, Gower).

Karn, V. *et al.* (1986) 'The Growing Crisis and Contradiction in Home Ownership', in Malpass, P. (ed.), *The Housing Crisis* (Croom Helm, London).

Kavanagh, D. (1990) *Thatcherism and British Politics* (Oxford University Press).

Keeble, D. (1976) *Industrial Location and Planning in the United Kingdom* (Methuen, London).

Keeble, D. (1980) 'Industrial Decline, Regional Policy and the Urban-Rural Manufacturing Shift in the United Kingdom', *Environment and Planning A*, vol. 12 (pp. 945–62).

Keeble, D. *et al.* (1991) 'Small Firms, Business Services Growth and Regional Development in the United Kingdom: Some empirical Findings', *Regional Studies*, vol. 25 (pp. 439–57).

Keegan, W. (1984) *Mrs Thatcher's Economic Experiment* (Penguin, Harmondsworth).

Keith, M. and Rogers, A. (1991) 'Hollow Promises? Policy, Theory and Practice in the Inner City', in Keith, M. and Rogers, A. (eds), *Hollow Promises* (Mansell, London).

Key, T. *et al.* (1990) 'Prospects for the Property Industry: An Overview', in Healey, P. and Nabarro, R. *Land and Property Development in a Changing Context* (Gower, Aldershot).

King, A. (1975) 'Overload: Problems of Government in the 1970s', *Political Studies*, vol. XXIII (pp. 162–296).

King, A. (1990) *Global Cities* (Routledge, London).

King, D. (1987) *The New Right* (Macmillan, London).

King, D. and Pierre, J. (eds) (1990) *Challenges to Local Government* (Sage, London).

Kingdom, J. (1991) *Local Government and Politics in Britain* (Philip Allan, London).

Kirby, A. and Lynch, K. (1987) 'A Ghost in the Growth Machine: The Aftermath of Rapid Population Growth in Houston', *Urban Studies*, vol. 24 (pp. 587–96).

Klosterman, R. (1985) 'Arguments For and Against Planning', *Town Planning Review*, vol. 56 (pp. 5–20).

Kolderie, T. (1986) 'The Two Different Concepts of Privatisation', *Public Administration Review*, vol. 46 (pp. 285–91).

Kynoch, R. (1989) 'King's Cross: A Rival for Canary Wharf?' *Chartered Surveyor's Weekly*, no. 33 (p. 9).

Lansley, S. *et al.* (1989) *Councils in Conflict* (Macmillan, London).

Law, C. (1988) 'Urban Revitalisation, Public Policy and the Redevelopment of Redundant Port Zones: Lessons from Baltimore and

Manchester', in Hoyle, B. *et al.* (eds), *Revitalising the Waterfront* (Bellhaven, London).

Lawless, P. (1979) *Urban Deprivation and Government Initiative* (Faber and Faber, London).

Lawless, P. (1980) 'Partnerships: A Critical Evaluation', *Local Government Studies*, vol. 6 (pp. 21–39).

Lawless, P. (1981) 'The Role of Some Central Government Agencies in Urban Economic Regeneration', *Regional Studies*, vol. 15 (pp. 1–14).

Lawless, P. (1986) *The Evolution of Spatial Policy* (Pion, London).

Lawless, P. (1988a) *Britain's Inner Cities* (Paul Chapman, Liverpool).

Lawless, P. (1988b) 'Urban Development Corporations and their Alternatives', *Cities*, vol. 5 (pp. 277–89).

Lawless, P. (1988c) 'British Inner Urban Policy Post 1979: A Critique', *Policy and Politics*, vol. 16 (pp. 261–75).

Lawless, P. and Ramsden, P. (1990) 'Sheffield in the 1980s', *Cities*, no. 7 (pp. 202–310).

Layton-Henry, Z. (1990) 'Black Electoral Participation', in Goulbourne, H. (ed.) *Black Politics in Britain* (Avebury, Aldershot).

Leach, S. and Game, C. (1991) 'English Metropolitan Government since Abolition', *Public Administration*, vol. 69 (pp. 141–70).

Lenon, B. (1987) 'The Geography of the "Big Bang": London's Office Building Boom', *Geography*, vol. 72 (pp. 56–9).

Lever, W. (ed.) (1987) *Industrial Change in the United Kingdom* (Longman, London).

Lewis, J. (1992) Land Aid, *New Statesman & Society*, 24 July (p. 23).

Lewis, O. (1966) 'The Culture of Poverty', *Scientific American*, vol. 215, no. 16 (pp. 19–25).

Lewis, R. (1988) *Anti-Racism: A Mania Exposed* (Quartet, London).

Lindblom, C. (1977) *Politics and Markets* (Basic Books, New York).

Llewellyn-Davies and Associates (1977) *Unequal City*, Final Report of Birmingham Inner Area Study (HMSO, London).

Lloyd, M. (1987) 'Simplified Planning Zones: The Privatisation of Land Use Control in the UK', *Land Use Policy*, January (pp. 2–17).

Lloyd, M. and Mcdougall, B. (1984) 'Free Zones in the United Kingdom', *Local Government Studies*, vol. 10 (pp. 39–51).

Lloyd, P. and Mason, C. (1984) 'Spatial Variations in New Firm Formation in the United Kingdom: Comparative Evidence from Merseyside, Greater Manchester and South Hampshire', *Regional Studies*, vol. 18 (pp. 207–20).

Logan, J. and Molotch, H. (1987) *Urban Fortunes* (University of California Press, Berkeley, CA).

London Docklands Development Corporation (LDDC) (1992) *London Docklands Development Corporation 1992 Corporate Plan* (LDDC, London).

Loney, M. (1983) *Community Against Government* (Heinemann, London).

Lunn, K. (1989) 'The British State and Immigration, 1945–51', *Immigrants and Minorities*, vol. 8 (pp. 161–74).

MacDonald, R. (1989) 'Liverpool North Docklands: The Potential for Urban Design and Industrial Regeneration', *Urban Design Quarterly*, vol. 29 (pp. 19–24).

MacGregor, S. and Pimlott, B. (eds) (1990) *Tackling the Cities* (Clarendon, Oxford).

Maclennan, D. (1987) 'Rehabilitating Older Housing', in Donnison, D. and Middleton, A. (eds), *Regenerating the Inner City* (RKP, London).

Maclennan, D. (1990) 'Urban Regneration Initiatives and Developments Other than Partnerships', *Urban Scotland into the 90s* (Scottish Office, Edinburgh).

Manley, J. (1983) 'Neo-pluralism: A Class Analysis of Pluralism I and Pluralism II', *American Political Science Review*, vol. 77 (pp. 368–83).

Marris, P. and Rein, M. (1973) *Dilemmas of Social Reform: Poverty and Action in the United States* (Aldine, Chicago).

Marsh, D. (1991) 'Privatisation under Mrs Thatcher: A Review of the Literature', *Public Administration*, vol. 69 (pp. 459–80).

Marsh, D. and Rhodes, R. (1989) *Implementing Thatcherism*, Essex Papers in Politics and Government, no. 62 (University of Essex, Colchester).

Marsh, D. and Rhodes, R. (eds) (1992) *Implementing Thatcherite Policies* (Open University Press, Milton Keynes).

Marshall, T. (1965) *Citizenship and Social Class* (Anchor, New York).

Marsland, D. (1988) 'The Welfare State as a Producer Monopoly', *Salisbury Review*, vol. 6 (pp. 4–9).

Martin, R. and Rowthorn, B. (eds) (1986) *The Geography of De-Industrialisation* (Macmillan, London).

Martin, S. (1990) 'City Grants, Urban Development Grants and Urban Regeneration Grants', in Campbell, M. (ed.), *Local Economic Policy* (Cassell, London).

Martin, S. and Pearce, G. (1992) 'The Internationalization of Local Authority Economic Development Strategies: Birmingham in the 1990s', *Regional Studies*, vol. 26 (pp. 499–509).

Marx, K. and Engels, F. (1968) *Selected Works* (Lawrence and Wishart, London).

Mason, C. (1987a) 'The Small Firm Sector', in Lever, W. (ed.), *Industrial Change in the United Kingdom* (Longman, London).

Mason, C. (1987c) 'The Geography of "Successful" Small Firms in the United Kingdom', *Environment and Planning A*, vol. 17 (pp. 1499–513).

Mason C. (1987b) 'Venture Capital in the United Kingdom: A Geographical Perspective', *National Westminster Bank Quarterly Review*, May (pp. 47–59).

Mason, C. and Harrison, R. (1986) 'The Regional Impact of Public Policy Towards Small Firms in the United Kingdom', in Keeble, D. and Weaver, E. (eds), *New Firms amd Regional Development in Europe* (Croom Helm, London).

Massey, D. (1982) 'Enterprise Zones: A Political Issue', *International Journal of Urban and Regional Research*, vol. 6 (pp. 429–34).

Massey, D. (1984) *Spatial Divisions of Labour* (Macmillan, London).

Massey, D. (1988) 'What is an Economy Anyway?' in Allen, J. and Massey, D. (eds), *The Economy in Question* (Sage, London).

Massey, D. (1990) 'Local Economic Strategies', in MacGregor, S. and Pimlott, B. (eds), *Tackling the Cities* (Clarendon, Oxford).

Massey, D. and Meegan, R. (1978) 'Industrial Restructuring versus the Cities', *Urban Studies*, vol. 15 (pp. 273–88).

Massey, D. and Wield, D. (1992) 'Evaluating Science Parks', *Local Economy*, vol. 7 (pp. 10–25).

Mawson, J. and Miller, D. (1986) 'Interventionist Approaches in Local Employment and Economic Development: The Experience of Labour Local Authorities', in Hausner, V. (ed.), *Critical Issues in Urban Economic Development*, vol. 1 (Clarendon, Oxford).

May, T. and McHugh, J. (1991) 'Government and Small Business in the UK: The Experience of the 1980s', paper presented to the Government/Business Relations Panel of the Annual Conference of the Political Studies Association, April 1991, University of Lancaster.

McArthur, A. (1987) 'Jobs and Incomes', in Donnison, D. and Middleton, A. (eds), *Regenerating the Inner City* (RKP, London).

McCarthy, M. (ed.), (1989) *The New Politics of Welfare* (Macmillan, London).

McCrone, G. (1973) *Regional Policy in Britain* (George Allen and Unwin, London).

McCrone, G. (1991) 'Urban Renewal: The Scottish Experience', *Urban Studies*, vol. 28 (pp. 919–38).

McKay, D. (1982) 'Regulative Planning in the Centralised British State, in McKay, D. (ed.), *Planning and Politics in Western Europe* (Macmillan, London).

McKay D and Cox A. (1979) *The Politics of Urban Change* (Croom Helm).

McLaren, D. (1989a) *Action for People* (Friends of the Earth, London).

McLaren, D. (1989b) '"Action for Cities" and the Urban Environment', *Local Economy*, vol. 4 (pp. 99–111).

McVicar, M. and Atkinson, R. (1985) 'Rate Capping and Local Government', *Social Policy and Administration*, vol. 19 (pp. 121–33).

Meacher, M. (1989) 'Employment', in McCarthy, M. (ed.), *The New Politics of Welfare* (Macmillan, London).

Merrett, S. (1979) *State Housing in Britain* (RKP, London).

Middlemas, K. (1991) *Power, Competition and the State 3: The End of the Post-War Era: Britain since 1974* (Macmillan, London).

Miles, R. (1984) 'The Riots of 1958: Notes on the Ideological Construction of "Race Relations" as a Political Issue in Britain', *Immigrants and Minorities*, vol. 3 (pp. 252–75).

Miles, R. (1990) 'The Racialisation of British Politics', *Political Studies*, vol. XXXVIII (pp. 277–85).

Miliband, R. (1970) *The State in Capitalist Society*, Weidenfeld and Nicolson, London).

Miliband, R. (1973) 'The Capitalist State: Reply to Nicos Poulantzas', in Urry, J. and Wakeford, J. (eds), *Power in Britain* (Heinemann, London).

Miller, S. (1978) 'The recapitalisation of capitalism', *International Journal of Urban and Regional Research*, vol. 2 (pp. 202–13).

Mills, C. W. (1956) *The Power Elite* (OUP, New York).

Mills, L. and Young, K. (1986) 'Local Authorities and Economic Development: A Preliminary Analysis', in Hausner, V. (ed.), *Critical Issues in Urban Economic Development*, vol. 1 (Clarendon, Oxford).

Ministry of Housing and Local Government (MHLG) (1962a) *Improvement of Houses*, Circular 42/62. HMSO, London).

Ministry of Housing and Local Government (MHLG) (1962b) *Town Centres: Approaches to Renewal* (HMSO, London).

Ministry of Housing and Local Government (MHLG) (1965) *The Future of Development Plans* (HMSO, London).

Ministry of Housing and Local Government (MHLG) (1969) *People and Plans* (HMSO, London).

Ministry of Transport (1963) *Traffic in Towns* (HMSO, London).

Mishan, E. (1989a) 'What Future for a Multiracial Britain?', Part 1, *Salisbury Review*, June (pp. 18–24).

Mishan, E. (1989b) 'What Future for a Multiracial Britain?', Part 2, *Salisbury Review*, September (pp. 4–11).

Mitchell, M. and Russell, D. (1989) 'Race, the New Right and State Policy in Britain', *Immigrants and Minorities*, vol. 8 (pp. 175–90).

Molle, W. (1990) *The Economics of European Integration* (Dartmouth, Aldershot).

Moon, G. and Parnell, R. (1986) 'Private Sector Involvement in Local Service Delivery', *Regional Studies*, no. 20 (pp. 253–7).

Moon, G. and Parnell, R. (1989) 'The Changing Role of Local Government: A Political Geographic Perspective', *Geographica Polonica*, vol. 56 (pp. 17–29).

Moore, C. (1990) 'Displacement, Partnership and Privatisation: Local Government and Urban Economic Regeneration in the 1980s', in King, D. and Pierre, J. (eds), *Challenges to Local Government* (Sage, London).

Moore, J. (1987) *The Welfare State: The Way Ahead* (Conservative Political Centre, London).

Morgan, K. (1985) *Labour in Power* (Oxford University Press).

Morley, S. *et al.* (1989) *Industrial and Business Space Development* (Spon, London).

Morse, S. (1993) 'Conquest of Space', *The Independent*, 12 March.

Mount, F. (1982) *The Subversive Family* (Counterpoint, London).

Mullins, D. (1989) 'Housing and Urban Policy', *New Community*, vol. 15 (pp. 475–82).

Munt, I. (1991) 'Race, Urban Policy and Urban Problems', *Urban Studies*, vol. 28 (pp. 183–203).

Munton, R. (1983) *London's Green Belt: Containment in Practice* (George Allen & Unwin, London).

Nabarro, R. (1980) 'Inner City Partnerships: An Assessment of the First Programmes', *Town Planning Review*, vol. 51 (pp. 25–38).

Nabarro, R. (1990) 'The Investment Market in Commercial and Industrial Development: Some Recent Trends', in Healey, P. and Nabarro, R., *Land and Property Development in a Changing Context* (Gower, Aldershot).

National Audit Office (NAO) (1988) *Department of the Environment: Urban Development Corporations* (HMSO, London).

National Audit Office (NAO) (1990) *Regenerating the Inner Cities* (HMSO, London).

Newby, H. (1987) 'Community and Urban Life', in Worsley, P. (ed.), *The New Introducing Sociology* (Pelican, London).

Newnham, A. (1986) *Employment, Unemployment and Black People* (Runnymeade, London).

Newton, K. (1976) *Second City Politics* (Oxford University Press).

Nicholson, B. *et al.* (1981) 'The Role of the Inner City in the Development of Manufacturing Industry', *Urban Studies*, vol. 18 (pp. 57–71).

Oatley, N. (1991) 'Streamlining the System', *Planning Practice and Research*, vol. 6 (pp. 19–28).

Office of Population Censuses and Surveys (OPCS) (1984) *Statistics for Urban Areas and Towns in Britain* (HMSO, London).

O'Gorman, F. (1986) *British Conservatism* (Longman, London).

Ohri, S. and Faruqi, S. (1988) 'Racism, Employment and Unemployment', in Bhat, A. *et al.* (eds), *Britain's Black Population* (Gower, Aldershot).

Opie, A. (1991) 'Compact Storms the Inner Cities', *Employment Gazette*, November (pp. 597–601).

Organisation for Economic Co-operation and Development (OECD) (1987) *Revitalising Urban Economies* (OECD, Paris).

Ouseley, H. (1984) 'Local Authority Race Initiatives', in Boddy, M. and Fudge, C. (eds), *Local Socialism* (Macmillan, London).

Ouseley, H. (1990) 'Resisting Institutional Change', in Ball, W. and Solomos, J. (eds), *Race and Local Politics* (Macmillan, London).

PA Cambridge Economic Consultants (1987) *An Evaluation of the Enterprise Zone Experiment* (HMSO, London).

Pacione, M. (1989) 'The Urban Crisis: Poverty and Deprivation in the Scottish City', *Scottish Geographical Magazine*, vol. 105 (pp. 101-15).

Pacione, M. (1990) 'A Tale of Two Cities', *Cities*, vol. 5 (pp. 304–14).

Pahl, R. (1966) 'The Rural–Urban Continuum', *Sociologica Ruralis*, vol. 6 (pp. 299–329).

Pahl, R. (1970) *Whose City*, 1st edition (Longman, London).

Pahl, R. (1975) *Whose City*, 2nd edition (Longman, London).

Pahl, R. (1977) 'Managers, Technical Experts and the State', in Harloe, M. (ed.), *Captive Cities* (John Wiley, Chichester).

Parker, D. (1990) 'The 1988 Local Government Act and Compulsory Competitive Tendering', *Urban Studies*, vol. 27 (pp. 653–68).

Parker, G. and Oatley, N. (1989) 'The Case Against the Proposed Urban Development Corporation for Bristol', *The Planner*, January (pp. 32–5).

Parkes, M. and Mouawad, D. (1991) *Towards a People's Plan* (King's Cross Railwaylands Group, London).

Parkinson, M. (1988a) 'Urban Regeneration and Development Corporations: Liverpool Style', *Local Economy*, vol. 3 (pp. 109–18).

Parkinson, M. (1988b) 'Dukakis the miracle worker?', *Town and Country Planning*, vol. 57 (pp. 312–13).

Parkinson, M. (1989) 'The Thatcher Governments' Urban Policy 1979–1989', *Town Planning Review*, vol. 60, 421–40).

Parkinson, M. and Evans, R. (1990) 'Urban Development Corporations', in Campbell, M. (ed.), *Local Economic Policy* (Cassell, London).

Parkinson, M. and Judd, D. (1988) 'Urban Revitalisation in America and the UK: The Politics of Uneven Development', in Judd, D. and Parkinson, M. (eds), *Leadership and Urban Rgeneration* (Sage, London).

Parkinson, M. and Wilks, S. (1983) 'Managing Urban Decline: The Case of Inner City Partnerships', *Local Government Studies*, vol. 9 (pp. 23–39).

Parkinson, M. and Wilks, S. (1986) 'The Politics of Inner City Partnerships', in Goldsmith, M. (ed.), *New Research in Central-Local Relations* (Gower, Aldershot).

Parsons, D. (1986) *The Political Economy of British Regional Policy* (Croom Helm, London).

Philips, D. (1987a) 'Searching for Decent Homes', *New Community*, vol. XIV (pp. 105–17).

Philips, D. (1987b) 'What Price Equality?', *GLC Housing Research and Policy Report*, no. 9 (GLC, London).

Philips, D. (1988) 'Race and Housing in London's East End', *New Community*, vol. XIV (pp. 356–69).

Phizacklea, A. and Miles, R. (1992) 'The British Trade Union Movement and Racism', in Braham, P. *et al.* (eds), *Racism and Antiracism* (Sage, London).

Phizacklea, A. and Miles, R. (1980) *Labour and Racism* (RKP, London).

Pickvance, C. (ed.), (1976) *Urban Sociology* (Methuen, London).

Pickvance, C. (1981) 'Policies as Chameleons: An Interpretation of Regional Policy and Office Policy in Britain', in Dear, M. and Scott, A. (eds), *Urbanisation and Urban Planning in Capitalist Society* (Methuen, London).

Pickvance, C. (1986) 'Regional Policy as Social Policy: A New Direction in British Regional Policy?', in Brenton, M. and Ungerson, C. (eds), *Year Book of Social Policy in Britain 1986* (RKP, London).

Pickvance, C. (1990) 'Is British Inner City Policy about Inner Cities?, revised version of paper read at a colloquium on Urban Regeneration in the UK, Ministère De La Recherche, Ancienne Ecole Polytechnique, Paris, 15–16 March.

Pickvance, C. (1991) 'The Difficulty of Control and the Ease of Structural Reform: British Local Government in the 1980s', in Pickvance, C. and Preteceille, E. (eds), *State Restructuring and Local Power* (Pinter, London).

Pinch, S. (1985) *Cities and Services* (RKP, London).

Pirie, M. (1985) *Privatisation in Theory and Practice* (ASI, London).

Piven, F. and Cloward, R. (1972) *Regulating the Poor* (Pantheon, New York).

Plender, J. (1992) 'Low-tech Risks for High Finance', *Financial Times*, 28 May.

Pollitt, C. (1990) *Mangerialism and the Public Services* (Blackwell, Oxford).

Poulantzas, N. (1969) *Political Power and Social Classes* (New Left Books, London).

Poulantzas, N. (1975) *Classes in Contemporary Capitalism* (New Left Books, London).

Poulantzas, N. (1973) 'The Problem of the Capitalist State', in Urry, J. and Wakeford, J. (eds), *Power in Britain* (Heinemann, London).

Prestwich, R. and Taylor, P. (1990) *Introduction to Regional and Urban Policy in the UK* (Longman, London).

Price, C. (1992) 'Dividends the Only Light in Property Gloom', *Financial Times*, 21 July.

Pryke, M. (1991) 'An International City Going "Global": Spatial Change in the City of London', *Environment and Planning D: Society and Space*, vol. 9 (pp. 197–222).

Purton, P. and Douglas, C. (1982) 'Enterprise Zones in the UK', *Journal of Planning & Environmental Law*, vol. 2 (pp. 412–22).

Ranelagh, J. (1991) *Thatcher's People* (HarperCollins, London).

Ratcliffe, P. (1992) 'Renewal, Regeneration and "Race": Issues in Urban Policy', *New Community*, no. 18 (pp. 387–400).

Ravetz, A. (1980) *Remaking Cities* (Croom Helm, London).

Redcliffe-Maud (1969) *Royal Commission on Local Government in England* (HMSO, London).

Redfern, P. (1982) 'Profile of Our Cities', *Population Trends*, no. 30 (pp. 21–33).

Rees, J. and Lambert, J. (1985) *Cities in Crisis* (Edward Arnold, London).

Rex, J. (1981) 'Urban Segregation and Inner City Policy in Great Britain', in Peach, C. *et al.* (eds), *Ethnic Segregation in Cities* (Croom Helm, London).

Rex, J. (1982) *Racial Conflict in the Inner City*, Working Papers in Ethnic Relations 16 (SSRC, London).

Rex, J. and Moore, R. (1969) *Race, Community and Conflict* (Oxford University Press).

Rhodes, R. (1988) *Beyond Westminster and Whitehall* (Unwin Hyman, London).

Rhodes, R. (1990) 'Policy Networks', *Journal of Theoretical Politics*, vol. 2 (pp. 293–317).

Rich, P. (1986) 'Conservative Ideology and Race in Modern British Politics', in Layton-Henry, Z. and Rich, P. (eds), *Race, Government and Politics* (Macmillan, London).

Richard Ellis (1990) *The Case for Property* (Richard Ellis Chartered Surveyors, London).

Riddell, P. (1983) *The Thatcher Government* (Martin Robertson, Oxford).

Ridge, M. and Smith, S. (1990) 'The First Months of the Community Charge', *Fiscal Studies*, vol. 11 (pp. 39–54).

Ridley, N. (1988) *The Local Right* (Centre for Policy Studies, London).

Robinson, P. (1989) 'Urban Unemployment and its Consequences', *Campaign for Work Research Report*, no. 6 (Campaign for Work, London).

Robinson, V. (1988) 'Economic Restructuring, the Urban Crisis and Britain's Black Population', in Herbert, D. and Smith, D. (eds), *Social Problems and the City* (Oxford University Press).

Robinson, V. (1991) 'Goodbye Yellow Brick Road: The Spatial Mobility and Immobility of Britain's Ethnic Population, 1971–81', *New Community*, vol. 17 (pp. 313–30).

Robson, B. (1988) *Those Inner Cities* (Clarendon, Oxford).

Roger Tym & Partners (1984) *Monitoring Enterprise Zones*, Year Three Report (Roger Tym & Partners, London).

Rose, E. (1986) 'Urban Development Grants, *Town Planning Review*, vol. 57 (pp. 440–57).

Rowthorn, B. (1986) 'Deindustrialisation in Britain', in Martin, R. and Rowthorn, B. (eds), *The Geography of Deindustrialisation* (Macmillan, London).

Rydin, Y. (1993) *The British Town Planning System* (Macmillan, London).

Salmon, H. (1992) 'Urban Regeneration and the Community: Birmingham Heartlands Mid-term Report', *Local Economy*, vol. 7 (pp. 26–38).

Saunders, P. (1974) 'They Make The Rules: Political Routines and the Generation of Political Bias, *Policy and Politics*, vol. 4 (pp. 31–58).

Saunders, P. (1978) *Urban Politics* (Penguin, Harmondsworth).

Saunders, P. (1981) *Social Theory and the Urban Question* (Hutchinson, London).

Saunders, P. (1985) 'Space, the City and Urban Sociology', in Gregory, D. and Urry, J. (eds), *Social Relations and Spatial Structure* (Macmillan, London).

Savage, S. and Robbins, L. (eds) (1990) *Public Policy under Thatcher* (Macmillan, London).

Savery, J. (1985) 'Anti-racism as Witchcraft', *Salisbury Review*, July (pp. 41–2).

Scarman (1981) *The British Disorders 10–12 April 1981*, The Scarman Inquiry (HMSO, London).

Scottish Office (1990) *Urban Scotland into the 90s* (Scottish Office, Edinburgh).

Scottish Office (1988) *New Life for Urban Scotland* (Scottish Office, Edinburgh).

Scrutton, R. (1980) *The Meaning of Conservatism* (Penguin, Harmondsworth).

Seldon, A. (1981) *Whither the Welfare State* (IEA, London).

Sellgren, J. (1990) 'Local Economic Development: An Assessment of Local Authority Economic Development Initiatives', *Local Government Studies*, vol. 16 (pp. 57–78).

SERPLAN (1989) *The South-East Regional Strategy* (SERPLAN, London).

Shankland, G. *et al.* (1977) *Inner London: Policies for Dispersal and Balance: Final Report of the Lambeth Inner Area Study* (HMSO, London).

Sharman, N. (1979) 'Inner City Partnership? The Docklands Experience', in Community Development Project Political Economy Collective (ed.), *The State and the Local Economy* (CDP, London).

Short, J. (1984) *The Urban Arena* (Macmillan, London).

Shutt, J. (1984) 'Tory Enterprise Zones and the Labour Movement', *Capital and Class*, no. 23 (pp. 19–44).

Siegan, B. (1972) *Land Use Without Zoning* (Lexington Books, Lexington).

Sills, A. *et al.* (1988) *The Politics of the Urban Crisis* (Hutchinson, London).

Simmie, J. (1974) *Citizens in Conflict* (Hutchinson, London).

Simmie, J. (1981) *Power, Property and Corporatism* (Methuen, London).

Sivanandan, A. (1976) 'Race, Class and the State', *Race and Class*, vol. XVII (pp. 347–68).

Smith, B. (1988) *Bureaucracy and Political Power* (Wheatsheaf, Brighton).

Smith, D. (1989) *North and South* (Penguin, Harmondsworth).

Smith, M. (1979) *The City and Social Theory* (Blackwell, Oxford).

Smith, S. (1993) 'Residential Segregation and the Politics of Racialization', in Cross, M. and Keith, M. (eds), *Racism, the City and the State* (Routledge, London).

Solesbury, W. (1990) 'Property Development and Urban Regeneration', in Healey, P. and Nabarro, R. *Land and Property Development in a Changing Context* (Gower, Aldershot).

Solomos, J. (1986) 'Training for What?', in Layton-Henry, Z. and Rich, P. (eds), *Race, Government and Politics* (Macmillan, London).

Solomos, J. (1988) *Black Youth, Racism and the State* (Cambridge University Press).

Solomos, J. (1989) *Race and Racism in Contemporary Britain* (Macmillan, London).

Solomos, J. (1991a) 'The Politics of Racial Equality and the Local State', *Local Government Studies*, vol. 17 (pp. 33–46).

Solomos, J. (1991b) 'The Politics of Race and Housing, *Policy & Politics*, vol. 19 (pp. 147–57).

Solomos, J. and Ball, W. (1990) 'New Initiatives and Possibilities of Reform', in Ball, W. and Solomos, J. (eds), *Race and Local Politics* (Macmillan, London).

Solomos, J. and Singh, G. (1990) 'Racial Equality, Housing and the Local State', in Ball, W. and Solomos, J. (eds), *Race and Local Politics* (Macmillan, London).

Sorensen, A. and Day, R. (1981) 'Libertarian Planning', *Town Planning Review*, vol. 52 (pp. 390–402).

Spencer, K. (1980) 'The Genesis of Comprehensive Community Programmes', *Local Government Studies*, vol. 6 (pp. 17–28).

Spencer, K. (1981) 'Comprehensive Community Programmes', *Local Government Studies*, vol. 7 (pp. 31–49).

Spencer, K. (1987) 'Developing an Urban Policy Focus in the 1990s', *Local Government Policy Making*, no. 14 (pp. 9–11).

Springay, P. (1989) 'King's Cross: Recreating the Landscape', *Chartered Surveyor*, June (pp. 20–3).

Steen, A. (1981) *New Life for Old Cities* (Aims of Industry, London).

Stewart, M. (1977) *The Jekyll and Hyde Years* (Dent and Sons, London).

Stewart, M. (1990) 'A View of Urban Policy in England', in *Urban Scotland into the 90s* (Scottish Office, Edinburgh).

Stewart, J. and Stoker, G. (eds) (1989) *The Future of Local Government* (Macmillan, London).

Stewart, M. and Whitting, G. (1983) *Ethnic Minorities and the Urban Programme* (SAUS, University of Bristol).

Stoker, G. (1989) 'Urban Development Corporations: A Review', *Regional Studies*, vol. 23 (pp. 159–73).

Stoker, G. (1990) 'Regulation Theory, Local Government and the Transition from Fordism', in King, D. and Pierre, J. (eds), *Challenges to Local Government* (Sage, London).

Stoker, G. (1991) *The Politics of Local Government* (Macmillan, London).

Stoney, P. (1987) 'Enterprise Zones: Incentive or Intervention?', *Economic Affairs*, October/November (pp. 28–30).

Storey, D. and Johnson, S. (1989) 'Are Small Firms the Answer to Unemployment?', in Shields, J. (ed.), *Making the Economy Work* (Macmillan, London).

Storey, D. and Strange, A. (1993) *Entrepreneurship in Cleveland*, Department of Employment Research Series no. 3 (HMSO, London).

Stungo, A. (1985) 'Simplified Planning Zones Explained', *Estates Gazette*, December (p. 14).

Syms, D. (1984) 'Urban Deprivation: Not Just the Inner City', *Area*, no. 16 (pp. 299–306).

Talbot, J. (1988) 'Have Enterprise Zones Encouraged Enterprise?' *Regional Studies*, vol. 22 (pp. 507–14).

Thomas, R. and Cresswell, P. (1973) *The New Town Idea* (Open University Press, Milton Keynes).

Thompson, J. (1986) *The Conservatives' Economic Policy* (Croom Helm, London).

Thornley, A. (1991) *Urban Planning under Thatcherism* (Routledge, London).

Thrift, N. (1987) 'The Fixers: The Urban Geography of International Commercial Capital', in Henderson, J. and Castells, M. (eds), *Global Restructuring and Territorial Development* (Sage, London).

Tilley, J. (1979) 'The Inner City Partnerships: An Assessment', in Loney, M. and Allen, M. (eds), *The Crisis of the Inner City* (Macmillan, London).

Townsend, P. (1962) 'The Meaning of Poverty', *British Journal of Sociology*, vol. 18 (pp. 210–27).

Trades Union Congress (TUC) (1984) *Contractors' Failures* (TUC, London).

Trades Union Congress (TUC) (1986) *More Contractors' Failures* (TUC, London).

Travers, T. (1986) *The Politics of Local Government Finance* (George Allen and Unwin, London).

Travers, T. (1990) 'London After Abolition', *Local Government Studies*, vol. 16 (pp. 105–16).

Treasury (1982) *Treasury Economic Report 1982* (HMSO, London).
Trippier, D. (1989) *New Life for Inner Cities* (Conservative Political Centre, London).
Trippier, D. (1988) *Urban Programme: Priorities for 1989/90*, Annex 2 to DoE (1990), *The Urban Programme Management Initiative: A Consultation Paper on Proposed Changes* (HMSO, London).
Turok, I. (1992) 'Property-led Urban Regeneration: Panacea or Placebo?', *Environment and Planning A*, vol. 24 (pp. 361–79).
Turok, I. and Wannop, U. (1990) *Targeting Urban Employment*, DoE Inner Cities Research Programme (HMSO, London).
Tweedale, I. (1988) 'Waterfront Redevelopment, Economic Restructuring and Social Impact', in Hoyle, B. *et al.* (eds), *Revitalising the Waterfront* (Bellhaven, London).
Vlessing, E. (1991) 'In the Market for Development', *Chartered Surveyor's Weekly*, no. 36 (pp. 42–3).
Walker, J. and Moor, R. (1983) *Privatisation in Local Government* (WEA, London).
Walters, A. *et al.* (1974) *Government and Land* (IEA, London).
Wannop, U. (1990) 'The Glasgow Eastern Area Renewal (GEAR) Project', *Town Planning Review*, vol. 61 (pp. 455–74).
Wannop, U. and Leclerc, R. (1987a) 'Urban Renewal and the Origins of GEAR', in Donnison, D. and Middleton, A. (eds), *Regenerating the Inner City* (RKP, London).
Wannop, U. and Leclerc, R. (1987b) 'The Management of GEAR', in Donnison, D. and Middleton, A. (eds), *Regenerating the Inner City* (RKP, London).
Ward, R. (1982) 'London's Docklands: The LDDCs Aims', *Planner News*, July (pp. 11–14).
Wedderburn, D. (1962) 'Poverty in Britain Today', *Sociological Review*, vol. 10 (pp. 257–82).
Willetts, D. (1992) *Modern Conservatism* (Penguin, Harmondsworth).
Wilson, D. *et al.* (1994) *Local Government in the UK* (Macmillan, London).
Wirth, L. (1938) 'Urbanism as a Way of Life', *American Journal of Sociology*, vol. 44 (pp. 1–24).
Worsthorne, P. (1988) 'Too Much Freedom', in Cowling, M. (ed.), *Conservative Essays* (Cassell, London).
Wray, A. (1987) 'Worth its Weight in Red Tape', *Architects Journal*, 25 May (p. 17).
Wrench, J. (1987) 'The Unfinished Bridge: YTS and Black Youth', in Troyna, B. (ed.), *Racial Inequality in Education* (Tavistock, London).
Young, K. (1983) 'Ethnic Pluralism and the Policy Agenda in Britain', in Glazer, N. and Young, K. (eds) (1983) *Ethnic Pluralism and Public Policy* (Heinemann, London).
Young, K. and Connelly, N. (1981) *Policy and Practice in the Multi-Racial City* (Policy Studies Institute, London).
Young, M. and Willmott, P. (1962) *Family and Kinship in East London*, revised edition (Penguin, Harmondsworth).
Zweig, F. (1961) *The Worker in an Affluent Society* (Heinemann, London).

# Index